STROLLING PLAYERS &
DRAMA IN THE
PROVINCES
1660–1765

A COUNTRY THEATRE

STROLLING PLAYERS &
DRAMA IN THE
PROVINCES
1660–1765

BY

SYBIL ROSENFELD
M.A.

1970

OCTAGON BOOKS

New York

First published 1939

Reprinted 1970
by permission of the Cambridge University Press

OCTAGON BOOKS
A DIVISION OF FARRAR, STRAUS & GIROUX, INC.
19 Union Square West
New York, N. Y. 10003

LIBRARY OF CONGRESS CATALOG CARD NUMBER: 78-96167

Printed in U.S.A. by
NOBLE OFFSET PRINTERS, INC.
NEW YORK 3, N. Y.

CONTENTS

ACKNOWLEDGMENTS

Writing this book has been an adventure. It brought contacts in different parts of the country with all manner of men. I never even knew the names of many of the people, such as innkeepers of inns in which the players had acted, whom I worried, but I should like them to know how grateful I am for their interest and courtesy in leaving their work to answer my many questions.

To the Librarians and Staffs of the Bath, Bristol, Canterbury, Greenwich, Hull, Margate, Norwich, Richmond and York Libraries, as well as to the Staff of the British Museum Reading Room and Newspaper Room, I owe a debt of gratitude for their unfailing patience and helpfulness.

I am also indebted to the courtesy of the Corporations of Norwich, York and Canterbury, and to the York Merchant Taylors for kind permission to quote from their records; and to the *Norwich Mercury* and *York Herald* for allowing me to examine in their offices their eighteenth-century files.

Chapters II and III on the Norwich Players first appeared in *The Review of English Studies*, Chapter XIII on Penkethman's GreenwichTheatre in *Notes and Queries*, and Chapter X on the Bristol Account Book is an enlargement of an article contributed to *The Times Literary Supplement*. I have much pleasure in acknowledging the courtesy of these journals in giving me leave to reprint the material.

For permission to reproduce the illustrations I have to thank the following: Mr Ifan Kyrle Fletcher for the Frontispiece; the Curator of the Christchurch House Museum, Ipswich, for the Tacket Street Theatre; the Keeper of the Prints, British Museum, for the York Actors and William Penkethman; the Dean and Chapter of York for the York Playbill; the authorities of the Bristol Public Library for the page from the Jacob's Wells Theatre Account Book; the Corporation of Sandwich for the Sandwich Theatre, and the Committee of the Richmond Library for the Richmond Hill Theatre.

I should also like to thank for the aid they in various ways gave this book: Miss Grace, Archivist of Norwich; Mr A. J. Quinton; Mr R. Noel-Hill; the Rev. Chancellor F. Harrison of the York Minster Library; Mr B. P. Johnson, of the York Merchant Taylors; Mr A. Mattison, of Leeds; the Rev. W. Coggill, Vicar of St Mary Sculcoates, Hull; the Rev. H. Cameron McNeil, Rector of St Michael's, Bath; Mr Byrne, Town Clerk of Sandwich; Miss Mabel Mills; Miss Edith Scroggs; Mr T. H. Smith, of Richmond; Mr Peter Davey.

S. R.

March 1939

ADDITIONS AND CORRECTIONS

Since the original edition of this book in 1939 a little more information has come to light which necessitates the following amendments.

P. 12. Add to list of books Thomas Snagg, *Recollections of Occurrences*, 1951.

P. 45. *Norwich*. Grompton Rhodes's Winston mss. now in Birmingham Public Library.

P. 50. 1711-12. Epilogue spoken by Cole on an ass.

P. 107. *York*. 1713. *Fall of Tarquin*, 1st ed. Newcastle (Dobell catalogue, 84, 1945). Fieldhouse and Pearson in cast; first actors known in York.

P. 112. 1727. Orfeur v. Huddy. Huddy had a London company which he proposed to bring to York at race week. It included Boheme and Spiller but the former denied that he was involved and the company probably never came (*Mist's Weekly Journal*, July 15, 20, 1727. Information from Mr. C. B. Hogan).

P. 116. 1733. Keregan's lease had been for ten years, not two.

P. 117. 1734. The Archbishop of York protested to Lord Irwin against the new playhouse (Temple Newsam, rent books and papers in Leeds Public Library. Information from Miss Foster, archivist).

P. 129. 1740. Keregan buried at St. Michael-le-Belfry on December 31, 1740 (York Parish Registers Society, Publications, XI, 255). His son was buried March 4, 1741 (*ibid*). Thomas Keregan left the use of his playhouse, clothes and scenes to his widow who from the profits was required to allow their son, Patrick, £1.7.0. a week for acting and assisting in the management. His daughter, Catherine Williams, was to be paid 6s. a week for help with the playhouse (Will in York Probate Office, vol. 87,f. 391.)

Pp. 145, 148. 1752, 1755-6. Dancer did not marry Miss Street, later Mrs. Barry and Mrs. Crawford, until 1754 in Bath. The Mrs. Dancer of 1752 must have been a former wife. But in 1755-6 he returned with his second wife.

P. 147. *Cornish Knights* by Samuel Foote.

P. 168. *Bath*. 1703. Company played in a converted tennis court (*Observator*, Aug. 21-5, 1703).

P. 169. 1703. The deserting comedian was probably Doggett who was at Bartholomew Fair that year.

P. 169. 1704. *Daily Courant* (April 22, 1704) reported that the new theatre was to open the first week of May. There is no further evidence that it opened before 1705.

P. 191. 1752-3. This was the first Mrs. Dancer, see note p. 145.

The London Stage. Pt. II ed. Emmett Avery; Pt. III ed. A. H. Scouten supplied the following additional performances.

P. 269. *Greenwich.* 1710, July 17. *Fair Quaker.*

P. 272. 1712, May 21. *Fatal Marriage.*

P. 285. *Richmond.* 1729, July 25. *Hob.* L.I.F. company in the gardens.

P. 285. *Richmond.* 1729. August 6. Unknown play. L.I.F. company in the gardens.

P. 286. 1730, June 27. *Spanish Friar.*

P. 288. 1733, Aug. 20. *Fop's Fortune* (*Love Makes a Man*).

P. 288. 1734, June 27. *Henry IV* (1).

P. 288. 1734, June 29. *Miser.*

P. 288. 1735, July 28. *Constant Couple.*

P. 288. 1735, Aug. 16. *Love for Love.* Theatre on the Green.

P. 299. 1762, July 31. *Rule a Wife.* Drunken officers from London caused a riot and were finally turned out (*St. James's Chronicle*, Aug. 5-7, 1762. Information from Prof. A. H. Scouten).

ILLUSTRATIONS

INTRODUCTION

It may be asked why one should isolate from the theatrical history of the provinces this particular century, ignoring those which went before and came after.

Two reasons can be cited in defence of this procedure. The first is the practical one that the period 1660–1760 has been comparatively neglected, whilst the earlier and later periods have received more than their fair share of the attention of scholars and dramatic historians. Sir E. K. Chambers's work on the Medieval and Elizabethan stage, Mr Tucker Murray's book on English Dramatic Companies, and a host of articles by local antiquarians, and chapters in local histories, have adequately covered the ground up to Cromwell's time. And, since a mass of material is readily available for the second half of the eighteenth century and onwards, this period, too, has not been ill served in theatrical chronicles of individual towns. It is true that no attempt has been made to write the theatrical history of a town like Canterbury, but, in the case of other centres, those interested can fairly easily lay hands on information which will provide them with an account of the beginning and end of the story. The point is that nearly all these histories have but passing references, or at most a scant and inadequate chapter to give, to the Restoration and first half of the eighteenth century. It is this gap that I have endeavoured, in some measure, to fill.

There is, however, a more weighty reason than mere practicability. It is that these hundred years are a unique and complete era in the long history of drama in the provinces. One is at once struck when studying the theatrical history of provincial towns, by the fact that everywhere during the decade 1755–65 new and imposing theatres were being built. Inn yards or rooms, booths and town halls were gradually replaced in the chief cities by playhouses, constructed only for purposes of acting, for the local company of players. They mark the end of a period of subterfuge and makeshift, the beginning of an era of recognition and acknowledgment; they were the harbingers of the emancipation of the drama from ban and restraint. Royal patents, in several instances,[1] soon followed, which gave a final stamp of authority and legality to the players in such towns as Bath, Norwich and York. The myriad lesser companies still remained unlicensed, and were therefore open to prohibition and arrest, but several town companies were henceforward assured in their position and needed no longer to work in constant fear of suppression; from being, in company with the poorer strollers, but homeless wanderers at the mercy of any informer, they attained, after the middle of the century, a certain amount of security against aggression and of status in society. Every fresh royal patent necessitated an Act of Parliament to exempt the players from the provisions of the law, and it soon became evident that a more embracing Act was needed to end this nuisance. As a result an Act was passed in 1788,[2] whereby Justices were given the power to license theatrical representations, in the provinces, of plays which had been presented at the patent theatres, for sixty days at a time, provided that the place was well outside London, Edinburgh, the King's residence or the Universities; the Act further provided that no second licence was to be granted to the same place until eight months after the first had elapsed, nor to a place within the same jurisdiction until six months had elapsed. This gave all strollers the chance of being able to exercise their calling legally; after a long and arduous struggle against puritanic prejudice the players had won for the cause of drama in the provinces a most deserved triumph.

These improved conditions were accompanied by a radical

---

[1] Bath and Norwich, 1768; York and Hull, 1769; Liverpool, 1771; Chester, 1777.
[2] Public General Acts, 28 George III, Cap. 30.

change in the organisation of the companies. The sharing system was abandoned in favour of salaries, and the major country companies aligned themselves in this respect with the London theatres. York had adopted salaries as early as 1730, and other companies employed occasional salaried performers in addition to the sharers. Many of the smaller troupes long clung, however, to the old tradition, so that Ryley,[1] writing of the 1770's, said that the sharing system was still 'nearly general'. Sharing troupes were proud of their conservatism, and Daggerwood[2] met one manager who expressed disgust at the suggestion that his was any 'paltry salary scheme'. Gradually sharing companies came to be considered inferior, and E. C. Everard,[3] strolling in the later days of the eighteenth century, did his best to avoid them. The middle decades of the century thus saw a definite break in theatrical conditions in the provinces. The new period which then opened was to close but recently, with the gradual disappearance of the touring company and the rise of the local repertory players.

Another question may be put as to the arbitrary selection of towns dealt with. This was admittedly in part dictated by the chance incidence of material. Those centres which produced early local newspapers are naturally more rewarding to the searcher after their theatrical history than those which did not. News items concerning the visits of the players and, later, advertisements of their performances, are the chief sources of our information about dramatic activities. It is thus almost impossible to dig out anything about a company such as Herbert's in Lincolnshire, whose circuit did not include a town which had a local paper. The players figure infrequently in town records, and it is because we have to rely on Mayors' Books and Chamberlains' Accounts for the years 1660–1700 that so little has come to light about

---

[1] *The Itinerant*, 1818, vol. I, p. 239.
[2] *Memoirs of Sylvester Daggerwood* [1806], p. 112.
[3] *Memoirs of an Unfortunate Son of Thespis*, 1808.

those early years. Contemporary diaries and correspondence give but glimpses and stray hints.

The choice of towns has not, however, been altogether without plan. I have selected what I considered to be the most productive centre for each point of the compass: Norwich for the east, York for the north, Bath for the west, and Canterbury for the south. These four towns were principal centres of theatrical activity in large districts, though there were, of course, others. Bristol, for instance, may claim to represent the west as well as Bath, but I give Bath the preference because the ground has been better covered at Bristol by several local theatrical histories. I have therefore confined myself to a description of the account book of the Jacob's Wells Theatre, a manuscript which, because it provides a unique opportunity of studying the working and financial methods of a strolling company, cannot be overlooked in any work on drama in the provinces.

In addition, I have dealt with the two summer theatres at Greenwich and Richmond because they are unique, in that their theatrical activity entirely depended, not on local companies, but on the visits of actors and actresses from the London theatres in vacation time.

We can form no idea at all of the number or quality of strollers in Restoration times, since only the Norwich records have anything to tell us of them. The Puritan opposition may have been strong enough to curtail their activities in most places or it may not. Even in the eighteenth century, with all the knowledge gained from the newspapers, it is impossible to estimate how many strolling companies there were. It seems as though the country was pretty well covered, and nearly every town of any size or importance must, I think, have been visited at assize, fair or race weeks. Mrs Charke and other strollers who have left us accounts of their adventures were always changing masters, yet seem to have experienced little difficulty in picking up with companies in whatever part of the country they happened to be. The provincial newspapers, too, frequently refer to companies outside their own particular circuits. Broadly speaking there were three main types of company: (1) the established comedians with headquarters at the chief town in the district, from which they generally took their name, and regular country circuits; (2) the innumerable small troupes, living very much from hand to mouth, which covered the lesser places but sometimes ventured on the bigger towns when the regular circuit company was elsewhere; and (3) the temporary bands which came from the London theatres during the long summer vacation to regale the provinces. Most information is available in connection with the first and last of these groups. The small companies crop up occasionally and quickly disappear into the unknown, leaving but a few names of plays and actors in their trail. As might indeed be expected, the provincial players resented the intrusion of the Londoners. In the *Memoirs of Sylvester Daggerwood*,[1] we read of how provincial managers were in the habit of contracting with London stars for a few performances at exorbitant rates. The actor from the metropolis had his name brandished in large letters on the playbill, and finally drew for himself a big benefit to the ruin of the regular country actor.

In 1737 the right of all provincial companies to act was abolished by the Licensing Act.[2] Until that time players had received permission to act in the provinces in the form either of letters patent from the sovereign, or a licence from the Master of the Revels or Lord Chamberlain. The patents sometimes took the form of a grant to a nobleman to maintain a troupe of players who then became his servants, and this custom lingered on until the Licensing Act came into force. Many advantages accrued to the players who were able to obtain this kind of protection; thus we shall find the

[1] *Op. cit.* p. 137. Though the author is writing of a later period, the same no doubt applies to the visits of Macklin to Norwich, etc.
[2] Public General Acts, 10 George II, p. 507.

Duke of Monmouth approaching the Vice-Chancellor of Cambridge University to grant his players permission to play at Stourbridge Fair, and Doggett obtaining preference over Power to play in Norwich because he held a patent from the Duke of Norfolk. In 1734 a Playhouse Bill[1] was introduced into the House of Commons with the purpose of suppressing the unlicensed theatre at Goodman's Fields, and of restricting the number of playhouses to the two patent theatres. Among petitions against the bill were those of Charles Lee and Lestrange Symes,[2] respectively Master and Comptroller of the Revels, whose right it was, under patent dating from the time of Charles II, to licence players of 'Interludes, Drolls, Country Shews and Entertainments', and who saw, if the bill passed, their occupation gone. They pleaded that such licences were subject to a stamp duty and that by them the players were restrained from profanity, obscenity, 'or any ways offensive to Piety and good Manners'. It is strange that the only country manager to protest was the notorious Tony Aston. On April 14, 1735, Aston asked that he might be heard personally, being poor, and having no money with which to fee counsel.[3] His petition was referred to the Committee of the whole House and we do not hear further of its fate, but Aston printed his version of it that same year. He points out that 'it would be a great Loss to the Country Gentry to be depriv'd of seeing Plays elsewhere than at the two Patent Playhouses', and foretells an outcry from frequenters of marts, fairs, horse races and cock matches, who would be robbed of their customary dramatic diversions. 'The country now', he states, 'is regularly entertain'd at great Expence with good Plays, and Waggon Loads of Scenes and adapted Habits.' He bears witness to the extent of dramatic activity in the country by his vivid quip that 'if all the Country Actors must promiscuously suffer by this Act, I question if there is Wood enough in England to hang

---

[1] For a draft of this Bill, see Brit. Mus. Dramatic Tracts and Papers, No. 5.
[2] *House of Commons Journals*, 1735, p. 459.   [3] *Ibid.* p. 459.

them all'. Nor does he see why a bill aimed against Good-man's Fields must result in total rural extirpation. According to Charles Dibdin,[1] it was largely owing to Aston's evidence that the bill was rejected. He is said to have given an exposition of the manner in which he had up till then evaded the laws, and to have pointed out the loopholes in the bill which would permit of his continuing to do so.

After this bill had been laid aside there was further trouble with regard to the performance of Fielding's satire *Pasquin* at the unlicensed Little Theatre in the Haymarket. This led, despite the eloquent protest of Lord Chesterfield,[2] to the passing of the Licensing Act which came into force on June 24, 1737. The Act was in the form of an amendment to the Act of Queen Anne relating to rogues and vagabonds.[3] As far as it touched itinerant players[4] the Act first of all adjudged players, who had no legal settlement in their place of acting, such as a royal patent or a licence from the Lord Chamberlain, to be rogues and vagabonds, and to be liable to the penalties inflicted on such. Then, in a later clause, it stated that no person was to be authorised by the King's patent or by licence of the Chamberlain to act for hire, gain or reward in any part of Great Britain except the City of Westminster or where the King was residing. In other words, playing in the provinces had no legal authority, and provincial players were therefore subject to be treated as vagrants. On the oath of creditable witnesses, or on his own confession, an offender was to be sentenced to a fine, and a distraint made upon his goods. If these proved insufficient to cover the fine he was to be committed to prison, without bail, and

[1] *A Complete History of the Stage*, 1800, vol. IV, p. 412.
[2] *The E- of Ch-F-D's Speech in the H-se of L-ds, Against the Bill for Licensing all Dramatic Performances*, Dublin, 1749.
[3] The patentees had previously summoned the actors at the Little Haymarket Theatre by virtue of this Act, but had lost their case because Harper could prove that he was a householder and therefore not subject to a law dealing with vagrants.
[4] The Act also contained provisions for the censorship of plays.

with hard labour, for a period not exceeding six months. Informers were encouraged by a reward of half the fine, and the other half was to go to the poor of the parish. The actor's one right of appeal from the Justices of the Peace was to the Quarter Sessions. Thus, whereas previously the magistrates would have found it difficult to refuse players with a proper licence leave to play,[1] henceforth they had every right to do so. Also if an informer lodged a protest against the performers the magistrate was bound to summon the offenders and close their theatre. Ryley[2] tells how one magistrate gladly gave him permission to play, but warned him that 'should anyone be vile enough, through malice, fanaticism, or from any other motive to lay an information', as a magistrate, he would be bound to take notice of it. The practice of the Justices seems to have been to grant licences to play in most cases, and only to prosecute under the law should a complaint or a disturbance ensue. They did not interpret it as part of their duty to suppress all players as having no legal right to act, nor to punish them as vagrants, but confined themselves to using the law as a restraint that could be invoked if necessary. So in practice the Act does not appear to have made very much difference to, or greatly to have hampered, the players' activities. It is true that actors from time to time were imprisoned, or a theatre shut down for a few weeks; thus Ryley[3] knew of one company that was carried miles to gaol in Carlisle 'with all the ignominy and insult attached to criminals', but we hear of comparatively few instances of this kind. Mrs Charke[4] was not a little astonished when she found herself in gaol on the advice of an informer; and the informer was, for his pains, almost hooted out of court and subsequently dropped by the best gentry.

---

[1] Sir Henry Herbert threatened to summon the Mayor of Maidstone for disobedience if he would not give some licensees leave to play (*Dramatic Records of Sir Henry Herbert*, ed. J. Q. Adams, 1917, p. 91).

[2] *Op. cit.* vol. II, p. 298.   [3] *Ibid.* vol. II, p. 297.

[4] *A Narrative of the Life of Mrs Charlotte Charke*, 1929, pp. 169–77.

Some companies, probably owing to prosecutions or threats of them, evolved the subterfuge of announcing concerts, at which the plays were to be given, between two parts of the concert, free of charge, and not therefore for hire, gain or reward. The earliest instance I have found of this method of self-protection is in Norwich in 1742, and many companies continued to act without employing any such procedure up to the 1760's; even then it was not used consistently. Indeed, such was the hold that the drama had at this time that the Act was, for the most part, ignored, and the strollers by their persistence won their way, in spite of it, from vagabondage to the recognition of Theatres Royal.

There remains a third and most searching question. Of what value to us to-day are these old records? From the point of view of the historian of the drama they have absorbing interest as chapters in the story of the long struggle, and eventual victory, of the drama over its old enemy puritanism. Another reason for their importance is that in the provincial companies are preserved, long after they had disappeared in London, the customs and traditions of an older age. We have seen how the strollers, though they liked to produce the latest London plays, were slow to adopt the methods and organisation of the London companies. They continued in fact to differ but little from the companies of Shakespeare's day, and can therefore throw light on the methods and manners of the Elizabethan theatre.

In addition, they were the training ground of many a famous player. In how many theatrical biographies do we read of the actor's career being launched by his running away with, or joining, a strolling troupe; how many celebrated players obtained in that hard life the variety of experience that helped them to greatness.[1]

From the repertoires, too, of these companies we can form

[1] George Parker says that Garrick used to send unfledged actors to Griffith's Company in Norwich for training (*A View of Society and Manners*, 1781, vol. I, p. 189).

some idea of the provincial taste. The most noticeable features are the widespread popularity of Shakespeare, albeit in adapted versions, the preference for comedy rather than tragedy, the large proportion of pathetic and romantic dramas, the rarity of classical tragedies such as *Cato*, and the craze for pantomime. It is exactly these tastes that Professor Nicoll finds among London audiences.[1] It would seem as though the stage were the one place where urbanity and restraint were not welcomed in the first half of the eighteenth century.

But it is not alone for the dramatic historian that these records have meaning. To-day when the touring system has failed and each town is having to provide its own drama, or face the possibility of having none, it must be an inspiration to know how the drama locally survived the trials and troubles of other days, and to feel the long tradition linking its present efforts to the past. In spite of the many attempts at frustration, in spite of what is worse—apathy—the players persisted then in their efforts to satisfy the perennial human need for dramatic expression; they must not fail in their persistence now.[2]

Lastly, the ways that men have lived in the past are of infinite human value; and there is no way of life any more quite like that of the old strollers, though that of the itinerant circus and fair comes perhaps nearest. In an unromantic age they lived a romantic, nomadic life. The wanderer has ever a primitive appeal to the imagination of men, and these 'Pedlars in Poetry and Gypsies of the Stage'[3] exercise, like the tramps and vagrants of to-day, their eternal fascination upon the adventuring mind.

[1] *A History of Early Eighteenth-Century Drama*, 1925, pp. 59 *et seq.*
[2] Tate Wilkinson as far back as 1790 complained that rival diversions were ruining the country theatres (*Memoirs*, vol. IV, p. 103).
[3] James Ralph, *The Taste of the Town*, p. 223.

Chapter I

THE STROLLING LIFE

'I saw an open waggon, with a woman and two or three children at the
top, some old boxes, with what appeared to be scenes and a green curtain;
and to confirm and crown the whole, a drum at the head; a picture of the
paraphernalia of a poor strolling company.'
            E. C. EVERARD, *Memoirs of an Unfortunate Son of Thespis.*

A general picture of the stroller's life and the conditions
under which he worked seemed necessary as a background
to the fuller details revealed in the subsequent chapters on
particular companies.[1] For this survey I have gone to the
memoirs written by the strollers themselves. The majority
of them actually describe times later than my period, but
such was the conservatism of the smaller companies, with
which they mostly deal, that the descriptions apply equally
well to preceding decades. And because most of the adventures of the memoir writers took place among these lesser
troupes they also supplement the information in the succeeding chapters, which are rather occupied with the
activities of the established and reputable companies.

The facts here presented are mainly culled from the
following classics of strolling:

GEORGE AKERBY, *Life of James Spiller*, 1729.

THOMAS MOZEEN, *Young Scarron*, 1752.

CHARLOTTE CHARKE, *A Narrative of the Life of Mrs Charlotte
    Charke* [1755].

OLIVER GOLDSMITH, 'Adventures of a Strolling Player', *Essays*,
    1765, Essay XXI.

GEORGE PARKER, *A View of Society and Manners*, 1781.

---

[1] Cf. Alwin Thaler, *Strolling Players and Provincial Drama after Shakespeare*, P.M.L.A. 1922, p. 243.

TATE WILKINSON, *Memoirs*, 1790.

JOHN WILLIAMS [pseud. Anthony Pasquin], *Eccentricities of John Edwin*, 1791.

TATE WILKINSON, *The Wandering Patentee*, 1795.

WILLIAM TEMPLETON, *The Strolling Player*, 1802.

CHARLES LEE LEWES, *Memoirs*, 1805.

PETER PANGLOS [pseud.], *Memoirs of Sylvester Daggerwood* [1806].

S. W. RYLEY, *The Itinerant*, 1808.

E. C. EVERARD, *Memoirs of an Unfortunate Son of Thespis*, 1818.

PIERCE EGAN, *The Life of an Actor*, 1824.

JOHN BERNARD, *Retrospections of the Stage*, 1830.

(a) Joining the Company

In London there were certain inns in the neighbourhood of Covent Garden which were used as houses of call where country managers could be sure of meeting unemployed comedians. They were frequented by actors of all ranks and kinds and you would find there 'a well-dressed gentleman of the Theatre-Royal in earnest conversation with a Country Player without a shirt'.[1] The manager in approaching a player would ask not only what parts he had played, but also the number of 'lengths' he could study nightly. A length was forty-two lines and the enquiry a most necessary one, since a country actor was often called upon to learn a long part at two or three days' notice. Sometimes the manager would not come himself to engage performers but would send out a member of his company to recruit them. Thus Wilkinson was commissioned by the manager of the Portsmouth Company to find a new actress, and obtained Miss Morrison from Bath,[2] and Linnett sent a special envoy to secure the services of Mrs Charke.[3]

Unscrupulous managers did not hesitate to misinform applicants as to the condition and profits of their troupes. In later days they would promise a certain salary, and when the

[1] Geo. Parker, *op. cit.* vol. I, p. 69.

[2] *Memoirs*, vol. II, p. 92.   [3] *Op. cit.* vol. I, p. 166.

actor had joined the company, would either reduce it, or even put him on the then despised sharing terms.[1]

A lively picture of the formation of a company of London actors to visit the provinces is given by Thomas Mozeen, who was writing from personal experience:

When the Time draws near that the Theatres Royal disband their Troops...each private Man becomes an Officer; and they who for nine Months before submitted to monarchical Government, now form themselves into several Republicks for the remaining three. Then each Hero takes the Path of his own Ambition; the different Parties assemble at different Places, where each has a Vote for Laws, a choice of Parts, and a Title to particular Dresses; and the Man that was but just of Consequence enough to make one of his Body Guard in December, is scarce contented with Alexander in June.[2]

A stock of scenes and clothes was obtainable from managers who had given up business and who rented them out on a small security. Hiring stock in this way was a regular trade in Monmouth Street. The disputes among the actors over the division of these clothes were long and bitter. Poor Mozeen tells us that his whole work for four days 'was not, as I design'd, to pick out proper Dresses for the Company, but to prevent the Company picking out one another's Eyes'. An actress would even demand a dress for every part she was to play though 'they would be more than a dozen Waggons could carry'. It was the same with parts. The actors suddenly acquired extraordinary opinions of their own merits 'and hardly one but what would sacrifice his best Friend, rather than give up a Part'. The tragedians wanted to try themselves out in comedy, and the comedians fancied themselves in tragedy; the task of reconciling the conflicting claims must have been an unenviable one.

Managers who had engaged actors were accustomed to send them money to defray their travelling expenses. Parker puts these 'charges', as they were called, for joining the

[1] *Memoirs of Sylvester Daggerwood*, vol. II, p. 82. [2] *Op. cit.* p. v.

company at one guinea per 100 miles, Weston[1] at a half a guinea plus the payment of carriage for the performer's belongings. Mrs Charke asked Elrington for three guineas to cover her journey, with that of her friend and daughter, from Corsham in Wilts. to Tiverton, and he sent two and a half guineas by a messenger on horseback. On the other hand, the actors in Mozeen's *Young Scarron* had to travel at their own expense though they were lent five guineas with which to hire carriages; the money thus advanced being stopped out of their shares. Some made the journey by coach, some by waggon, and yet others on horseback. John Edwin and Tate Wilkinson could even afford to join companies by post chaise. But the poorer sort tramped. Mrs Charke walked from London to Dartford, a distance of about 15 miles, in five hours, and played that evening. On another occasion she journeyed from Devizes to Romsey on 4*s.*, mostly on foot, though she was given a lift in a waggon for five miles for 1½*d.* This was the most usual mode of travel for those actors who had not been definitely engaged, but tramped the roads in the hope of falling in with some itinerants who would admit them as sharers.

(b) *Managers, Actors and Others*

Managers or masters of companies varied considerably. We hear a great deal of their rapacity and the hard treatment they meted out to their companies, a matter to be more fully dealt with under benefits. Parker speaks of a company in which the actors were in rags whilst the manager strutted in a blue-and-gold lace coat and waistcoat, red breeches, a silver-laced hat and black stockings. In the *Memoirs of Sylvester Daggerwood* we read that 'these sharing managers are all alike—all sad scoundrels', and Mrs Charke,[2] who has not a good word to say for the strolling life, inveighs against their 'impertinent power'. Unscrupulous managers there

---

[1] *Memoirs of Tom Weston*, 1776.   [2] Charke, *op. cit.* p. 167.

were in plenty. Elrington deserted his company without a word for a London engagement, leaving them stranded without enough money to pay their carriage to the next town; Mossop was in the habit of never announcing his last night and stealing out of town with his bills unpaid.[1] Dennis Herbert, on the other hand, though he was accustomed to drink ninety-three half pints of beer in a day, luckily had a provident wife who kept a hold on the cash, and paid his tradespeople's bills punctually every morning after play night.[2]

There is, however, a brighter side to the picture. We hear of good and respected masters and of many acts of generosity. Powell had an agreement with Everard whereby that latter could sell £5 worth of tickets for his benefit without deduction; if he sold more, half was to go to the management; though he sold £20 worth Powell never deducted a penny. Kemble sent a poor performer whose benefit failed £10, with a receipt in full for the charges which he had not paid.[3] Once, when Everard was in great straits he applied for a job to Herbert at Lynn; Herbert had no vacancy but, seeing his condition, slipped half a guinea into his hand. Another manager, having inherited a fortune, gave liberal presents to his company.[4] Neither were the managers always well dressed whilst the company went in rags. Ryley describes the shabbiness of one Davis, and his philosophic attitude: 'If he had money, which was rarely the case, he laughed and lent it; if he had none he laughed and did without it.' A manager had to be a jack of all trades as he might be called upon to do anything; Ryley describes how amazed he was to find one, in his shirt sleeves, printing the bills whilst his wife washed the property clothes.

About the actors themselves the most prominent and reiterated fact is their poverty. Parker describes one company as being 'in a deplorable pickle, ragged and emaciated; yet

---

[1] *Eccentricities of John Edwin*, vol. I, p. 33.   [2] Lewes, *op. cit.* vol. I, p. 70.
[3] Ryley, *op. cit.* vol. III, p. 335.   [4] Templeton, *op. cit.* vol. II, p. 73.

some shreds of old lace were visible either in the hats, breeches, or petticoats of these poor deplorable mortals'. Templeton contrasts the happy, secure lot of the London actor with that of the poor strollers whose attire was often little better than a beggar's so that 'I often', he says, 'sickened at the prospect of their distress.' Frequently they went without food and, after a week's work, their only profit might be a stock supper 'which was generally ended in a Quarrel by Way of Desert'.[1] It it not to be wondered at that bad business, as Mrs Charke relates, frayed the tempers and undermined the morale of the company: 'for, as they grow hungry, they naturally grow peevish, and fall out with one another, without considering that each bears a proportionable Part of the Distress, the Manager excepted'.

If they had not enough to eat, they often had too much to drink. The women of one company drank themselves into fainting fits on the stage.[2] One actress in Elrington's Company was dead drunk in bed when she should have been playing Lucy in *The Beggar's Opera* on the opening night at Tiverton, and Mrs Elrington had to step in and contrive to double the parts of Lucy and Polly.[3]

Another outcome of the shocking poverty of many strollers was debt. James Spiller, the low comedian, though comparatively well off, was often in arrears, 'especially at the Tap', and was once seized by bailiffs just as he was going on the stage. As he was to act the Country Squire in *Æsop*, he prevailed on the bailiffs to lead the hounds on the stage and, whilst they were so engaged, successfully made his escape.[4]

Such pranks of the comedians must have saved many a situation and helped the company to endure. A good humour, bonhomie and comradeship often prevailed, so that Everard was once shocked to come upon a 'company...so refractory, so opposite, so obstinate, so unlike comedians'. Ryley was told by an actor: 'We players are a set of merry,

[1] Mrs Charke, *op. cit.* p. 161.   [2] *Eccentricities of John Edwin*, vol. I, p. 19.
[3] Mrs Charke, *op. cit.* p. 161.   [4] G. Akerby, *op. cit.* p. 8.

undone dogs, and though we often want the means of life, we are seldom without the means of mirth. We are philosophers...and laugh at misfortune; even the ridiculous situations we are sometimes placed in, are more generally the cause of mirth than misery.' Meeting a strolling company on the road, the same writer comments on their imperturbable good humour, the liveliness of their continual sallies, and their 'free, easy, and unembarrassed' air. Bernard, too, remarked of a poverty-stricken troupe: 'never under all the inflictions of empty pockets and empty bellies were a merrier, more care-despising group.' On the other hand, jealousy, petty spite and envy as frequently riddled a company with dissension. Mrs Charke says,

The least Glimmering or Shade of Acting, in Man or Woman, is a sure Motive of Envy in the rest; and, if their Malice can't perswade the Town's-People into a Dislike of their Performance, they'll cruelly endeavour to taint their Characters; so that I think going a Strolling is engaging in a little, dirty Kind of War...And to say Truth, I am not only sick, but heartily ashamed of it, as I have had nine Years Experience of its being a very contemptible Life; rendred so, through the impudent and ignorant Behaviours of the Generality of those who pursue it.

Templeton blames the actors on other grounds: 'No people expose themselves so much: they talk loud in the streets, are overbearing in public company, and at the theatre break out into all the insolence of self-importance.' Yet later he grieves that even the most respectable country actor had to demean himself in degrading fashion to the gentry, to secure a tolerable benefit: 'he must go cap in hand, and with the humblest demeanour, paint his distress, and solicit their support: or he must attend their nocturnal revels, wait upon their smiles, and feed them with his jests. He must spout, sing, and be every way subservient to their wishes, and, after thus debasing human dignity, it is well if he finds himself enriched with a few guineas.' In a later chapter we shall see how Tate Wilkinson rebelled against similar practices at York.

Here and there we have glimpses of other members of the
company who were not actors,[1] although they might be
called upon, at need, to take a part on the stage. Parker
describes stage-keepers as 'usually...as greasy and black as
lamplighters'. Candle-snuffing was a despised position,
sometimes undertaken by the local ostler,[2] but even the
candle-snuffer might, at a pinch, be given a part,[3] and
managers such as Burton and Hippisley began their theatrical
careers in this capacity; so, too, might the prompter, whose
business it sometimes was, in addition, to engage the menials
of the theatre.[4] Door-keepers or checkers were so notoriously
swindlers that they gave rise to the cant term 'player queer
checkers'. Their method of cheating is described by Parker,[5]
who tells how one woman maintained a family for many
years on her ill-gotten gains, and confessed on her deathbed
to having swindled the company to the tune of £1200.

The better companies had their own musicians who were
also used as actors. They and the dancers sometimes eked out
a living by giving lessons in the towns where they played,[6]
just as later some actors took to giving recitations or lectures.
When the company travelled without musicians they had to
rely on local talent, which led to embarrassments and difficulties. In one village, visited by Ryley, only two blind
fiddlers 'who set harmony at defiance' could be produced,
in another the help of a doctor had to be enlisted, who was
subsequently insulted by a playful audience at the performance.[7] The circulating of playbills was undertaken in the
small companies by inferior actors who were sometimes
called orators and were paid 1s. a day for the town and 2s.
for the country.[8]

---

[1] See chapter X for information as to salaries, etc.
[2] See *post*, p. 265.   [3] Goldsmith, *op. cit.*
[4] Parker, *op. cit.* vol. I, p. 64.   [5] *Ibid.* vol. II, p. 123.
[6] Everard, *op. cit.* p. 131.   [7] *Op. cit.* vol. III, pp. 10, 227.
[8] Ryley, *op. cit.* vol. II, p. 176.

(c) On the Road

We have already seen how individuals travelled to join companies. The companies themselves moved from town to town in just as many ways, depending on their circumstances. The quotation at the head of the chapter gives a vivid picture of a company's progression. The York comedian, Joseph Yarrow, provides another in 'An Epilogue, made by a Gentleman of Hereford, occasion'd by meeting a Company of Strolers on the Road':[1]

> From Hereford the Jovial Crew departed,
> Kings walk'd on Foot, and Princesses were Carted:
> In pure Compassion to the Maiden Queen
> That wanted but a Month of Lying-In.
> Thus on a Heap lay pil'd; there the Brandy Bottle,
> Here the Child.—
> Great Montezuma hir'd an humble Hack,
> And he that grasp'd the World bestrid a Pack:
> Great Oroonoko from his Privy Purse,
> Cou'd not afford Imoinda poor a Horse:
> Young Ammon, staying late behind the rest,
> Was in great Danger too of being prest.
> But Faith it would have made the Greatest laugh,
> To see the Truncheon[2] knuckle to the Staff.
> Thus, on the Road, no more but common Men,
> Once got to Ludlow, then all Kings again.

At worst the company tramped with their belongings on their shoulders: 'each member took a portion of the scenery or wardrobe on his back, and trudged on to where they next intended to establish themselves;...nor were the Ladies excused on such occasions.'[3] Parker mentions the 'Village Hunters' of one night stands who 'each carried the poles and canvass which constituted their Theatre, in their hands; and the first barn which received them answered their purpose'.

---

[1] A Choice Collection of Poetry, 1738, p. 47.
[2] The accompaniment of the tragedian.
[3] Petronius Arbiter [pseud.], Memoirs of the Present Countess of Derby.

Another company walked every week from Poole to Wimborne and back for the sake of one night's performance at the latter.[1] Only in the more prosperous companies could coaches be afforded. The manager, and those who were unable to walk, travelled with the baggage by waggon. There were often accidents on the road. Owing to the carelessness of a waggoner the Bath Company once lost by fire all their properties, together with the personal gear of the actors. Waggons sometimes overturned, burying their human load among the properties.[2]

Usually the troupe would have some bright distinction in their dress to mark them off from ordinary mortals. At Newby Bridge Ryley's eye was caught by a band of itinerants: one was adorned with a gold-laced cocked hat and long ruffles, another wore scarlet, all had tarnished gold on their waistcoats and silk stockings; the women, too, were 'removed from plainness' and made a smart, showy appearance. Especially when entering towns the actors would appear in some striking habit or finery. One family dressed their eight children in scarlet to attract attention;[3] Jimmy Whitely, when entering a town of importance, donned his Don Felix suit of pink silk and white satin, spangled and slashed, and paraded an enormously long feather and a rapier; thus arrayed, and accompanied by a boy with a bell, he was wont to announce his performances from the market place.[4] We hear, too, of a bill deliverer sporting a suit of blue and gold, with a gold-laced hat and a gold-headed cane.[5] Even when the company were reduced to tatters, some remnants of gold or lace usually remained on their clothes.

Two actors were generally sent ahead to get leave to play, since a licence had to be obtained from the mayor or magistrates at every town or village. Sometimes permission

[1] *Memoirs of Sylvester Daggerwood*, p. 155.
[2] Ryley, *op. cit.* vol. I, p. 250. Goldsmith, *op. cit.*
[3] Ryley, *op. cit.* vol. I, p. 250.
[4] Bernard, *op. cit.* vol. I, p. 159.   [5] *Ibid.* p. 102.

was granted on condition that a benefit was to be given, or money paid for the poor of the parish. A friendly mayor would occasionally bespeak a performance. The visiting of the authorities, together with the hiring of the barn or other suitable accommodation, was known as 'taking the town', and managers would pride themselves on their ability to achieve this successfully. One, for instance, explained to Ryley[1] that the best way of winning the magistrate was to visit him at 4.30, when his worship was taking his wine in his easy chair, and to take a glass with him. In the accounts of a small strolling company preserved in the British Museum 'Taking the Town' is put down among the expenses at 1s. or 1s. 6d.[2]

The first business of the company, on arrival in a town, was to beat the drum, gather a crowd together, and distribute playbills. When Herbert's Company omitted the ceremony of the drum at Grantham, they played, in consequence, to empty houses; and it was not until they resumed the customary practice, at the request of the Marquis of Granby, that they retrieved their fortunes.[3]

The actors lodged at inns, or in rooms with the butcher, the baker and the candle-stick maker. Landlords were well accustomed to give credit when performances failed. In Lincolnshire Everard lodged and boarded for 8s. a week; elsewhere he and his wife were comfortably boarded for 4s. a week.

(d) Theatres and Properties

Almost any room might serve as a theatre. The more reputable companies, as we shall see, were housed in inns, inn-yards, town halls, public rooms, and the like. The poorer itinerants had to make do with barns, stables, cowsheds and haylofts. Parker mentions acting in a half-clean stable in which the pigsty, 'not entirely free from the scent of its old

[1] Op. cit. vol. II, p. 289.   [2] Add. MS. 33,488.
[3] Wilkinson, Memoirs, vol. III, p. 130.

inhabitants', was the dressing-room. On another occasion it was 'a horrid wreck of a barn, with a few bits of candle stuck in clay to light the dismal hole'. The rain often poured through the broken roof of such wrecks, and one was half carried away by a storm.[1] Wooden booths, temporarily erected in the fields on the edge of the town, often served the purposes of a theatre. One such shelter had only a wooden bar to divide the pit from the gallery, and the boxes had the air of being flour bins adorned with green baize.[2] The hayloft in a barn sometimes formed a gallery; the boxes were made by nailing rough boards on to uprights; and the stage was divided from the pit by a board with holes as sockets for the footlights.[3] The frontispiece gives an excellent idea of the inconveniences of a barn theatre, as does Hogarth's more famous picture of 'Actresses Dressing in a Barn'.

Inns, too, were not always very convenient. Everard writes indignantly of how 'in a paltry public house, we played in a paltry room up two stories high, with a few seats put down miscalled pit and gallery'. Parker describes a village performance at which the alehouse served as the ladies' dressing-room, the blacksmith's shop as the men's; the doors of alehouse and forge were entrances to the theatre, the curtain consisted of bed curtains strung on pack thread and the back cloth was made out of furniture paper. Bernard's first experience of the stage was in a large inn room in which the manager had

suspended a collection of green tatters along its middle for a curtain, erected a pair of paper screens right-hand and left for wings; arranged four candles in front of said wings to divide the stage from the orchestra (the fiddlers' chairs being legitimate division of the orchestra from the Pit), and with all the spare benches of the inn to form boxes, and a hoop suspended from the ceiling (perforated with a dozen nails, to receive as many tallow candles) to suggest the idea of a chandelier; he had constructed and embellished what he denominated a Theatre.

[1] Parker, *op. cit.* vol. I, p. 222.
[2] Templeton, *op. cit.* vol. III, p. 107.   [3] Bernard, *op. cit.* p. 241.

The scenery consisted of two drops 'simply and comprehen-
sively divisible into the inside of a house, and the outside of a
house'. It is interesting to note that even when the curtains
were but tatters they had to be the traditional green.

Properties were apt to be few and far between, though they
were made to sound imposing enough on the bills. In
Breval's farce *The Strolers*, printed in 1727, one of the
characters boasts: 'we have a Mustard Bowl to make
Thunder, and our Fidlers can find us Rosin for Lightening...
we have a Second-hand Dragon, that lost a Wing and two
Claws in an opera last Winter.' Though written in mockery,
this is probably not far from the truth, for we remember that
Mrs Charke estimated the contents of a heavy property box
as 'scabardless, rusty Swords, and departed Mopsticks, trans-
migrated into Tragedy Truncheons'. Yarrow laments in a
prologue[1] the lack of means with which to imitate London
spectacles:

> To aggravate the Case, we have not one,
> Of all the new Refinements of the Town:
> No moving Statues, no lewd Harlequins,
> No Pastboard Play'rs, no Heroes in Machines.
> No Rosin to flash Light'ning—'twould exhaust us,
> To buy a Devil, or a Doctor Faustus.
> No Windmills, Dragons, Millers, Conjurers,
> To exercise your Eyes, and spare your Ears.
> No Paper Seas, no Thunder from the Skies,
> No Witches to descend, no Stage to rise.

As for costumes, there were never enough to go round;
with the consequence that bitter wrangles continually arose.
In Mozeen's story there were but four tragedy dresses for
women in the whole wardrobe. These were seized by two
actresses, one of whom wore a second as an under-petticoat,
the other ripped her second one up to make a train. Nothing
then was left for the heroine but 'common Gowns and

---

[1] *Op. cit.* Spence, *Anecdotes*, 1858, p. 294, quotes this prologue as by
Charles Pitt for the Blandford strollers.

Petticoats...scarce grand enough for Comedy'. A deprived fury thereupon flew at one of the offenders, tore her head-dress to pieces and rushed out of the theatre so that her part had to be omitted and the play maimed. Another night the company was compelled to perform *Tamerlane* in modern dress for lack of eastern habits, and Bajazet had to make do with 'a Tallow-chandler's Frock, for an Under-Dress, ty'd round with a Serjeant's Sash; and over it, a blue Stuff Night-Gown, which was design'd to pass for a Robe'; these rags were ornamented with white paper spotted with ink to imitate ermine. The devices to which the actors were forced to resort in the matter of costume are ridiculed by Goldsmith, who describes how 'the same coat that served Romeo, turned with a blue lining outwards, served for his friend Mercutio: a large piece of crape sufficed at once for Juliet's petticoat and pall: a pestle and mortar from a neighbouring apothecary's answered all the purposes of a bell; and our landlord's own family, wrapped in white sheets, served to fill up the procession'. Mrs Charke had actually seen 'a Queen with one Ruffle on, and Lord Townly without shoes, or at least but an Apology for them'. She also tells how an actress, who played the Queen in *The Spanish Fryar*, lent her stockings to the actor who played Torrismond, as his were full of holes, and had to go through the performance stooping to hide her bare legs. The company which Edwin joined, that acted *Romeo and Juliet* in dresses of coloured frieze edged with gilt leather, were comparatively well off, though their music consisted of but two fiddlers who stood on the left side of the barn stage and accompanied the songs between the acts. It often happened that the principal performers wore reason-ably good costumes whilst those of the subordinates were despicable.[1] Occasionally an actor or actress would be possessed of an excellent wardrobe: Mrs Barrington, for ex-ample, played in Maidstone with Peg Woffington's tragedy jewels;[2] but this was the exception, not the rule.

[1] Templeton, *op. cit.* vol. II, p. 12.   [2] Wilkinson, *Memoirs*, vol. I, p. 134.

Nevertheless the more established companies, as we shall see, could attempt quite elaborate spectacles, and, even discounting the big talk of the playbills and advertisements, their resources were evidently far and away superior to those of the humbler itinerants with whom the memoirs are mostly concerned.

(e) The Acting

Many smaller companies were as short of actors as they were of properties. Parker was once with a troupe in which there were only five men, so that the actress who took Lady Townly had to perform John Moody too, a doubling which involved quick changes of clothes. Templeton remarks that it was 'no novelty for the same person to perform two, or even three characters in the same piece, proceeding from the scarcity of performers; while the principal actors have perhaps five or six parts assigned them for each successive night'. King once told how, when he had been but a short time on the stage, he 'performed one night King Richard, gave two comic songs, played in an interlude, danced a horn pipe, spoke a prologue, afterwards Harlequin, in a sharing company, and, after all this fatigue, my share came to three pence, and two pieces of candle'.[1] Bernard opened his career in a troupe in which there were three men: one played tyrants in tragedies and the French horn in the 'orchestra', the manager was prompter, money taker, scene painter, machinist and fiddle player and would play two parts a night behind the scenes, the third played the lovers, sang, danced and performed tricks; yet three times a week this brave band 'put William Shakespeare on the rack, to the delight of the red-headed bumpkins of Hampshire'. He further speaks of the strange situation which arose when, from paucity of players, Romeo had to toll the bell for his own death and dead Juliet had to sing her own dirge! A foolish manager, too, would cause unnecessary difficulties by assigning one

[1] E. C. Everard, op. cit. p. 62.

part to several actors and thus find himself without anyone to take another part in the same play. Everard remembers an instance where there were seven Archers and no Aimwell for a performance of *The Beaux Stratagem*. A comedian sometimes wished, and sometimes was compelled, to take tragic roles. James Spiller, a low comedian, played in the country, where heroes were not plentiful, Mithridates and Alexander, 'although it must needs be confessed, excellent as he was in his own Way these Parts were but burlesqu'd by him'.[1]

The shortage of actors meant hard work and great versatility: it also entailed rapid studying of parts. Parker knew an actor who was given the part of Iago on Monday and had to play it on Wednesday; another, we learn, had two days in which to prepare Sir George Airy and no rehearsal,[2] a third three days for Lord Townly.[3] The consequence was that country actors were known to be imperfect in their parts. There is an incident in *Young Scarron* of an actor in the role of Moneses in *Tamerlane* who, 'though he had cut above Half his Part, was not able to repeat the little Matter that was left....This set the Audience a hissing, which so provok'd Arpasia (who was perfect in the whole Play) that she could not help shewing it was not her Fault, by prompting Mr Broad to every Line'; whereupon the indignant culprit told her he knew what he was about, and, turning to the audience, assured them that he was perfect in the character but disconcerted by the prompting; then, lugging on the prompter, he desired his opinion. Mrs Charke says that 'were the Spirits of departed Poets to see their Works mangled and butchered, as I have too often been a melancholy Witness of, they would certainly kick the depredating Heroes out of this World into the next'. It was not unknown for the company to indulge in mixing several plays together when they thought their audience would be none the wiser. Mrs Charke was in

[1] Akerby, *op. cit.* p. 7.   [2] *Memoirs of Sylvester Daggerwood*, p. 153.
[3] Mozeen, *op. cit.* p. 181.

a performance of *The Beaux Stratagem* at which, because the audience consisted of drunken butchers and their wives, the performers had a grand lark, breaking into a 'Wild-goose Chace through all the dramatic Authors we could recollect, taking particular Care not to let any single Speech bear in the Answer the least Affinity; and, while I was making Love from Jaffeir, she tenderly approv'd my Passion with the Soliloquy of Cato'. On another occasion, the initiative came from a member of the audience who desired her, when she was tragedising as Pyrrhus in *The Distress'd Mother*, to mix a few of Scrub's speeches from *The Beaux Stratagem* in that play. Ryley tells us of a performance of *Pizarro* that was received with applause, though 'to find out what they were at, or what play it was they were representing, would have puzzled the oldest performer on the stage,... the parts were composed of speeches from various plays—Hamlet, Douglas, Macbeth, Jane Shore, Othello, etc.'

Mrs Charke's complaint, that the wretchedness of country acting was, in part, due to the unsuitability for the stage of the tradesmen, prentices and journeymen who tried their fortunes on it, is confirmed by Mozeen who says: 'The Strolling Companies are commonly a Set of undutiful 'Prentices, idle Artificers, and Boys run mad with reading what they don't understand.' Even after long practice in the country they never, he continues, prove more than useful performers in the London theatres. He avers further that you can tell a country from a town actor, 'For they all bring home a Whine of their Education.' According to Mrs Charke 'the Difference of them is upon an Equality with a Mouse-trap and a Mountain'. An actor, Pasquin remarks, that is good in York will be but indifferent in London. We know, however, that this is not altogether true and that a few actors who started their careers in the country made their name in London. Indeed Templeton, on the contrary, expressly tells us that he saw little of the supposed distinction and would acknowledge pre-eminence only in a very few leading per-

formers at Drury Lane. One advantage the stroller certainly
had—a wider variety of experience. Knipe once told Barry
that he would not be worth half a share in a country company because he would not play Othello and Jobson, in the
afterpiece, on the same evening without a murmur.[1]

Nevertheless London experience was carefully advertised
by managers in their playbills, and was certainly looked up
to by the audience. We read in the *Memoirs of Sylvester
Daggerwood* that you were sure of approbation if you came
from a London theatre, though you had been but an under-
ling there; and, according to Goldsmith, an actress of nine
months' London experience was deferred to as a judge.

Rehearsals usually took place in the morning. After
Herbert's company had been reflected upon for the slovenly
manner in which they conducted their rehearsals, they agreed
to begin every day, Sundays excepted, at 10 a.m. and to
allow only ten minutes' grace to late comers. As is evident
from the Bristol Account Book non-attendance at rehearsals
meant a forfeiting of one's share at the performance, though
whether or not this was the general practice, it is not possible
to tell.[2]

(f) The Sharing System and Benefits

A more detailed consideration of the sharing system, on
which nearly all country companies were in those times run,
will be found in the chapter on the Bristol Account Book.
A brief outline and a few additional points only will be given
here.

At the end of every performance a list of expenses was
made out; these were deducted from the evening's total
receipts, and the remaining profit was shared out among the
actors and actresses of the company in equal shares. It did not
matter whether you had been in the play or not, or whether
you had a small or a large part in it: all received the same

[1] *Eccentricities of John Edwin*, vol. i, p. 187.
[2] See *post*, p. 213. Everard says it was usual in salaried companies.

amount. All, that is to say, except the manager, who took five shares, one for acting, the other four, known as dead shares, for his expenses in connection with scenery, wardrobe and general running of the company. Weston says it was the manager's duty, too, to act as treasurer and keep the stock book in which the accounts were set down, to share out the money, and to fix the plays. Even the remains of the candles were shared.[1]

Most of the later memoir writers have not a good word to say for the sharing system, which was then in the decline. Ryley calls it 'an iniquitous business, by which the manager laid his hands upon everything and gave the poor actor a paltry, scanty subsistence'. In fact rascally managers could, and no doubt did, cheat their companies by trumping up what was known as the stock debt. The stock debt was the accumulation of big bills that the management owed. Sometimes the manager would discharge these out of his own pocket at the conclusion of a season and would then assume the right to take the money from future successful nights. This was fair enough if the manager played fair, but it became proverbial that the stock debt was never paid. Ryley knew of a company where the stock debt had been £400 for years, though he was convinced that it had been paid off over and over again. It thus was capable of becoming, as he points out, a stalking horse 'under semblance of which the manager, can rob and plunder at pleasure'. Ryley also felt that the system was unjust. He once shared for three weeks without playing at all, and, though he only played twice in the following five weeks, his share was equal to that of those who had played long and arduously every night.

Yet, for all the abuses which attended it, there is a great deal to be said for this sharing principle. Not only did it make every actor vitally interested in the proceeds of every performance, but it gave him a feeling of equality and

[1] *Ante*, p. 25. At benefits the candles were given to the actor whose benefit it was (*Eccentricities of John Edwin*, vol. i, p. 197 and *post*, p. 255).

fellowship with the other players, and a responsibility towards them. By virtue of it a company had the rights and advantages of a commonwealth.

Actors did not depend so much on the shares as on their benefits. Parker, when engaged in an Irish company, was told that his benefits would bring him more than £200 a year, while his shares would merely serve as pocket money. Bernard says it was customary for sharers to live on credit until their benefit, as the receipts rarely did more than meet ordinary expenses. The first question that was asked of a London actor when he returned from a summer in the country was: 'How did your benefit turn out?'[1]

All kinds of arrangements were made about benefits. Actors were careful to contract for the number they could have and whether they should be single or double (i.e. solus or shared). A tax imposed by the manager on benefits was called a 'saddle' and was much resented. Parker says that a certain Winchester manager extorted two guineas on each person's benefit, and in addition charged some of the stock debt on the benefits.In the *Memoirs of Sylvester Daggerwood* it is hinted that when the benefit drew a full house the manager would, as likely as not, trump up a stock debt and thus deprive the actor, whose benefit it was, of much of his earnings. As we have seen, an actor was sometimes allowed to sell for clear profit a given amount's worth of tickets; any money that he brought in after that sum had to be shared with the management. According to another arrangement, the manager would charge £10 for benefit expenses for which the actor had to give his note of hand. If he chose to have a double benefit it was £5 down and 'half over'—that is, half any further profits to be shared with the manager—for which both actors must give a joint security up to £10.[2] Occasionally when the charges of the house exceeded the receipts both from the actor's sale of tickets and the cash taken at the door,

---

[1] E. C. Everard, *op. cit.* p. 42.
[2] *Memoirs of Sylvester Daggerwood*, vol. I, p. 157.

the actor might have to pay the deficit.[1] A scoundrelly manager had even been known to dismiss an actor as soon as he had paid his benefit charges. On the other hand we hear, too, of actors who, having money in their pockets from their benefit, 'fled from their Company in a tarnished lace waistcoat and a gold button and loop, dressed like fiddlers, squandering their money in dissipation'.[2]

The whole benefit system put the actor in a position of inferiority and dependence. He had to go begging from door to door, visiting the gentry for the favour of their patronage, and cringing in gratitude thereafter. Tate Wilkinson was one of the first to make a stand against these customs. He found it was the practice in Norwich, York and Hull for the performer, whose benefit it was, to attend the playbill man round the town, knocking at every door, and stopping at every shop and stall to leave a bill. Templeton once distributed nine hundred bills for his benefit. Nor were the women exempt from trudging from door to door in any weather.

Fortunate was the actor who could get a bespeak for his benefit. He would tramp miles out to the mansion of a local worthy in the attempt to get his night bespoken. The worthy would then sell the tickets among his friends and have what was tantamount to a private performance of any play he chose from the company's repertoire. Thus Parker joined a poor company at Taunton-Dean and went at once into the country, with a bill to Lady Willoughby, who bespoke *The Provok'd Husband*. More often than not the actor was met with a rebuff. Ryley has one or two stories of the rude and offensive treatment that he received at the hands of the gentry when he went to beg the favour of a bespeak; not, in this instance, for his benefit but for the sake of a more or less starving company. Sometimes an actor was lucky, as

[1] E. C. Everard, *op. cit.* p. 42. Kemble never exacted more in charges than was in the house.

[2] Parker, *op. cit.* vol. I, p. 69.

Everard was when the manager Powell gave him an introduction to some families who purchased many tickets from
him at one guinea or half a guinea each. It often happened
that the cash for the tickets was not immediately forthcoming
and the actor had to walk out and gather in the money. He
was anyway expected to wait on his friends and patrons the
morning after the benefit, to return thanks.[1]

The actor was allowed to choose the play for his benefit,
but often came to his decision in consultation with his friends,
or with those who were taking tickets. The manager and
more prominent members of the company frequently
arranged to have a new play or afterpiece, or both, produced
on their nights.

(g) The Audience

In a letter from Elizabeth Montagu[2] to the Duchess of Portland, dated October 15, 1738, we have a picture of the
country gentry going to visit a play: 'Lady T— bespoke a
play at a town eight miles from us, and summoned us to it;
and two of my brothers, my sister, and your humble servant,
went according to her Ladyship's commands, and after the
play the gentlemen invited all the women to a supper at the
inn, where we staid till two o'clock in the morning.... We
had seven coaches at the play'; on the way home two of the
coaches overturned and many of the company caught colds
and other ailments. Going to the theatre in the country was
an adventure, yet sometimes people came from many miles
away. We hear of the actors being joined at supper at the
inn by the townspeople after the performance,[3] or of the
principal ladies and gentlemen of the place coming to compliment a particular actor on his success.[4]

The strollers were dependent on the local gentry to fill the
boxes. The presence of people of quality also naturally

[1] E. C. Everard, *op. cit.* p. 63.
[2] *The Letters of Mrs Elizabeth Montagu*, 1809, p. 47.
[3] Mozeen, *op. cit.* p. 116.   [4] Goldsmith, *op. cit.*

attracted the rest of the town. On the other hand they often made themselves a nuisance by sitting on the stage. As the pantomime and spectacle developed, their presence there became more of an embarrassment than ever, and there are continual notices regretting that permission could not be given to go behind the scenes or on the stage, as it interfered with the scene shifting, processions and other actions. Lee Lewes[1] once met with an accident whilst playing Harlequin, because the scenes were overcrowded with those who could not get into the front of the house, and were standing on the stage. A woman was stationed at the place where he was to escape and, though he succeeded in leaping over her head into the hole, he missed the carpet prepared to catch him and fell on the floor.

Mrs Charke thought that strollers did not pay enough attention to the tastes of the country gentry—among whom she considered there were great judges: 'It is for want of this Consideration in the Players, which makes the Favours they receive from Families of Distinction rather a Charity, than a genteel Reward.' She admits, however, that 'the lower Sort are foolish enough to be pleased with Buffoonery in Comedy, and Bellowing in Tragedy, without a Regard to Sense or Nature in either'. Not only was the majority of the audience completely undiscriminating, but they were liable to behave themselves very badly. When Parker acted at Gosport the sailors used to sing and drink flip during the performance, and would even occasionally hand bowls of punch to the actors. At York, Tate Wilkinson tells us, the upper gallery became so noisy and overcrowded on Shrove Tuesday that the company had to raise the prices on that night. Interruptions were apt to be embarrassing, as when Mrs Kirby as Anne in *Richard III* spoke her line, 'Oh when shall I have rest?' and was answered by a ruthless grocer, 'Not till you have paid me my one pound, one and tenpence, Ma'am.'[2] Often a simple spectator, unused to dramatic representations,

[1] *Op. cit.* vol. I, p. 67.   [2] Bernard, *op. cit.* vol. I, p. 53.

took the actor at his word: thus a grazier hearing Griffiths exclaiming 'My kingdom for a horse', immediately offered to supply him.[1]

In some of the regular circuit towns, as we shall see, societies bespoke evenings. The military and the freemasons, in particular, were often staunch supporters of the theatre in this way, and the actors responded by devising special songs and prologues for the occasion, much as to-day happens on Oxford and Cambridge boat-race night.

With all this variety how true it must have been that, as Ryley says in defence of the stroller, 'We see the world, and, by study and observation, acquire a greater knowledge of men and manners, than twice the number of years would give to a person tied to one situation.'

[1] Bernard, vol. I, p. 141.

Chapter II

THE PLAYERS IN NORWICH 1669–1709

The actor who spoke the prologue to Etherege's *Comical Revenge* in 1664 warned the audience that, if they continued to submit to the judgment of hostile critics,

> we and our Comedies
> Must trip to Norwich, or for Ireland go.

Norwich, then, was an acknowledged centre of theatrical activity, and it has in fact been shown that four companies of players, among them that of George Jolly, visited the city between 1660 and 1665.[1] The frequency with which puppet shows and other diversions invaded the town led to a complaint being made to the King in 1663, in which he was informed that one of the ill consequences of their visits was that 'the meaner sort of people' were diverted from their work. As a result the King granted to the Mayor and Sheriffs of Norwich and their successors power to determine the length of stay of such shows in the city, notwithstanding any licences from His Majesty or the Master of the Revels.[2] The players, before they could act, had, as usual, to present their licence and obtain permission from the Mayor's Court. An examination of the Court Books for the years 1669–1709[3] reveals that Norwich was well served for dramatic entertainment and presents us with a cross-section of the activities of

[1] See 'George Jolly at Norwich', by B. M. Wagner, *Review of English Studies*, 1930, p. 449.

[2] *Cal. S.P. Dom.* 1663, p. 200.

[3] Permission to quote from them is by courtesy of the Corporation of Norwich. Some items have already appeared in Walter Rye's *Extracts from the Court Books of the City of Norwich*, 1666–1688 (1905).

the strolling players at a period when little trace of them can be found elsewhere.

During the plague years no company is recorded as visiting Norwich but on September 22, 1669, the adventurous George Jolly reappears on a familiar scene in an entry: 'Liberty is given unto George Jolly of London gent & such persons as he shall choose and thinke fit to practise and make show of to exercise such plays opperas maskes showes scenes and ffasses [farces] & all other representations of the stage whatsoever in any convenient place wthin the City of Norwich.'[1] Jolly was at this time patentee of the London Nursery for training actors and he may have been travelling with a company from there.

Jolly, once established, was a difficult man to get rid of and on December 8 'Mr. Townclarke is desired to use all possible endeavers to obteyne an order to prevent ye acting of stage plaies in ye City'.[2] Soon after the corporation set about obtaining another order from the King empowering them to limit the stay of their unwelcome guests. A letter dated December 24, 1669, from Thomas Corie, the Recorder, to Sir Joseph Williamson[3] sets out the town's grievances: 'While attending Lord Arlington at Thetford, on Wednesday last, I presented a letter to him from the mayor and aldermen of Norwich, praying his assistance in obtaining a letter from his Majesty, authorising them and their successors to limit a time to stage and puppet players, lotteries and shows; by frequently resorting to Norwich, they divert the meaner sort of people from their labour in the manufactories, thereby occasioning a vain expense of time and money. His lordship has promised to comply, and desired me to request you to hasten the letter, as the players intend returning within 14 days.' The letter to Lord Arlington which is annexed puts the case even more forcibly against the players: 'by the frequent resort to which of the meaner sort of people, we

[1] Court Book, 1666–77, f. 121.   [2] *Ibid.* f. 127.
[3] *Cal. S.P. Dom.* October 1668–December 1669, p. 627.

have been much damnified in our manufactures...they drain too much money from the inhabitants, and the place is being daily impoverished by decay of trade, and the charge of maintaining the poor.' 'Remember my application,' Corie wrote to Williamson on January 5 and gave as an additional reason, 'the small pox still rages'.[1] 'Moved by the importunity of those who addressed Lord Arlington', Corie renewed his solicitations on January 28, 1670,[2] but the letter from the King, authorising 'you to determine the time during which the said players shall stay in the city, and they are to remain no longer, any licence from us or the Master of the Revels notwithstanding', was not sent until February 17.[3] Nevertheless a gratified Mayor's Court subscribed to a letter of thanks to Lord Arlington.[4] It is interesting to compare their complaint, which is mainly based on financial considerations, with that of the authorities in Bristol who were perturbed chiefly by fears of immorality and corruption.[5]

Whilst this was happening in Norwich, Edward Bedford, manager of the Nursery in London of which Jolly was patentee, obtained a licence from the King to act in the provinces with the Duke of Monmouth's Company. Professor Nicoll quotes from the Chamberlain's papers a warrant desiring the Clerk of the Signet to prepare a bill for the King's signature, licensing Bedford and the Duke of Monmouth's Company.[6] Professor Nicoll conjectures that this licence was used by Jolly's travelling company which then became the Duke of Monmouth's, and substance is given to this surmise by the fact that the warrant speaks of plays which the company 'have already studied or used' as though they were already in existence. But if Bedford were taking his Nursery Company on the road this would equally well apply to his troupe. The warrant is dated November 25,

[1] *Cal. S.P. Dom.* 1670, p. 5.   [2] *Ibid.* p. 39.
[3] *Ibid.* p. 71.   [4] Court Book, 1666–77, f. 132.
[5] See G. T. Watts, *Theatrical Bristol*, 1915.
[6] *Restoration Drama*, 1923, p. 279; L/C/5/12, p. 185.

1669, and it does not seem likely that Jolly had been acting in Norwich since September without a licence. Yet it is equally possible that he may merely have wanted a confirmation from the King of a licence already held from the Master of the Revels, since we know that in 1663 he had both. We cannot, however, be quite sure that Jolly's Company and that of the Duke of Monmouth were the same troupes.

After the trouble that they had experienced with Jolly the Court exercised the caution of granting only a week on May 25, 1672, to Cornelius Saffery and his associates in which 'to Act Comedies tragedies pastoralls & interludes'.[1] The players, however, obtained a week's extension on June 8, 'and they gave to the Hamper 20s.', a further licence on June 12 and a final one on June 19 for another week.[2] A contribution to 'the hamper' for the poor of the city was an alternative to the Mayor's play, by which the company gave a benefit performance for the same purpose.

On August 6 of the same year (1672) we first come across John Coysh and his company who are granted a week in which to play '& upon Aplication to Mr Maior at the end of this tyme, he may if he thinke fit give them a longer tyme'. This he did on August 14 and Coysh paid 40s. to the hamper.[3]

Coysh, too, had been at the Nursery. About 1667 he had induced Joseph Haines to join his company at Cambridge and, after visiting many towns, both actors joined Edward Bedford at the newly opened Nursery in Hatton Garden.[4] In a later reference, as we shall see, he is spoken of as the successor to Jolly's patent.

The connection with the Nursery continues the next year when John Perin appears, since Perin was Bedford's successor as manager of the Nursery. Apparently he also succeeded

[1] Court Book, 1666–77, f. 204.
[2] *Ibid.* ff. 205, 206.   [3] *Ibid.* ff. 212 v., 213 v.
[4] Tobias Thomas, *The Life of the Late Famous Comedian Jo. Haynes*, 1701.

Bedford as manager of his strolling company. 'Mr Perin who brought ye D. of Monmouths Patent' was granted a two weeks' licence on December 10, 1673 and another week's grace on January 10, 1674.[1] A further application on January 17 was refused: 'It is agreed that no longer time be allowed to Mr Perryn to make shew of any Playes after ye day and that some persons be apointed to see if he transgress ye Order'.[2]

The next company to visit Norwich was that of Robert Parker[3] who, on October 14, 1676, 'had lycence to act Peices of plaies and drolls according to a Lycence under the Seale of the Office of Revels for Tenn-dayes from Monday next at ye Redd Lion in St. Stevens'. An extension for another week was allowed on November 4.[4] The Red Lion, on the site of which now stands the Cricketers' Arms, had been used by the players of Queen Elizabeth's time. Parker played there again the following year for two weeks and then secured a further licence on November 3, 'they observinge good order & breake up by 8 of ye Clocke'; which evidently they did as a third licence 'till saterday senight' is recorded on November 14.[5]

The same kind of condition was laid down on October 26, 1678: 'Mr. Robert Parker Master of the Players had Lycence to Act plaies Comedies & Tragedies &c as by his Patent, for 14 daies from Monday next he observing good orders & howres, and not to act or keepe Companie together after 9 at night'.[6]

The following spring Cornelius Saffery reappears and is given 'untill this day senight or further order' 'to make

---

[1] Court Book, 1666–77, ff. 262 v., 265.

[2] *Ibid.* f. 266. On August 29, 1676, the Duke of Monmouth recommended Perin, 'Master of his Grace's Company of Actors', to have leave to play during Stourbridge Fair (*S.P. Dom. Entry Book* 41, p. 54).

[3] Parker had been apprehended in 1670 for acting without a licence (Nicoll, *op. cit.* p. 279).

[4] Court Book, 1666–77, f. 369 v.

[5] Court Book, 1677–95, ff. 9, 10, 11.   [6] *Ibid.* f. 35.

shew of part of playes, Interludes &c.';[1] but Parker returned the next year when the entry under November 13, 1680, reads: 'Mr Parker Master of Newmarket Companie of Players had lycence to Act Playes &c in ye City at ye redd lion for 14 daies from Monday next making use of ye City musig.'[2] It seems likely that it was this Newmarket Company which acted, before the King and Court at the races, those three farces or drolls which were printed in 1680 as *The Muse of New-Market*.

It was a great concession for the Mayor's Court to allow the city musicians to co-operate with the players. Another instance of their good humour is recorded under December 15, 1680: 'The Players in respecte of ye bad season of ye weather, have leave to stay 10 daies from ye 26th of ye month, they absteyning every day next weeke except monday next.'[3]

Coysh, who reappeared on March 12, 1683, succeeded in securing no less than five extensions to act at the Red Lion, these being granted on April 3, 18, 21, May 2, 30;[4] he was thus enabled to stay to perform 'the whole Guild weeke'. On April 21 the sword bearer, or city treasurer, is bidden 'take of him what monies he can gett which is to be paid into ye hamper'. In the entry of March 12 the leader is referred to as 'Jo: Coysh assignee of yᵉ Patent of Georg Jolly deceased'.

This statement appears rather to favour the theory that Jolly's Company was a different one from that of the Duke of Monmouth, since the patent is alluded to as Jolly's whereas Perin's patent is spoken of as the Duke's. On the other hand if Jolly's Company and the Duke of Monmouth's were the same then Coysh's Company and Perin's were also one and the same, and the mastership of it must have passed from Coysh in 1672 to Perin 1673–4 and back to Coysh in 1683. That this is indeed what happened is supported by the fact that Coysh was certainly employed at

[1] Court Book, f. 44 v., April 19, 1679.   [2] *Ibid.* f. 78.
[3] *Ibid.* f. 80 v.   [4] *Ibid.* ff. 126, 127 v., 128, 130.

Drury Lane from 1674 to 1681. The balance of evidence is therefore in favour of the theory that the Duke of Monmouth's patent was the same as Jolly's. It is unfortunate that copies of the licences granted to these travelling troupes do not seem to have been preserved either among the Lord Chamberlain's papers or among those still extant of Sir Henry Herbert, Master of the Revels.

In 1684 Parker acted at the Red Lion for fourteen days from Easter Monday.[1] On February 14, 1685, 'Henrie Gayne ser^t to Mr Coysh not produceing satisfactorie Authority to act plaies or showes is to make his application where requisite to have sufficient authority', and on February 25 Coysh produced the necessary 'instrument under the hand of King Charles ye second'.[2]

Coysh was already in favour with the Duke of Norfolk when on October 16, 1686, he had leave 'to act Playes in ye City dureinge the stay of his grace ye Duke of Norff: in ye Citie',[3] but thereafter he disappears from the records for ten years and two new managers make their appearance.

The first of these is the strangely named Moundford Ballydon who was granted leave to act for ten days at the Red Lion on March 9, 1687,[4] and who does not reappear; the second is the more important John Power to whom leave was given 'to make show of a Play called the new Market Company for the space of 14 days keeping good howres and behaving themselves civily'.[5] Perhaps there was a play of that name or perhaps it was the clerk's misunderstanding for the name of the company, but whichever is the case we may conjecture that Power had taken over the Newmarket Company from Parker, whose name does not henceforward appear. About Christmas time of this same year the soldiers of Col. Hefford's regiment gave an amateur performance of an unknown play called *The Critics*.

Between 1688–91, possibly on account of the Revolution,

---

[1] Court Book, f. 151 v., March 26.   [2] *Ibid.* ff. 168, 168 v.
[3] *Ibid.* f. 187.   [4] *Ibid.* f. 214.   [5] *Ibid.* f. 243 v.

there is no record of any company having visited Norwich; but on November 25, 1691, Power had 'libertie to Act playes, drolles, ffarces and interludes with Musicke and Sixteen Servants att the Red Lion' for a fortnight.[1] The company had swelled to twenty by November 16, 1692. On this occasion, too, they acted 'att the Angell in St. Peter of Mancroft' and the custom of the Mayor's play was revived.[2] Under December 17, 1692, it is 'Ordered That Mr Power and his Company giveing to the poor the profit of a play such as the Major shall appoint upon such day as Mr Major shall allso appoint They have leave to Act their plays til the next Court day'. On December 8, 1694, Power was allowed three weeks in which to perform but he seems to have abused his privilege and outstayed his welcome since, on January 26, 1695, it is 'Ordered that the sword bearer give notice to Mr Power and other the players That they forbeare playing any more And that if they shall presume to play after notice of this Order They shall be proceeded against according to Law'.[3] A rather cryptic entry under the same date: 'Ordered That the Players be allowed Twenty shillings towards the charge of their Hous and that Munday sevennight be the day That the players give a Play for the bft of the poor For the libberty of their stay in the Towne', may refer to another company, though this is unlikely, or may mean that the Court so far relented as to allow Power to stay provided he gave the Mayor's play. He was still in Norwich on February 22, 1695, when he was again warned: 'Ordered that notice be given to Mr Power and the rest of the players by the swordbearer That they presume not to play any longer at their perrill.'[4]

Coysh arrived on the scene again on September 23, 1696, this time 'having his Grace the Duke of Norfolk's patent', and was permitted to act comedies in a convenient place for a month from about Christmas.[5]

[1] Court Book, 1677–95, f. 286.   [2] Ibid. ff. 299, 300v.
[3] Ibid. f. 332v.   [4] Ibid. 1695–1709, f. 9v.   [5] Ibid. f. 18v.

The Duke of Norfolk now had his own company and the next year, on October 13, 'Upon reading this day a Lre from his Grace the Duke of Norfolk It is Ordered that Mr Doggett have leave to make show of his Comedy in this Citty behaving themselves decently paying the officers Fees.'[1] The same day a similar licence was granted to Power for two weeks but there was not room in the city for two companies and Doggett, armed with the authority of the Duke, won the day: 27 November, 1697, 'Whereas at a Court of Maioralty held the 13th day of October last leave was given to Mr Dogget & Mr Power to make shew of Comedies persuant to their respective pattents In regard that Mr Doggett was recommended by his Grace the Duke of Norffolk & that leave was first granted to him It is ordered that the sd Mr Dogget have Libertie first to make shew of his Comedy and that Mr Power doe not make shew of his till Mr Dogget hath done.' Doggett even obtained an extension on January 12.[2]

Thomas Doggett, who had been having his troubles with the Lord Chamberlain and the patentees in London, had evidently taken over the company from Coysh. Tony Aston joined the company when Coysh still led it and tells us that he 'travell'd with Mr. Cash, Dogget, Booker, Mins'.[3] Elsewhere Aston says that he stayed a year with Doggett and that 'each Sharer kept his Horse, and was every where respected as a Gentleman'.[4]

Doggett was in Norwich again on September 24, 1698, and obtained the usual licence. He tried to find new quarters, and an entry under October 8 runs:[5] 'Ordered upon Reading Mr Doggetts Petition that he have the leave of this Court to apply himselfe to the Comittee that were appointed last Assembly to treat for all or any part of the Granary For a

<hr />

[1] Court Book, 1695–1709, f. 36.   [2] *Ibid.* ff. 38, 40.
[3] 'A Sketch of the Life of Mr Anthony Aston' appended to *The Fools Opera*, 1731.   [4] *A Brief Supplement to Colley Cibber,*[1747?].
[5] Court Book, 1695–1709, ff. 50v, 51v.

Lease of such part of the Granary as hee petitions for.' The granary was no less a place than the fine St Andrews Hall where performances had been given in Elizabeth's time.[1] Doggett could not have succeeded in his object as the following disaster is recorded in Dawks's *News Letter*, February 4, 1699: 'Letters from Norwich say that on Friday the 27th of January, there was a Play Acted at the Angel-Inn by Mr. Dogget and his Company; the House being very full, it broke down the Gallery, which kill'd a young Woman outright, and, dangerously bruised and wounded a great many people.'[2] This accident may account for the fact that the next year Doggett found quarters in the Duke's palace. Leave to act was granted to him and his company 'being his Grace the Duke of Norfolkes Servants' on September 29, 1699,[3] and on December 29 Humphrey Prideaux, Bishop of Norwich, wrote: 'The D[uke] of N[orfolk] hath been here; and some will have it that his only business was to fix Dogget and his players here, who have now their stage up at yᵉ Dukes place, and are helping all they can to undoe this place wch on yᵉ decay of their weaveing trade, now sinks apace. But I suppose his Grace had some other designe on this journey than for yᵉ sake of these varletts.'[4] The players were still the scapegoat for the town's misfortunes.

During this season the company staged an ambitious production which it was even thought worth while to advertise in *The Flying Post* for January 20–23, 1700: 'On the 17th of January the Opera *Dioclesian*,[5] was acted at Norwich, by

[1] In 1696 it was used as a mint, and in the summer of 1699 a committee had been appointed to treat 'for all or any part of the Granary which was formerly used as a Mint' (Norwich Assembly Book, 1668–1707, p. 221).

[2] Noted by Watson Nicholson, *Anthony Aston, Stroller and Adventurer*, 1920.

[3] Court Book, 1695–1709, f. 69.

[4] *Letters of Humphrey Prideaux to John Ellis*, Camden Soc., 1875, p. 193.

[5] Betterton's *The Prophetess or the History of Dioclesian*. It is noteworthy that *Dioclesian* is referred to in *The Post Boy*, May 14–16, 1700, as 'hitherto the greatest [opera] that the English Stage has produced'.

Mr Dogget's Company, the Duke of Norfolk's Servants, with great Applause, being the first that ever was attempted out of London.' Doggett must have had means as well as enterprise.

Doggett's last recorded appearance in Norwich was when he obtained a licence on October 23, 1700.[1] Power visited the city and had licences to play on September 26, 1702, November 20, 1703, October 14, 1704, November 7, 1705,[2] on the first occasion for an unspecified time, on the other three for a period of three weeks. We do not know where he held performances from 1702 to 1704, but in 1705 he was at the King's Arms.

Power's Company was also visiting, and getting into trouble at Bristol.[3] We may surmise that among the plays performed at Norwich were *Timon of Athens, Love for Love* and *The Provok'd Wife* which we know to have been in his Bristol repertoire. In 1706 Mrs Centlivre's *Love at a Venture* was printed 'As it is Acted By his Grace the Duke of Grafton's Servants at the New Theatre in Bath'. Since we know that Power visited Bath, and since the epilogue to the play is spoken by Miss Jacobella Power, we may safely assume that the Duke of Grafton's men were Power's Company. This accords with R. Crompton Rhodes's statement, in a note[4] based on the James Winston MSS. formerly in his collection, that in the early eighteenth century the Norwich Company of Comedians was known as 'the Duke of Grafton's men, servants to the Lord Chamberlain'. He adds that they acted under this style at Windsor before Queen Anne about 1706,[5]

[1] Court Book, 1695–1709, f. 69.   [2] *Ibid.* ff. 134, 162, 186, 208.

[3] He erected a theatrical booth there in 1704, returned despite the protests of the Common Council in 1705, but on August 10, 1706, was presented to the Grand Jury and ordered to be suppressed. See *post,* p. 170.

[4] 'The King's Players at Oxford, 1661–1712', *T.L.S.* February 21, 1929.

[5] It was whilst acting with the company here that Mrs Carol met Joseph Centlivre. Whincop, *A List of all the English Dramatic Poets,* 1747, says: 'about the Year 1706, the Court being at Windsor she there put on her Breeches again and acted the Part of Alexander the Great, in the Tragedy of that Name. She played this Part, it seems, to great Perfection.'

and quotes a letter from Cambridge that 'the Norwich Company of Comedians come here and act every evening, during the fair [Stourbridge] and collect to £60 and £70 a night'.

Power's Company may possibly have visited Stourbridge, but it was Doggett's Company that was suppressed in 1701 by Dr Bentley. The Mayor and Corporation gave Doggett leave to play without obtaining the sanction of the Vice-Chancellor, an omission that enabled Bentley to commit Doggett to gaol and have the theatrical booth demolished.[1]

Whether the actual term 'Norwich Company of Comedians'[2] was in use at all so early is doubtful, but it is clear that the Duke of Norfolk and the Duke of Grafton, who had his seat at Euston near Thetford, were patrons of rival companies. In 1707 there was another clash. One Thomas Ager was granted permission to act for a month on September 20, and on November 19 occurs an entry: 'Ordered that Mr. John Power comedian have leave to Act Plays for the Space of ffourteen days and so forwards (untill Mr Aiger comes to Towne to play).'[3] Ager was Doggett's successor as manager of the Duke of Norfolk's Company.

There is a story,[4] whose origin I have been unable to trace, that in 1708 the Mayor, Thomas Havers, forbade Thomas, Duke of Norfolk, to enter the city preceded by his comedians playing on their trumpets; in consequence of which the Duke left Norwich in a rage and allowed his palace to go to ruin.

Part of this, at least, is untrue for, as we shall see, in the winter of 1711-12, 'his Grace the Duke of Norfolk's

[1] C. H. Cooper, *Annals of Cambridge*, 1852, p. 45. Defoe praises Bentley for his action (*A Review of the State of the English Nation*, August 16, 1706). Defoe mentions several attempts of the players to 'set up under Pretence of superior Licenses' at Cambridge.

[2] The earliest use of it I have traced in the local newspapers is 1726. It was the Duke of Norfolk's Company which survived and was acting 1710-12.

[3] Court Book, 1695-1709, ff. 252, 255v. For Ager's subsequent activities in York, see post, pp. 107 *et seq.*

[4] See Mark Knights's *Highways and Byways of Old Norwich*, 1887.

Servants' were once more acting at the palace.[1] Neither is there any reference to this dramatic episode in the Court Books, only on January 11, 1709, an entry 'Ordered that for the future no stage play or Comedy or Mountibanks Drolls or other shows or Plays shall be allowed in this Citty but by Order of the Court of Majoralty'.[2] Curiously enough plays and players disappear henceforward from the Court Books and the entry marks the end of a period in the annals of the Norwich stage.

It was a period for the players of continual struggle with the town authorities who would but grudgingly admit them. Their chief friends seem to have been the working classes, until they were taken under the patronage of two local noblemen. It is impossible to estimate the number of strolling companies which then existed, but of the goodly number that visited Norwich it is noteworthy that three were led by men connected with the London Nursery and probably recruited from the ranks of those training there. We have found something about the size of the companies, a little about the plays and drolls they acted, hints of their connections with other towns and a good deal about the difficulties they encountered. Had it not been for them Norwich would have had no higher form of entertainment than the many shows, varying from freaks to acrobatic feats, which the Mayor's Court was so frequently called upon to license and at which the crowd no doubt delighted to gape.

[1] *Norwich Gazettes* in the Colman library at Crown Point, kindly examined for me by Mr A. J. Quinton.
[2] Court Book, 1709–19, f. 17.

Chapter III

THE PLAYERS IN NORWICH 1710–1750

The local newspapers now take up the story of the drama in Norwich. Fortunately there is an almost complete series of *Norwich Gazettes* for the period 1710–1750; and this paper not only regularly advertised performances in great detail but often provided news paragraphs of the movements of the Norwich Company on tour. The Norwich Public Library possesses copies of *Cross-grove's News or the Norwich Gazette* from November 16, 1728, and the *Norwich Mercury* for 1727. For the earlier years I am indebted to the courtesy of Mr A. J. Quinton who has been good enough to search the volumes of the *Norwich Gazette* from December 1710 to January 1712, January 1716 to March 1718, and January 1721 to 1727 in the Colman Library at Crown Point for items of theatrical interest; and to Mr Noel-Hill who has kindly sent extracts from his collection of *Norwich Gazettes* for December 1722 to July 1723. Except then for the gaps 1712–16 and 1718–21, the records are complete. I have thought it best to deal with the years up to 1718 in detail, since nothing has been written on this early time; the later period I have treated as a unity under headings of: (*a*) The Companies, (*b*) Theatres and Staging, (*c*) The Audience, (*d*) Plays.

1710–1718

The first available advertisement is that of the *Norwich Gazette* of December 9–16, 1710, which reads: 'At the Queen's Arms on Monday next will be acted a Trajedy call'd Mackbeth, with all the Witches, Songs and Dances as they were originally perform'd at the Theatre Royal in London. Beginning at Five a Clock. Vivat Regina.'

There are several points of interest. It is the first time we hear of acting taking place at the Queen's Arms; in the preceding period we have mention of the King's Arms, Red Lion, Angel and the Duke of Norfolk's palace. The performance began at five o'clock, an hour or two earlier than in following years. As for the play, the decorations appear to have been the chief attraction in Davenant's operatic version of *Macbeth*. That Norwich as well as London was to be lured by song and dance is borne out by an advertisement of the first performance there of Settle's *Heir of Morocco* in the same season: 'With several Entertainments of Singing, particularly that pleasant Entertainment of the Country Wedding, and the Song of Genius of England.' Whether these entertainments were performed between the acts of the tragedy or after it or both, it is not possible to say, but they prepare the way for the vicious practice of the afterpiece and of song and dance turns between the acts. In this same season, at the presentation of Trapp's *Abra-Mule* 'our last new farce called the Walking Statue' was given before the tragedy. Aaron Hill's *Walking Statue* had only been produced in London in January 1710, so that Norwich did not have to wait long to see the latest hit. Other plays advertised are *The Committee*, Shadwell's adaptation of *Timon of Athens* and *King Lear and his three Daughters* in Tate's version. The predominance of Shakespeare in the repertoire is noticeable.

The company, which stayed about six weeks, included one Keregan, who acted the part of 'Mad Tom' in *King Lear* for his own benefit. Keregan appears again in Norwich in the winter season 1711–12 with 'the Duke of Norfolk's Servants'. From this, and from the fact that their repertoire is partly the same, we may conclude that it was likewise the Duke's Company that had been playing in 1710–11. But in 1711–12 they acted at the Duke's palace for five weeks, playing four or five days in the week. They presented *The*

Indian Emperor (twice), *The Rover*, Rowe's *Tamerlane the Great*, *The Tender Husband*, *Abra-Mule*, *The Busy Body*, *The Heir of Morocco*, *The Recruiting Officer*, *Othello*, *Love for Love*, *Injured Love* (which had only been brought out at Drury Lane in April 1711), *Macbeth*, *The Country Wit*, *Hamlet*, *Tunbridge Walks* (twice), *Amphitryon*, *The Unhappy Favourite*, in which Keregan played Essex, *The Rival Queens* and 'a Masque of Musick call'd the Country Wedding'. Ravenscroft's *London Cuckolds* was down for the last night 'unless any other be desired'. It is a large and comprehensive repertoire in which tragedy and comedy are well balanced.

Among the actors was Benjamin Griffin who ran away from his apprenticeship with a glazier in Norwich, and thence joined the strollers, 'with whom and in other companies, he arrived at considerable excellence' until, in 1714, he was engaged at Lincoln's Inn Fields and made a name as a low comedy actor and as an author of farces.[1]

The next season in which we can trace the players[2] is that of 1716 when they acted at the King's Arms, on January 16, J. Phillips's new farce, *The Earl of Mar Marr'd*, which had been printed in 1715 but of whose production in London we have no record. This performance provoked a Jacobite riot, described in the *Gazette*, December 14–16, 1716:

When the Part of Proclaiming the Pretender as King was acted on the Stage and the Players gave a Formal Huzza at it, the People also in the Galleries gave a great Shout; whereupon Capt. Hall and some other Gentlemen well affected to King George, began to Hiss at 'em, at which they not only shouted louder but clapp'd their Hands, and stampp'd with their Feet to that Degree, that the House rang again: Upon that the Gentlemen drew their Swords, and cry'd out, Down with the Rebels! Down with them! Damn 'em we'll Marr 'em. Which set the Ladies a shrieking, and put all the House in Disorder. On Tuesday Night

[1] See *Biographia Dramatica*.
[2] Sometime between 1711 and 1713 the company visited York (see *post*, p. 107). For Keregan's connections with York and Canterbury see the chapters on these towns.

the said Farce was play'd again, and the Audience in the Galleries not only shouted as they did before, but had the Impudence to Hiss at what was spoken of his Most Sacred Majesty King George. Good Lord what a sad age we live in.

It was presumably an amateur company that acted, at the King's Arms on July 3, Walker's *Marry or Do Worse*, 'at the Request of the Gentlemen in Town', for the benefit of the charity schools,[1] but we do not know who was responsible for the 'Two New and very Diverting Farces the one The Lunatic, the other, The Rival Fool, or Witty Factor', the performance of which at the King's Arms was advertised for November 6. Singing and dancing between the plays and 'a new humorsome Epilogue spoken by Two Persons, which was made and presented to the Company by a young Lady' were additional attractions on the latter occasion.

In 1717 the Duke of Norfolk's Company of Comedians gave at 'the White-Horse at Troas' (viz. Trowse, just outside the city) from February 25–29, five plays: *Sir Courtly Nice*, *Sir Harry Wildair*, *The Fair Penitent*, *Don Quixote* and *The Distress'd Mother*.

The 1718 season lasted from January 27 until March 17 and opened at the King's Arms at 'the Request of divers Gentlemen and Ladies' with 'the celebrated Play of Hamlet, Prince of Denmark'. *The Inconstant* was given the second week at the request of 'the Young Gentlemen of this City who lately Play'd several Comedies for their Diversion and converted Money arising from the same to Charitable uses'. *The Rival Queens* was revived 'With all new Habits proper to the Play being the Finest and Richest that were ever seen upon a Stage in this City'. Keregan chose for his benefit *Love and a Bottle*, which had never been played in Norwich. The announcement adds, 'They will begin early by Reason the House will be Extream full; this being the last week of their acting in Town.' After performing *The Recruiting Officer* on the Saturday they finished the season with J. D.

[1] See *infra*.

Breval's *The Play is the Plot*, which had been first given at Drury Lane only a month previously. The company then, though it acted mostly old plays, was also able to present from time to time the latest from London.

Companies 1721–50

In 1721 we find a company calling themselves the Duke of Richmond's Servants at the King's Arms. Beyond the fact that this company had produced Tony Aston's *Pastora: or, The Coy Shepherdess*[1] in Tunbridge Wells as far back as 1712, we know nothing of them. At the same time Tollett and Thompson's medley was giving puppet shows at the White Swan Playhouse. An unnamed company, possibly again the Duke of Richmond's, was at the King's Arms the following winter, presented *Caius Marius* for the first time in Norwich, and revived *Venice Preserv'd*, which was advertised as 'not play'd here these 20 years'. Since *Caius Marius* was again in the repertoire it was probably the same company which returned the next winter and acted at the Angel. They also presented Steele's *Conscious Lovers*, 'Never acted out of London.... With a New Prologue and Epilogue, written by a Gentleman of this Town.' By 1723 Tollett of the puppets had started a legitimate company:

Norwich Feb. 23. I have an Account, That Mr. Tollett is Coming with a New Company of Comedians to Act in this City, having obtain'd Mr. Mayor's leave for that End: By Reports of Divers Persons who have seen them perform in Boston, Lincoln and other places, they are the Completest Company that ever Stroled: I hear that there are among them the famous Mr. SPILLER and his wife, and several other fine actors from the Playhouse in London, besides the most Curious Dancers that ever travelled. It seems they were last at Rochester, where they perform'd with great Applause, and on the 13th instant hired a ship to bring them to Norwich, and they are hourly now expected.[2]

[1] See title page, 1712 edition.   [2] *Norwich Gazette*, February 16–23, 1723.

Acts of God prevented their appearance until June, as we learn from the *Gazette* of May 25–June 1:

Notice is hereby given, That Mr. Tollett's Company of Comedians embarqu'd last Sunday at Whitstable for Norwich, and then waited only for a fair wind, being desirous the City should see how much a completer Company they are....They intended to have been at Norwich last February but meeting with a terrible Storm at Sea, they were then prevented....Henry Tollett.

The company opened at the King's Arms on June 10 and stayed until August 10, the longest season that Norwich had yet known. James Spiller, the low comedian from L.I.F., played, among other parts, those of the Elder Clincher in *The Constant Couple*, Young Hobbs in Doggett's farce of *The Country Wake*, and the Sham Doctor in *The Anatomist*. The new play of the season was *Whig and Tory*, a comedy by Benjamin Griffin.[1]

Three months after Tollett had departed 'Mr. Keregan's Company of Comedians' opened at the White Swan Playhouse. Tollett, who seems to have had the knack of self-advertisement, thereupon put a notice in the *Gazette* of November 30–December 3:

Being Credibly inform'd, That my adversaries have rais'd malicious Falsehoods of me in order to promote their own Ends and that they report, that my Company will not be in Norwich this Christmas season; This is to satisfie the Publick, That I have hired a Vessel for that Purpose, and hope to be at Norwich in a few Days; and question not but to give the City greater Satisfaction, than any Company has ever done since Mr. Doggett's time.

He in fact opened at the King's Arms on December 30 and stayed until April 11, 1724. In the company were Morris, James, Jones, Dyer, Price, Paul, Williams, Mrs Dyer, Mrs Clark, Mrs Gale, Mrs Howard and Mrs Tollett. Norwich profited in dramatic entertainment out of the rival companies.

[1] See *ante*, p. 50.

A company not named but presumably Tollett's, since he was at Beccles the week after, played during Assize week from July 25 at the White Swan, but Keregan was acting there as Justice in *Æsop* on October 3. In 1725 Keregan had a final winter season at the King's Arms and appears thereafter to have abandoned Norwich for Canterbury and York. A company which included Paul, Collier, Green, Penkethman,[1] and Mrs Frisby from the Dublin Theatre, played 'with an entire Sett of New Scenes never before put up' during Assize week at the White Swan. Mrs Bedingfield thus describes her visit to the play to Mrs Howard and incidentally illustrates the inconveniences of allowing the audience to sit on the stage:[2] 'The house was too small for the actors; but a trap-door opened, and four of the company fell in—one a particular man, who was high-sheriff last year, fell upon a pretty woman, and liked his situation so well, that they could not get him out.'

The following year 'the Norwich Company of Comedians' acted the winter season at the White Swan. Frisby, Buck,[3] James, Mrs Frisby, Mrs Plomer from L.I.F., Green and Marshall were the chief actors. They returned 'at the Request of a great number of Gentlemen and Ladies' during Assize week and, 'all possible Care' being 'taken to secure a very strong, commodious Building for their Reception', performed at the King's Arms. Here at last was a permanent company which played almost every winter season and Assize week, and were trumpeted in the *Gazette* of December 17–24, 1726, by the paragraph: 'I hear that Preparations are

---

[1] This could hardly have been William Penkethman, who was running his Richmond Theatre at the time, see *post*, p. 285. Though he did not marry until 1714 it may have been his son of whom otherwise we first hear at L.I.F., April 19, 1729.

[2] *Letters to and from Henrietta, Countess of Suffolk*, 1824, vol. I, p. 257.

[3] Timothy Buck appears in a list of actors at L.I.F., April 1722 (see P. Fitzgerald, *A New History of the English Stage*, vol. I, p. 416). In July, 1715, a benefit had been given there to release him from prison (see Genest, *Some Account of the English Stage*).

making for the Reception of our Norwich Company of Comedians at the King's Arms Playhouse in this City and that (according to the Provisions they are making for themselves) 'tis the general opinion they will make the most splendid Appearance that was ever seen on the Norwich Stage.'

On the last night of Assize Week, 1727, at the King's Arms, the company presented Welsted's *Dissembled Wanton*, advertised as having had a London run of fifteen nights. In the October of this year the *Ipswich Journal* announces (October 7–14): 'The Norwich Company of Comedians are Divided.' The Greens' party, which kept the name of the Norwich Company, was the first to play in the city at the White Swan in 1728. With the Greens were the Pauls, and the Bowmans,[1] and in addition the company included the Merediths, West, Duckworth, Mynn (who had been in Doggett's company), Barret, Mrs Bray and Mrs Potter. The new plays presented were Frowde's *Fall of Saguntum*, *The Provok'd Husband*, advertised as having been performed for thirty-two successive nights at Drury Lane, and *The Beggar's Opera* 'With the Scenes, Musick, Singing and Dancing as perform'd at the Theatre in London'.

During Assize week 'The Norwich OLD Company of Comedians (late separated from Mr Green)' were billed to appear. This troupe included the Frisbys, the Bucks, the Milwards, the James's, Marshall, Mrs Plomer, and the Pauls

[1] It is unlikely that this was Betterton's adopted daughter and her husband as has been supposed. In favour of the supposition is the fact that Bowman's name disappears after 1738, and we know he died, aged 88, in March 1739 (*London Daily Post*, March 26). He is referred to as 'belonging to Drury Lane Theatre' in this notice. Bowman was acting at Drury Lane as the Ghost in *Timoleon*, January 26, 1730, and the Norwich Bowman as Iago on January 18. The Norwich actor again played Iago on January 20, 1735, whilst his Drury Lane namesake played Count Baldwin in *The Fatal Marriage* on January 23. It is difficult to believe that a man over eighty would rush from one theatre to another in this way, or that his wife would be playing such parts as Millamant or Shakespeare's Isabella in 1748. The Norwich actor was possibly the 'Young Bowman' who was acting at Drury Lane in 1715–16.

who had deserted the Greens sometime before.[1] The quarrel had been made up by October,[2] and on November 23 a reporter in the *Gazette* writes: 'I am inform'd that our Norwich Company of Comedians have (since their Union) perform'd the Beggar's Opera after the new Manner...and some who pretend to be Judges, and have seen the same Performance at London, give our Company the Preference.' The united company was playing in Ipswich from November 11 and included Frisbys, James's, Pauls, Bowmans, West, Marshall, Platt, Mrs Bray and Mrs Jackson; the Greens do not appear again.

During 1729 at the White Swan *The False Friend*, 'With a Prologue to the Town (particularly applicable to the Trade of this City)', *The Quaker's Opera*, which had originated in a booth in Southwark Fair, and *The Victim* were given first performances, and in July *The Village Opera*, 'With all the proper Decorations and Musick as lately Performed at the New-House', was announced.

The next year the company styled itself 'Servants to His Grace the Duke of Grafton, Lord Chamberlain of His Majesty's Household'.[3] They played at the King's Head, but thereafter made the White Swan their permanent playhouse. Pitt from the Theatre Royal, who was with the company as late as 1743, and one Woodward[4] 'from London', joined the

---

[1] By March 27 when Paul played Polonius at Ipswich with the old company (*Ipswich Journal*, March 18–23).

[2] When a united company was acting at Colchester (*Ipswich Journal*, October 19–26).

[3] The Duke had been a patron of a Norwich company in the early years of the century (see *ante*, pp. 45–6); he became Lord Chamberlain in 1724.

[4] It has generally been assumed that this was the famous Henry Woodward. This, however, is not possible, as his name appears regularly with the Norwich Company until 1743, whereas Henry Woodward joined the Drury Lane Company in 1738 and played there regularly until 1741 when he transferred to Covent Garden. Henry Woodward played Spruce in *The Independent Patriot* at L.I.F. on February 12, 1737, whilst the Norwich actor had his benefit on February 14.

troupe in the 1730–1 winter season. The only new play was B. Martyn's *Timoleon*. During 1732 Betterton's *Amorous Widow*[1] and Mallett's *Eurydice* were given. 1733 was a notable year in the company's annals: "'tis believed they will be more splendid than for many Years past', reports the *Norwich Mercury* for December 16–23, 1732. They introduced to Norwich Banks's *Mary Queen of Scots*, Steele's *The Tender Husband* and Kelly's *Married Philosopher* and, for the first time in their history, though not for the first time in Norwich, played Tate's version of *King Lear*. In June the company lost West, who died, aged thirty-two, and was buried in the churchyard of St Peter Mancroft. The company had a month's summer season, starting during Sessions week, in which they produced Fielding's *The Miser*.

The activities of a rival company gave cause for the following declaration to appear in the *Gazette* of July 6–13, 1734:

Whereas for some Time past, a small Body of People have been at Several Towns in the County of Norfolk, and call themselves a Company of Comedians, and report that they have some Concerns with the Proprietor of his Grace the Duke of Grafton's Company, in order to gain Credit, and impose upon the Publick: These are therefore to prevent such Abuses for the future (by signifying to his Majesty's Justices of the Peace, Bayliffs, High Constables, etc. to whom such Persons may apply for leave to Play) That no Company or Body of People who travel about in this Country, have any Protection or Patent from his Grace the Duke of Grafton (or any other Authority) but those who for many Years past have been call'd the Norwich Company, of which Mr. William James is now Manager thereof.

The other company was probably that of Bainbridge, in which Upton, the Wheelers and Mrs Daniel played at Holt in July, having 'lately had the Honour to be Encouraged

---

[1] Though advertised as 'never played in the City before', it had been given by Tollett's Company, December 30, 1723: 'not play'd in this City for a great many Years last past.'

by several Noblemen and Persons of Distinction in this County'.

Mrs Schoolding's name first appears in 1734, and in January 1735 "'tis assur'd that Mr. Roberts (from the Theatre-Royal) will perform the Character of Justice Ballance:[1] for which 'tis reasonable to believe that the Character was never so well personated in this City before'. Roberts also played Othello to the Iago of Bowman and the Desdemona of Mrs Bowman, and spoke a new Prologue to the City before *Abra-Mule*.

Giles, Bawtree and Mr and Mrs St Nicholas are the new actors in 1736, whilst Aaron Hill's *Zara* and Fielding's *Pasquin*, which had 'met with the greatest Encouragement of any other [entertainment] on the English Stage in the Memory of Man, having exceeded the Beggar's Opera in its Run by 5 Nights', are the new plays.

In 1737 the company lost by death Henrietta Maria Bray, aged sixty, who was buried in St Peter Mancroft in November, and Ann Buck, aged thirty-two, whose quaint epitaph at Colchester reads:

> Having acted a good Part
> On the Stage of Life for 32 Years,
> And on that of the Theatre for 14 Years....
> She made a most decent Exit.

An accident to Mrs Bowman is reported on December 15–17: 'The Report of the Death of Mrs. Bowman, the fam'd Actress in the Norwich Company of Comedians, is not true, for since the Waggon went over her Body going from Bury Fair to Colchester, she is so well recover'd as to Play almost every Night.'

In spite of these misfortunes the company gave the following new plays: Mrs Haywood's *Wife to be Let*, Young's *The Revenge* and Havard's *King Charles I*. The company did not open until January 31 in 1738, and Norwich had to console

[1] In *The Recruiting Officer*.

itself for the delay with Woodham and Frost's waxworks at the Star, and Sheppard's puppets at the Red Lion. James, too, was evidently dead, as henceforward there is always a benefit performance for the Widow James. Upton from Bainbridge's company was a new recruit. New plays were Popple's *Lady's Revenge*, Miller's hash of *Much Ado* with *La Princesse d'Élide* called *The Universal Passion*, and *Oroonoko*.

The year 1739 was another outstanding one in the company's history. On January 6–13 the *Gazette* announces that the comedians 'will shortly be here, and open the House in a very grand Manner, with the Play of King Henry the Fourth'. Great preparations for new scenery were in hand at the White Swan, and money was lavished on scenes and clothes for the new plays: Rowe's *The Royal Convert*, Lillo's *Fatal Curiosity* and Mallett's *Mustapha*. Drury and the Slaters had joined the company.

In 1740 no less than five new pieces came out: E. Smith's *Phaedra and Hippolytus*, *Measure for Measure*, Sewell's *Sir Walter Raleigh*, Centlivre's *The Man's Bewitched* and Lillo's *Elmerick*. Whoever was James's successor as manager of the company was an enterprising man.

As You Like It and *Twelfth Night* were given for the first time in Norwich in 1741, and Crouse who, according to Lee Lewes,[1] was 'a very imperfect performer' made his début at the White Swan as Hamlet. Buck, who used to supplement his income by teaching small sword and quarter-staff to the gentlemen of the cities which he visited, must have died about 1741–2 as a benefit was given for his orphan in January 1742. Trouble must have arisen or been anticipated under the Licensing Act[2] of 1737, and for the Assize season the White Swan was adapted for concerts, and plays were advertised as being performed gratis between the two parts of the concert. This procedure, however, was dropped the following winter season. The names of Pierce from Good-

[1] *Op. cit.* vol. i, p. 81.   [2] See Introduction, p. 7.

man's Fields, Stevens, Stone and the Waldegraves,[1] appear in the casts and Roberts again played in the company. Anne Roberts died in this year aged thirty. Cibber's *Lady's Last Stake* and Fielding's *The Wedding Day* were the only new presentations in 1743. In 1744 Stevens played Macbeth and in 1745 Beaufort and Brock first appeared. Of Brock Lee Lewes[2] says: 'he was not only esteemed the best comedian in the country, but was also plentifully endowed with a more than ordinary share of wit'. In the latter year Hurst's *Roman Maid* and Thomson's *Sophonisba* were given. For some reason there does not seem to have been a winter season in Norwich in 1746, but in this year Pearson, Peterson,[3] Hicks and Mrs Hill, and in 1747 Julian and Mrs Sunderland, joined the company.

In June 1747 with fresh scenes and rich clothes, Macklin came from Drury Lane with part of his London company to entertain Norwich in a newly fitted out White Swan. The company, which included Taswell, Cashel,[4] Luke and Isaac Sparks, Mills, Mrs Elmy[5] and the Mozeens,[6] stayed, acting every Monday, Wednesday and Friday, until the beginning

[1] There was a Waldegrave in the company in 1728. Stone joined the York Company in 1744.

[2] *Op. cit.* vol. I, p. 76. Brock died May 17, 1763, and is buried at King's Lynn.

[3] For his previous career with the York Company see *post,* p. 127. The Pearsons had also come from the York Company.

[4] Oliver Cashel, an Irishman and a personal friend of Macklin's, died during the season at Norwich, being 'taken speechless on the Stage in the Part of Frankly, in a Comedy call'd *The Suspicious Husband.* He was carried to his Lodgings where Physicians and Surgeons attended but to no Purpose; for he expired in a few Hours' (W. R. Chetwood, *A General History of the Stage,* 1749, p. 125). See also *Norwich Gazette,* August 15–22, which gives the date of his seizure as August 17.

[5] See Genest, *op. cit.* II, p. 653, for her career.

[6] Mozeen, according to Chetwood, *op. cit.,* had 'a good Person join'd to a genteel Education, Judgment, Voice and Understanding'. Mrs Mozeen, formerly Miss Edwards, was a protégée of Mrs Clive's and an adept in music; she is said to have been graced with a charming manner and voice.

of September. Among Macklin's parts were those of Ben in *Love for Love*, the Miser, Teague in *The Committee*, Shylock, Polidore in *The Orphan*, Brass in *The City Wives Confederacy*, Lord Foppington in *The Careless Husband*, Sir Harry Wildair in *The Constant Couple*, Sir Gilbert Wrangle in *The Refusal*, and Fondlewife in *The Old Batchelor*. It is interesting to read that Macklin took the part of a carrier in *Henry IV*, leaving Hotspur to Cashel and the Prince to Mills.

In November 1747 at the return of the Norwich Company, a benefit was given for Mr and Mrs Dancy 'formerly belonging to Mr. Carragan's Company of Comedians who are reduced very low by long Sickness'; old stagers were not forgotten.

During 1748 *Henry V*, as altered by Hill, was first performed in Norwich with Peterson as the King. For the July season the company 'fitted up the Play-House at the Red-Lyon in St Stephen's in a Commodious Manner...and as the Company is altered much to Advantage in their Performances they make no doubt of giving intire Satisfaction'. The following year they returned to the White Swan producing there *A New Way to Pay Old Debts* and *Œdipus*.[1]

The Company used, then, to play in Norwich for about three or four months at the beginning of the year, and from a week to three weeks during the Assizes in July and August. Their visitations to other towns were frequently arranged to coincide with fairs or races when multitudes would gather. During the period the towns in the circuit varied. In 1727 after leaving Norwich in March, the comedians spent part of April in North Walsham, May in Aylsham, June at the Holt races, then, after revisiting Norwich in August during Assize week, there came the split; the old company proceeded to Woodbridge, and Green's company to Colchester in November for two weeks and then to Ipswich. It was the practice of the company to leave Norwich for a week during the winter season to attend 'Lynn Mart'. Beccles was usually

---

[1] Most likely Dryden and Lee's, but possibly Theobald's.

visited about May for the races, Ipswich in June or July, and
Bury for the fair in September. The circuit in 1749, which
must be almost complete, was as follows:

January–May ..	..	..	Norwich	
June ..	..	..	..	Dereham for 3 weeks
July ..	..	..	..	Ipswich (races)
August ..	..	..	..	Beccles
September–October ..	..	Bury (fair)		
October–December ..	..	Colchester		
December ..	..	..	Ipswich	

In the early part of the period Yarmouth was a regular
circuit town, but there is no mention of it after 1742 until
1750. Other places to which we can trace the company are
Framlingham (1728), Cambridge (1731), where they performed for the benefit of sufferers by fire, and gave £12 in
addition to profits to the cause to make up an acceptable
sum, Harleston (1734, 1737, 1748), Swaffham (1735), Thetford (1736), Woodbridge (1742), Fakenham (1743), Saxmundham (1743, 1745, 1747), Sudbury (1744), Hingham
(1744), Walsingham (1748). Their stay varied from one
week to four, but two to three weeks was the usual time
allotted. These towns were no doubt visited more often than
I have found trace of, but they do not seem to have been
regularly included in the yearly tour. In one advertisement
for Dereham, for instance, it is definitely stated that the
company would not appear there for another two years.

The company played in Norwich four or five times a
week, except during Lent, when they played only twice. In
the smaller towns they generally confined themselves to three
days a week, but often advertised their willingness to give
additional performances by special request. Benefits were
regularly given for the actors and sometimes for victims of
fire and other accidents. Command performances by local
people of importance were an habitual feature both in
Norwich and in other towns, and towards the end of the

period the masons and other societies and clubs had special request performances.

There were other companies active in the district. We have already met that of Bainbridge at Holt in 1734. This company included a Mrs Daniel, and was probably that subsequently known as Daniel's Company which acted at Holt in September 1738 during the time of the races. A troupe including the Daniels, the Cuthberts, the Hasleups, the Whitakers, and Freeman who joined the Norwich Company in 1744, acted at the Tankard Street Theatre, Ipswich, for a month at the beginning of 1741. There was also Mr Herbert's Company[1] which presented at St George's Hall, King's Lynn, on March 7, 1743, the operatic version of *The Tempest* with Barret as Prospero, Wignell as Ferdinand and Mrs Wignell as Miranda, and with 'decorations all entirely new'. In December 1744 this company was in Yarmouth playing *She Wou'd and She Wou'd Not*, and they reappeared at King's Lynn in February 1745, February 1746, and April 1748. Besides the Herberts, the company included the Wheelers, who had been with Bainbridge, the Slaters, who were with the Norwich Company 1739–41, and Brock who joined the Norwich Company in 1745. Lastly, a third company, known as Smith's, was acting at Hingham in July 1749. It is of interest to note the interchange of actors between these lesser strollers and the Norwich Company.

A word must be added about the many companies of puppets and medleys that visited Norwich. Some of these came from the London fairs and entertained Norwich at Christmas time. That they were popular is attested by the statement on December 27, 1740, that 100 people were turned away every night from Frost and Rayner's puppet show though two others were running concurrently in town. In the winter of 1733–4, too, the Italian rope dancer, Signora Violante, and company were at the Angel, John

---

[1] This company acted mostly in Lincolnshire. See J. Winston, *The Theatric Tourist* under Grantham, also *post*, p. 113.

Karby and his puppets at the Red Lion, and Plat and Godwin's medley from London at the Rampant Horse. Waxworks, drolls, dancing, acrobatic feats and conjuring were
the staple entertainments offered by these companies. Drolls
such as *Jephtha's Rash Vow* or *Princess Elizabeth*, acts from
operas or from comedies, and one-act ballad operas like
Damon and Phillida were performed.

Theatres and Staging

The chief theatre in Norwich was the White Swan Playhouse,[1] which was situated near the west end of St Peter
Mancroft. The auditorium consisted of the stage, pit, and
first or under, and upper galleries. In 1739 great improvements were made: 'I hear that great Preparations are making
for Opening the White-Swan Playhouse on Monday Se'n-
night next: and that the Fine Sett of Scenes Painted by the
Famous French Painter Devoto[2] are arriv'd, in order to be
put up against that Time: the Motto on which is Speculum
Vitae' (January 20–27). The opening performance had to be
postponed until the Tuesday because 'the Paintings would
scarcely be dry before that Time; when every Person may
expect to see the most compleat Appearance that was ever
seen in this Town'. Commodious boxes were erected for the
ladies. In 1742 further alterations were made: 'the White
Swan Play-House is finished up so well, as to make it capable
of entertaining the finest Musical Hands for Concerts, as well
as Playing' (July 31–August 7). In the winter we learn 'the
House is ceiled, and made very warm'. For Macklin's visit
in 1747 the playhouse was again improved: 'Their Scenes
are painted by the best Hands in London, and are entirely

[1] For a view of the exterior see frontispiece to T. L. G. Burley's *Playhouses and Players in East Anglia*. The inn has long since been pulled down.

[2] John Devoto, born in France, of Italian parents, was appointed scene
painter to L.I.F. by Rich and was later employed to paint the scenery and
decorations at Goodman's Fields (Henry Angelo, *Reminiscences*, 1828,
vol. I, p. 11).

New; their Clothes Rich and Elegant; and for the better Accommodation of the Audience, they have alter'd and fitted up the House in a Commodious and Theatrical Manner' (June 13–23). In 1749 occurs the first mention of upper boxes. The White Swan continued to be the regular playhouse of the Norwich Company until the new theatre was built in 1758.

The Angel, the gallery of which had fallen down at a performance in 1699, was reconstructed in 1722 and an announcement appeared on December 15: 'The Play House at the Angel in the Market Place being new built by Mr. Starling the Carpenter, for the reception of Gentlemen, Ladies and others; This is to give notice that such care is taken by the said Mr. Starling for the Strength and security of the Galleries, etc., that there will be no reason to fear any Danger, as has been maliciously insinuated: and he, the said Mr. Starling, will give further Satisfaction to any person or persons who desire it.' The Angel was thereafter used by puppet shows and medleys.

The matter of heating was a vital one and notices similar to the following for the Red Lion, 1734, are of frequent occurrence in the *Gazette*: 'That the Gentry may not be incommoded with Cold, there are Contrivances to keep the House Warm.' That this was done in very simple fashion is evident from an advertisement from a *Norwich Gazette* of 1725:[1] 'The pit is lined, and there are boxes on the stage for the better reception of gentlemen and ladies. There will be two fires kept on the stage during the time of performance that the room may be warm.' In 1729 the room at the Red Lion was made 'more commodious than ever', and in 1748 it was again refitted for the Norwich Company to perform there during the Assizes.

The one reference to lighting is in a notice of Tollett's Company at the King's Arms in December 1723, wherein it

[1] Quoted by the *Norfolk Weekly Standard and Argus*, September 29, 1894.

is stated that 'Mrs. Tollett...has been at the Charge of fixing Lamps, and other Conveniences more commodious than has formerly been'.

We know that the company performed in Yarmouth in a warehouse until, in 1736, a theatre was fitted up for them in the Town Chamber;[1] in Colchester at the Moot Hall; and in Ipswich in the Shire Hall in 1728, in a playhouse in St Nicholas Street in 1733, in another in Griffin Yard in 1736, until one Betts built the New Theatre in Tankard Street. This was first used by puppet shows and then in 1739 by the players. Town Halls were in use at Sudbury, Woodbridge and Beccles; the latter, as advertised in 1745, being 'fitted up in an Elegant Manner' for the players' reception. A New Theatre arose in Saxmundham in 1745,[2] and the company announce in the *Ipswich Journal*, October 14, 1749, 'that they intend to pleasure themselves by waiting on' the gentlemen and ladies of Bungay 'to open their theatre'. Elsewhere the players had to make do with barns and booths, the latter often erected specially for them as at Holt Races in 1735.

The company's resources with regard to scenery and clothes are typical of those of the more established circuit companies. Throughout the period there are constant announcements both of new plays and revivals 'with Scenes and Clothes entirely new' or with 'all new scenes and decorations' or 'with proper Dresses for the Play entirely New'. In 1726 *Mithridates* was newly dressed 'with Scenes and other Decorations as perform'd in the Royal Theatre at London'; in 1729, *The Victim* was brought out, not only 'With the Original Sacrifice Scene new set to Musick', but 'with Habits entirely new, by much the Richest ever seen in the Country'; flyings and sinkings were used in *Amphitryon* in 1736;[3] in 1739 *Henry IV* was performed in the 'grand manner' and new scenes and clothes were provided

[1] E. J. Palmer, *Perlustration of Great Yarmouth*, 1872, vol. I, p. 352.
[2] See *Ipswich Journal*, August 10.
[3] Chambers, *A General History of the County of Norfolk*, vol. II, p. 1120.

for *King John*, *The Way of the World*, *The Royal Convert*, and *The Merry Wives of Windsor*. Ten years later *The Siege of Damascus* was 'decorated with the Elegance of these Times' whilst *Œdipus* was 'decorated after an entire New Method' and included a grand procession, transparent paintings, scenes, machines, flyings and sinkings; and in 1744 the actors reminded their patrons that they had been 'at an Extraordinary Expence for Machinery'.

Adventitious music and dancing were popular. *Macbeth* was done 'With all the Witches,[1] Musick, Singing, Dancing and all other Decorations as performed at the Theatre Royal'; in 1735 *Theodosius* was accompanied by 'all the Musick, Vocal and Instrumental as perform'd at the Theatre in London', and *Henry IV* in 1743 'With the Prologue, Epilogue, and all the Songs as usually perform'd at the Theatres in London on the like Occasion'. Attempts at historical accuracy were occasionally made. The *Ipswich Journal* advertises *Cato* on June 30, 1739, as 'With New Roman and Numidian Dresses proper to the Play', and *The Rival Queens* on September 2, 1749, with a procession 'adorn'd with Lictors with their Fasces, Trophies, Standard-Bearers, Prisoners of War and all other pompous Solemnities suitable to the Occasion'. The services of supers must have been enlisted for this and similar spectacles. Neither were prologues and epilogues neglected, and in Restoration fashion, Miss Frisby spoke epilogues in boys' clothes and Giles, in 1736, delivered Haines's notorious epilogue riding on an ass. Special epilogues of thanks were usually addressed to the town before departure.

When a great scenic effort had been made prices were often raised. It is, however, impossible to say what the normal charges were, since the cost of seats was only advertised on special occasions such as first and last nights of the season, first performances of plays and benefits. Probably

---

[1] The Witches were performed by men in 1728, by three men and two women in 1733. The music was Leveridge's.

these prices were augmented ones, at any rate as far as stage and pit were concerned. We find the stage advertised at 3s. or 2s. 6d., the pit at 2s. 6d., and once at 2s., the first gallery at 1s. but once at 1s. 6d., and the upper gallery at 6d. That neither of these scales represented normal charges is evident from the note to the first performance of *Mary Queen of Scots* in which the company begged leave 'to make the Price of the stage 3s. to prevent the Scenes being overcrowded', and from that for the production of *Henry IV* in 1739 which reads: 'On account of the extraordinary Expence, and that Commodious Boxes are made for the Ladies the Price of the Stage will be 2s. 6d. Pit 2s. First Gallery 1s. and Upper Gallery 6d.' We have a first mention of boxes for Macklin's season in 1747 when 3s. was charged for them, but in 1749 they were only 2s. 6d., and there were upper boxes at 1s. 6d. in addition to the usual first gallery at 1s. At Bury the prices were stage 3s., pit 2s. 6d., first gallery 1s. 6d., upper gallery 1s. At Aylsham and the smaller towns the pit and stage together were 2s. 6d. and the gallery was 1s. Puppet shows charged only 1s. for the stage and provided other seats at 6d., 3d. and 2d. Tickets for plays were obtainable at the playhouses themselves or at other taverns and coffee-houses or sometimes at tradesmen's.

The Audience

Disturbing customs similar to those that marred performances in the London theatres afflicted the provincial stage also.

Every endeavour was, however, made by local authorities to have good hours kept. Performances began at 6, 6.30 or 7 o'clock, never later. The advertisements often announce the time of starting as being by command: 'By positive command' reads one 'we are oblig'd to begin exactly at Six', or again, 'By command we shall either begin or shut up the Doors exactly at Six o'clock during the whole Season.' Tollett in 1723 'resolved to begin constantly at

7 o'clock that the company may not be kept from going home too late'. When the company visited a town during the races they started performing as soon as the racing was over in order to be done in time for the assembly. At other, smaller towns, care was taken to announce, with unconscious poetry, that gentlemen and ladies at a distance would 'in their Return have the Opportunity of the Moon'.

Doors usually opened at 4 o'clock, sometimes at 3 o'clock, and during Macklin's season not until 5 o'clock. Ladies sent servants to keep places and one notice even reads, 'Servants will be allowed to keep Places on the Stage.' The iniquitous system of admitting people for half price or less after the second or third act prevailed, but efforts were made to put a stop to it later in the period. In 1741 an announcement appeared that 'Nothing less than the full Price will be taken till after the 3rd Act', and the following year it was given out that 'No less than the whole Money will be taken during the Performance'. In 1745 nothing under half price was accepted after the end of the third act, and Macklin would not permit entrance under full price at any time.

Another nuisance was the admission of spectators behind the scenes to sit on the stage. Though many and various were the prohibitions the practice continued to flourish. In 1722 at a performance of *Venice Preserv'd* an announcement read: 'The hurry of the play obliges us to desire no person to be on the Stage.'[1] Notices at first were rather peremptory: 'None to be admitted on the Stage' or 'No Persons to be admitted behind the Scenes', but later the attitude was deferential and apologetic and the players 'hope the Gentlemen and Ladies will not take it ill, if no one can be admitted on the Stage, more than the Seats will contain'; on another occasion the same formula was used when gentlemen were not to be admitted behind the scenes whilst the boxes were at liberty.

Sometimes, when only a small audience was assembled the players did not act, but this practice seems to have had the

[1] Chambers, *op. cit.*

natural effect of keeping people away; so that on one occasion a notice appeared that in order not to disappoint those living at a distance 'the Company are resolv'd never to dismiss'.[1] Another inconvenience was the last-minute alteration of the programme so that an audience who had come to see one play sometimes found the curtain rising on another; the actors were at last forced to announce that 'As many Inconveniences have arose by altering Plays, or Entertainments, at a short Notice; these are to acquaint the Gentlemen and Ladies, that no other Play, or Farce can possibly be represented, after those publish'd in the Ipswich Journal, or specified in the Bills of the Day.'[2]

The players were wont to be regulated in their choice of plays to some extent by requests. Innumerable performances are by the desire of ladies and gentlemen; in 1734, for example, the company was requested to return from Colchester 'to their New Theatre at Bury, to perform a small Number of bespoke Plays'. On occasion some city gallant would have a fancy to take part in the performance; thus one played 'for his Diversion' Leontine in *Theodosius* on August 4, 1735, and doubtless paid for the privilege.

At Colchester the comedians performed before the Princess of Orange and a great audience. Patronised by royalty and leading county families such as the Berniers and Pettus's, the company's standard must have been fairly high. It is not likely that the gentry would have encouraged mere tattered strollers. Though the nobility and quality figure most freely in the advertisements there is evidence that merchants, too, were patrons; thus *George Barnwell* was advertised as meeting with 'great Encouragement from the Merchants and Citizens of London', and Norwich trade was made the subject of a special prologue.

[1] *Ipswich Journal*, October 28, 1749.   [2] *Ibid.* December 2, 1749.

Plays

New plays were often given soon after they had seen the light in London. Thus Fielding's *The Wedding Day*, given at Norwich in May 1743 was announced as 'acted at London, this winter with Applause'; Havard's *King Charles I*, given in London on March 1, 1737, appeared in Norwich, 'As it is now Acting in London with great Applause', on April 11; *The Beggar's Opera*, which London had acclaimed in January 1728, was presented in Norwich by April and, 'after the New Manner, at Bury, Colchester and Ipswich, with very great Applause', by November of that year.

Within the period 1721–50 seventeen of Shakespeare's plays were acted by the company, sixteen at Norwich, and *Romeo and Juliet* at Beccles. This includes the adaptations of *Macbeth*, *Timon*, *King Lear* and others, but does not take account of such a hotch-potch as *The Universal Passion*. I can trace twelve performances[1] of *Macbeth*, eight of *Hamlet*, seven of *Timon*, five of *Henry IV*, *Richard III* and *Othello*, and four of *King Lear*, *The Merchant* or *Jew of Venice* and *As You Like It*. During these years *Henry IV*, *King John*, *Measure for Measure*, *As You Like It*, *Twelfth Night* and *Henry V* were given first performances at Norwich. It is to be noted that the tragedies were more popular than the comedies, and that more performances of *Macbeth* can be traced than of any full-length eighteenth-century play. It was no mean achievement to keep Shakespeare so constantly alive in the provinces.

Other Elizabethan plays that were performed were *The Maid's Tragedy*, *The Scornful Lady*, *The Chances*, *Rule a Wife*, *A New Way to Pay Old Debts* and *The Royal Merchant*.[2]

---

[1] In estimating number of performances one must remember that the newspapers generally advertised the play only for the first day of the week. Very many more representations were given than we know of, but the proportion of times any particular play was given probably remains about the same. Unless otherwise stated I have counted performances in Norwich only.

[2] Altered by Henry Norris.

Forty-one Restoration plays[1] were given during these years, of which we can trace the following number of performances: *The Constant Couple*, ten; *The Rival Queens*, nine (seven consecutive); *Love's Last Shift*, eight; *The Committee*, *Love for Love* and *Oroonoko*, seven; *The Mourning Bride*, six; *The Relapse*, *The Provok'd Wife*, *The Cheats of Scapin*, five; *Theodosius*, *The Spanish Fryar* and *Œdipus*, four. Comedy here was rightly preferred.

I have found mention of seventy-five full-length eighteenth-century plays, of which Steele's *The Conscious Lovers* had eleven performances; *The Miser*, ten; *The Provok'd Husband* and *The Careless Husband*, nine; *The Beggar's Opera* and *The Country Lasses*, eight; *The Beaux Stratagem*, seven; *The Recruiting Officer*, *Jane Shore* and *King Charles I*, six; *Cato*, *The Wife's Relief*, *Love Makes a Man* and Thomson's *Sophonisba*, five; *The City Wives Confederacy*, *A Bold Stroke for a Wife* and *The Double Gallant*, four.

Afterpieces were sometimes included in the programme as early as 1711, but were not advertised as a regular feature until 1730, when the success of *The Beggar's Opera* had established a vogue for ballad operas such as *Damon and Phillida* and *Flora*, which could be called 'after the manner of *The Beggar's Opera*'. There is evidence of the performance of sixty-one afterpieces in Norwich, and of these Carey's *Honest Yorkshireman* recurs most often with eighteen representations, followed by *The Devil to Pay*, thirteen; *The King and the Miller of Mansfield*, *Damon and Phillida*,[2] *The Contrivances*, eleven; *The Rival Milliners*, nine; *The Lying Valet*, *The Stage-Coach*, *The What D'ye Call It*, eight; *Intrigues of Harlequin*, seven; *Bridegroom Bilked*, *Tom Thumb*, *The Mock Doctor* and *Miss in Her Teens*, six.

Norwich did not lack variety in plays or players. Actors

---

[1] Taken here and elsewhere to cover the period 1660–1700.

[2] The 1730 edition of Cibber's ballad opera 'As perform'd by His Grace the Duke of Grafton's Servants, at the Theatre at Norwich' was altered by Frisby (*Gazette*, January 24–31, 1730).

from London did not scorn to play in the company, and scenery and costumes were from time to time obtained from London theatres. The city was well served, not by an itinerant band of impoverished strollers, but by a company capable of showing its citizens the best in old and the latest in new drama.

Chapter IV

THE PLAYERS IN NORWICH, 1750–1758

There is really no break at the half century in the history of the Norwich players; it is merely a matter of chapter convenience. But the closing of the White Swan Playhouse and the opening of the new theatre on January 31, 1758, do mark the end of an era. The 'fifties and 'sixties of the century were decades in which, as we have noted, several of the permanent theatrical companies were established in new, and comparatively luxurious, theatres; an acknowledgment long due to their untiring efforts.

For the last eight years of this period we have almost full records from the files of the *Norwich Gazette*, *Norwich Mercury* and *Ipswich Journal* in the British Museum, Norwich Public Library and offices of the *Norwich Mercury*. These enable us to trace the company to all the towns it visited in Norfolk and Suffolk and therefore to learn, more fully than in the case of other centres, details of a major company's activities, not only in its chief town, but in all the smaller places included in its itinerary.

In February 1750 the Norwich Company performed for some three weeks at St George's Hall, King's Lynn. This hall, whose theatrical history dates from 1592, still stands, and may be viewed by kind permission of Messrs G. M. Bridges and Son, who use it as a repository for scenery. It was described[1] in 1738, as 'a large spacious Room cover'd with a high Roof of Irish Oak'. The writer continues: 'it is used but seldom; as at the Quarterly-Sessions of the Peace for the County of Norfolk, during the Time of the Mart, and sometimes it hath

[1] B. Mackerell, *The History and Antiquities of King's Lynn*, 1738, p. 251.

been granted to a Company of Strolling-Players during the
Time of the Mart, and somewhat longer, according as Mr.
Mayor pleases'. In the next century William Richards[1]
records that it 'is said to be very convenient and neat, neither
profusely ornamented nor disgustingly plain; and although
not free from faults, yet they are, it seems, what resulted
from the architect having to fill up the shell of an old
building which had been erected for another purpose'.
Built originally as a guildhall for St George's Guild, it was,
subsequent to its use as a theatre, employed as a granary and
wool warehouse. To-day, it remains a fine, spacious hall with
a large seating capacity, and it has returned to theatrical
purposes.

Here the company presented their new production of
Hill's adaptation of *Henry V*, *A New Way to Pay Old Debts*,
and Garrick's version of *Romeo and Juliet*, with a new ballad,
entitled Les Plaisirs de Jeunesse, introduced into the mas-
querade scene. Shakespeare was followed by *The Pleasures of
the Town*, described as 'a satyrical, burlesque, whimsical,
operatical Piece'. 'In this Farce', runs the announcement,
'the Company will be entertained from the low Grimace of
Punch, up to the elevating Sensation of the lulling Italian.
As this is the most extraordinary Piece that ever was represented by a Company of living Puppets, we dont doubt but
the Goddess [of nonsense] who hath so long reign'd pre-
dominant will still continue her Influence...that the Ladies
be charm'd...and the Gentlemen pleas'd...and the whole
Audience satisfied.' For this great occasion, which was for
the benefit of the Pearsons, the boxes and pit were laid
together at 2*s*. 6*d*., the gallery was 1*s*., and 'It is humbly
hop'd that the Gentlemen and Ladies will not think it an
Imposition, (or that it was merely calculated for this Town)
that the Prices are raised; it having been the Method the
Norwich Company have proceeded in ever since their first
Establishment; and which hath been kept up by mutual

[1] *History of Lynn*, 1815, p. 1172.

Agreement at every annual Benefit; for which Reason there is but one during their Residence in any Town.'

From Lynn the company returned to Norwich, where they played until the end of April. The chief features of this season were the acting of Richard III by a gentleman of the city; the first performance there by this company of *The Old Batchelor*; the production of *Measure for Measure* with the following cast: Duke—Peterson, Angelo—Pearson, Escalus—Hicks, Provost—Mrs Sunderland, Lucio—Freeman, Barnardine—Crouse, Pompey—Morgan, Claudio—Bawtree, Mariana—Mrs Pearson, Juliet—Mrs Hill, Francisca—Mrs Freeman, Mrs Overdone—Mrs Plomer, Isabella—Mrs Bowman. Mrs Bowman could still play a young part though she had been years in the company; and although she was compelled to beg to be excused a personal application to the ladies and gentlemen for her benefit, owing to 'being very much afflicted with Rheumatism', yet, on the night itself, she played Angelica in *Love for Love*.

The Garrick *Romeo and Juliet* was advertised as having been played for twenty successive nights at Drury Lane, and was given the following cast: Romeo—Peterson, Escalus—Bawtree, Paris—Mansfield, Montagu—Hicks, Benvolio—Mrs Sunderland, Capulet—Crouse, Friar—Pearson, Apothecary—Morgan, Peter—Miss Frisby, Watchman—Girling, Mercutio—Freeman, Lady Capulet—Mrs Bowman, Nurse—Mrs Plomer, Juliet—Mrs Pearson.

Mrs Sunderland had played Paris in Ipswich and, since she so often filled male parts, must have had what was known as a 'breeches figure'.

The month of May was spent in Aylsham, where the company promised never to disappoint their patrons by dismissing without playing, when audiences were sparse. There they acted Cunningham's farce *Love in a Mist*, which had been brought out in Dublin in 1747. Thence they removed to Harleston for June, advertising that 'The House will be fitted up in an entire new Manner, and the Stage

adorn'd with Side Boxes'. This practice of fitting up boxes
along the sides of the stage had been started in the London
theatres about 1738,[1] and was in constant use throughout the
period 1750–8, at most of the towns in the Norwich circuit.
Thus in Walsingham in 1751, the stage was formed into side
boxes in an elegant manner 'so as to render it airy and agreeable, as well as to prevent any Obstruction in the Performance'; in Yarmouth the stage was made into an 'amphitheatre
...so as to render it warm and Commodious'. The arrangement, in fact, could be made to suit every season of the year!
It seems to have been confined to special occasions, when
either a great crowd was expected, or some elaborate piece
of staging was toward, its main object being to prevent
people from overcrowding the stage to the detriment of the
performance.

At Harleston, *The Petticoat Plotter*,[2] by the York comedian
Henry Ward, was produced, and was subsequently pre-
sented at Ipswich and at Norwich during Assize week. The
company acted at the Tankard Street Theatre in Ipswich for
three weeks in July, and then proceeded to Woodbridge
Town Hall, where they played Mondays, Wednesdays and
Fridays from July 20 to August 8. Thence they returned to
Norwich for the Assizes where, in a revival of Mrs Cent-
livre's *The Man's Bewitch'd*, we first hear of the Prigmores;
Prigmore doubled the parts of Sir Jeffrey Constant and
Slouch, and Mrs Prigmore played Laura.

From Norwich the company toured to North Walsham,
remaining there from August 27 to September 15. On the
last night Harlequin not only escaped into the Quart Bottle,
'as for 60 nights successively at Covent Garden', but 'for the
farther Satisfaction of the Audience' came out of the same.
The comedians then visited Bury and Colchester, performing

[1] Odell, *Shakespeare from Betterton to Irving*, vol. I, p. 284.
[2] This farce, taken from an older one of Hamilton's, was acted in York
(see *post*, p. 135), but does not appear to have been given in London.
Ward's *Widow's Wish* was also in the company's repertoire.

every night but Saturday for three weeks in the latter town. Here on the last night, for the benefit of the Pearsons, White-head's *The Roman Father* was produced, 'decorated in an elegant Manner, with all the Pomp suitable to so grand an occasion.... The Approbation this Piece met with from crowded Audiences at the Theatre-Royal in Drury-Lane, is the Motive which induced us to offer it to our general Benefactors.'

It is interesting to note that the company did not reserve for Norwich their first performances but gave them im-partially, sometimes at one town, sometimes at another. The tragedy was followed by a new and otherwise unknown farce called *A Lover's Resolution*. A short stay in Ipswich followed, after which the company betook themselves to Yarmouth for the month of December. Here again they acted every night but Saturday, and there was but one benefit. The company begged that gentlemen would not be offended if not admitted behind the scenes while there was room in the front of the house. Full prices were taken until the end of the third act, and, thereafter, nothing under half price 'during the Time of the Action'.

The itinerary of the company varied from year to year, but the more important towns were visited regularly every year about the same time. Thus Norwich had the company for the first four months of the year, and for a week or two in July and August during the Assizes. The Ipswich seasons were three weeks in June or July (in 1756 it was as late as August) during the races, and the end of November or beginning of December. Bury in September or October, followed by Colchester in October or November and Yarmouth at the turn of the year, were regular circuit calls. The smaller towns were visited somewhat haphazardly. Aylsham had the Company in May 1750, 1751, 1752, 1754, and June 1757; Walsingham in August 1751, July 1753, May to July 1755,[1] July 1757; Bungay July 1752, June to August

---

[1] In consequence of this long stay the company omitted their summer visit to Ipswich this year.

1754, June 1756; North Walsham August to September 1750, September 1752, 1754; Woodbridge July 1750, September 1752, 1754; Dereham May 1751, 1753; Harleston June 1750; Beccles August 1752. An additional visit was paid to Bury in May 1755.

During the spring season at Norwich 1751, the company gave the Shakespeare-Hill *Henry V* with the following cast: Henry V—Peterson, Exeter—Pearson, York—Prigmore, Cambridge—Williams, Scroop—Bawtree, Harriet—Mrs Pearson, K. of France—Crouse, Dauphin—Freeman, Bourbon—Hicks, Charlotte—Mrs Sunderland, Katharine—Mrs Bowman. The production included 'A new scene of a Bridge, where the English and French Monarchs had an Interview.... The Meeting', the announcement continues, 'will be adorn'd with a Procession of both Nations, their separate Standards, and all other Decorations proper'. *The Roman Father* and *A Lover's Resolution* were given their first performance in Norwich. The Petersons chose Tate's version of *King Lear* for their benefit, with a cast as follows: Lear—Peterson, Gloster—Crouse, Kent—Pearson, Bastard—Bawtree, Edgar—Freeman, Albany—Hicks, Cornwall—Wignell, Burgundy—Williams, Physician—Prigmore, Usher—Mrs Sunderland, Old Man—Girling, Goneril—Mrs Bowman, Regan—Mrs Prigmore, Arante—Mrs Wignell, Cordelia—Mrs Pearson.

Macbeth was selected by Hicks and Mrs Plomer: Macbeth—Peterson, Macduff—Crouse, Duncan—Prigmore, Malcolm—Bawtree, Donalbain—Williams, Banquo—Wignell, Lenox—Freeman, Seyward—Hicks, Seyton—Pearson, Fleance—Miss Frisby, Lady Macduff—Mrs Bowman, Woman to Lady Macbeth—Mrs Wignell, Woman to Lady Macduff—Mrs Plomer, Lady Macbeth—Mrs Pearson, Witches—Mrs Freeman, Mrs Crouse, Mrs Sunderland, Mrs Prigmore, Hecate—Mrs Hill. *Romeo and Juliet* was still popular and now announced as with the 'Grand Scene of the Tomb' (Garrick's scene), and 'other Decorations entirely New and proper to the Play'. In *The Way of the World* Mrs Bowman played Millamant to the Mirabel of Peterson. Wignell made a first appearance as Lord Hastings in *Jane Shore* on February 25, and Mrs Wignell as the Landlady in *The Suspicious Husband* two days later. The Wignells had been in Herbert's Company in 1743 and in the York Company in 1748; they remained but a year with the Norwich comedians.[1] The last night of the season was reserved for their benefit, at which, after the play of *Love for Love*, Wignell spoke the customary epilogue of thanks to the city on leaving it.

Many nights were bespoken by masonic fraternities; among them the society of Gregorians, the 'most Ancient and Honourable Fraternity of Free and Accepted Masons', and the Bear and Green Dragon Lodges. On the occasion of the bespeak of the last named, the brethren were 'desir'd to be at Brother Lindsey's by Five o'Clock precisely, in order to go Cloath'd as Masons in Procession to the Theatre', where boxes on the stage were railed in for their reception. Masons' songs and a special prologue and epilogue were generally introduced into the performance on such nights. The actors even became masons, and we find Brother Peterson speaking a prologue, Sister Pearson an epilogue and Brother Hind executing a dance. The players must have welcomed these masonic bespeaks, which increased in number as time went on. Masonic processions to the theatre became the fashion, and many notices were appended to theatrical advertisements, advising the masons of their starting place. One lodge announced that 'the Appearance of any of the Brethren of the other Lodges will be esteemed a Favour'. Frequently only masons were admitted to seats on the stage, 'they having taken them for that Purpose: And proper Persons will be appointed to guard the Stage Door to prevent Disorder'. The company chose the race season at Ipswich in which to produce Moore's *The Foundling* with Mrs Pearson in the title role. At Colchester *The Fair Penitent* was played with

[1] For their subsequent career in Kent, see *post*, pp. 251, 254.

Mrs Davis as Calista, and the new production of *The Foundling* was followed by Yarrow's ballad opera, *Love at First Sight*. Yarrow was another York comedian,[1] so that this is the third piece from York to be given by the Norwich Company, a fact which testifies to the continued theatrical connection between the two towns. Mrs Davis appeared as Polly in *The Beggar's Opera* in December at Ipswich, and at this performance one Budd, a new addition to the company, danced a hornpipe in the third act. *Richard III* and *Lethe* were given at the desire of the Young Ladies at the Boarding School, the comedians thus tapping a fresh audience. But the great occasion of this season was the production of Hill's tragedy *Merope*, with an additional scene, with Mrs Pearson as the heroine and Peterson as Dorilas. The advertisement reads:

> The Beauty of this Piece induc'd the Managers of Drury Lane Theatre to purchase it of the Author for a very large Sum; which has answer'd their Expectations by the Approbation it met with from The Town: It being the first Season of its Appearance perform'd fifteen Nights (and the Season following reviv'd) to crowded Audiences, with general Applause. The Play will be conducted with Decorations to each Scene, in particular, the Tomb of Cresphontes, with a solemn Procession, and in the additional Scene, the Temple embellish'd with the Statue of Hercules.

Juliet's tomb no doubt served also for Cresphontes. It was on occasions such as this that the stage was formed into side boxes.

At Yarmouth the playhouse was 'new seated, and the Stage entirely new decorated'. The last night was reserved for *Merope* and *Love at First Sight*, at which Crouse, who shared the benefit with Mrs Sunderland, spoke an epilogue to the ladies and gentlemen of the town.

The company heralded their visit to Norwich in 1752 by the promise of 'several New Performances' and 'Cloaths and Scenes entirely New'. *The Foundling*, *Merope* and an

---

[1] See *post*, p. 131. Mrs Davis was possibly his daughter who married Tom Davies (*post*, p. 141).

otherwise unknown farce called *The Merry Counterfeit*, were the new offerings; *The Fair Quaker of Deal* was revived after an absence of twenty years. *The Foundling* was 'entirely new Dress'd', and 'the Stage New Decorated'; gentlemen were not admitted behind the scenes as long as room could be found in the pit or boxes.

The Hindes, and a dancer named Staples, joined the company this season. Mrs Hinde played Portia at her début with a supporting cast as follows: Antonio—Freeman, Bassanio—Bawtree, Salanio—Pearson, Salarino—Hinde, Morochius—Wignell, Launcelot—Hicks, Gratiano—Crouse, Lorenzo with songs—Mrs Sunderland, Shylock—Peterson, Nerissa—Mrs Crouse, Jessica—Mrs Freeman.

Mr and Mrs Hinde played Macheath and Polly at Ipswich, and Mrs Hinde also played the Fair Quaker to the Mizen of Peterson.

At Bungay, Hoadley's *The Suspicious Husband* was revived with new dresses. Though the company was housed only in a 'Great Theatrical Booth', yet the stage was formed into a complete set of side boxes. *The Relapse* was revived at Colchester: Foppington—Peterson, Amanda—Mrs Pearson, Berinthia—Mrs Bowman.

Mr and Mrs Knipe, who replace the Wignells, first appear in November at Ipswich in the roles of Oroonoko and Lucy Welldon, and later as Archer and Cherry in *The Beaux Stratagem*. The Young Ladies at the French Boarding School this year bespoke *The Conscious Lovers* and *Pygmalion*. On the last night *All's Well* was produced with the following cast: K. of France—Freeman, D. of Florence—Wm. Hinde, Bertram—Bawtree, Lafeu—Pearson, Levatch (Clown)—Crouse, Dumain—Hinde, Dumain jun.—Knipe, Gentleman—Mrs Sunderland, Steward—Hicks, Parolles—Peterson, Countess of Rousillon—Mrs Bowman, Helena—Mrs Pearson.[1] Freeman as the King spoke the original epilogue and

[1] This cast is actually taken from a performance at Yarmouth, January 29, 1753.

Peterson the epilogue of thanks to the town. At Yarmouth
All's Well was followed by a new afterpiece called *Sawney
the Scot; or A Cure for a Scold*, adapted from *The Taming
of the Shrew*. This was probably Worsdale's ballad opera
A Cure for a Scold, which was in fact taken from Lacy's
Sawney the Scot, though Sawney is left out of the piece.

For their 1753 season in Norwich the company announced:
'By Particular Order...the Doors will not be open'd till
Four o'clock, and to begin each Evening exactly at Six.'
Richard III was given: Richard—Peterson, Henry VI—
Freeman, Prince of Wales—Mrs Knipe, D. of York—Miss
Hinde, Tressel—Bawtree, Ld. Mayor—Pearson, Bucking-
ham—Crouse, Richmond—Knipe, Catesby—Hicks, Ratcliff
—Hinde, Queen—Mrs Bowman, Duchess of York—Mrs
Hinde, Lady Anne—Mrs Pearson. Miss Hinde also appeared
in the traditional child's role of the page in *The Orphan*.
Moore's *The Gamester* was produced on March 29, seven
weeks after its appearance at Drury Lane.

At Dereham the company made a point of advertising that
they would stay only three weeks, being due at the Ipswich
Races, and therefore they hoped 'the Gentlemen and Ladies,
our Benefactors, will on our Arrival, be Early in their
Commands, which Favours will greatly be acknowledged
by their most Humble Servants'; a necessary precaution,
since, in the smaller towns, a large proportion of the performances were bespoken by the local gentry.

Norwich first saw Jones's *The Earl of Essex* during Assize
week. Founded on Banks's play, with emendations, 'It was
recommended to the Stage by some of the most eminent
Personages of this Kingdom, who afterwards gave their
general Concurrence for the Performance, and was highly
received by Crowded Audiences Twenty Nights successively'
at Covent Garden in February.

At North Walsham the company acted Mondays, Wednesdays and Fridays, unless altered by request, at the Theatre in
the Bear Yard. *Merope's* scenery had grown more elaborate:

'The Tomb of Cresphontes will be adorn'd with Two Statues of Hercules, representing his Labour and Rest, and the Temple with a Group of Figures, regularly dispers'd and design'd proper to the Occasion; with other Adornments necessary to conducting the Whole.' An additional note assures 'the Gentlemen and Ladies, that proper Musick will be provided, to render their Entertainment as compleat as possible'.

When the company went on to Bury it was reported in a news item in the *Norwich Gazette* that the stage of their theatre there, which stood in the Market Place, would be adorned with new side boxes 'and decorated in an elegant Manner'. *The Earl of Essex* was further described here as Banks's 'Drama regulated', with 'a strict Adherence to History'. It was followed by a revival of *Tom Thumb* in which Miss Hinde, five years old, played Tom. This child also spoke the epilogue of thanks at Colchester at her parents' benefit. At Colchester, too, James Thomson's *Tancred and Sigismunda* was given for the first time.

In 1754 at Norwich no person was to be admitted behind the scenes or on the stage, except in the boxes. It is further announced that 'Liquors of any sort will not be suffered to be sold or brought into the Theatre after the Curtain is drawn up'. It might seem, from the former of these fiats, that the stage boxes were permanent erections. That this, however, was not the case is proved by the facts that, at the revival of *King Lear*, a note was specially made that they would be 'left' for the better reception of patrons, and that, for the Pearsons' benefit, it was announced that the stage would be enclosed and formed into side boxes and 'places may be taken in it as usual'.

At Aylsham an otherwise unknown afterpiece called *The Medley* was produced. During race week in Ipswich Sanders made his first appearance as Teague in *The Committee*. The last night in Ipswich Peterson played Tancred to Mrs Pearson's Sigismunda for the benefit of the Freemans; tickets could be had from them at the Tankard Inn adjoining the theatre, 'where all Commands for Places will be punctually complied with'. Features of Assize week at Norwich were the playing of violin solos in the entr'actes by one Hughes, and the production of William Shirley's *Edward the Black Prince*. This tragedy is said to have received uncommon applause for nineteen successive nights at Drury Lane and to have been revived subsequently to polite and crowded audiences. Its great attraction was the patriotic one of witnessing the English beat the French in battle ten to one: 'The Representation of so glorious an Action must afford to every true Lover of his Country, a Satisfaction of Joy and Mind rather to be felt than express'd. The Colours, Standards, and other Decorations both for the English and French Camp, are all entirely New.' It was followed by the first production in Norwich of Chetwood's *The Lover's Opera*.

A new actress, Mrs Sanders, appeared as Alicia in *Jane Shore* in Bury and as Ophelia with the following cast: Hamlet—Peterson, Ghost—Crouse, King—Pearson, Polonius—Hicks, Laertes—Freeman, Horatio—Bawtree, Osric—Mrs Sunderland, Rosencrantz—Hinde, Player King—Wm. Hinde, Gravediggers—Crouse, Sanders, Player Queen—Mrs Bowman, Queen—Mrs Pearson. The cast of *King Lear* varied from that of 1751 in these particulars: Cornwall—Hinde, Burgundy—W. Hinde, Usher—Sanders, Regan—Mrs Sanders. Of the former cast the Wignells, the Prigmores and Williams were no longer with the company. At Colchester one Briggs played Chamont in *The Orphan*, and Lothario in *Don Quixote in England* for his diversion. On November 29 the New Theatre in Tankard Street was opened at Ipswich for the benefit of Betts, the builder of the house.[1]

In Yarmouth on December 30, we first come across the well-known actor John Moody, who played Careless in *The Committee*.[2] The new play for the last night here was Brown's

---

[1] See *post*, p. 104.
[2] For his subsequent long career under Garrick see *D.N.B.*

Barbarossa, which had been produced about five weeks previously at Drury Lane and was still running there. Peterson
played the title role to the Zaphira of Mrs Pearson and the
Othman of Moody.

The opening of the season of 1755 at Norwich was uneventful except for the production of *Barbarossa* which was
reported to be in rehearsal on March 22, and was given on
March 31, Easter Monday. Vanbrugh's *The Cornish Squire*,
which had been tried out at Bury, was the only other new
piece given. Hughes still played violin solos, accompanied
by one Love. The masons continued to be good patrons, and
the New Enter'd Prentice's and Grand Treasurer's Songs were
sung on one of their nights; on another Moody rendered a
New Occasional True Blue Song, and on the Jockey Club's
night that society's song was introduced into *The Devil to Pay*.

It was announced in the *Gazette* of March 15 that 'the
Norwich Comedians (on their Norfolk Circuit this Season)
intend entertaining the Gentlemen and Ladies, with several
new Performances lately exhibited at the Theatres in London'.

Moody played Macheath to Mrs Sanders's Polly in May
race week at Bury. To Walsingham, *The Medley*, *The Fair
Quaker*, *Henry V*, *Barbarossa* and *The Cornish Squire* were all
new pieces. *King John* was the plum of Assize week in
Norwich, 'As reviv'd lately in the Theatre Royal in Drury
Lane, to crowded Audiences.' 'It will be decorated', continues the advertisement, 'with New Scenes. One whereof
will represent the Walls of Angiers, with the Gates through
which the English and French King make their Entrance
into the Town. The Coronation of King John, will be adorn'd
with the Regalia, and everything proper to the Grandeur
thereof; nor will any Embellishment be omitted that may be
necessary to set off the Play in the Lustre it so justly Merits.'

At North Walsham, where the company played three
times a week, the Gentlemen Bowlers bespoke an evening.
In *The Beaux Stratagem* Peterson, the leading man, chose to
play Scrub in preference to Archer, which was taken by

Crouse. Moody's name does not reappear until April 1757, so that it looks as though he temporarily left the company.

Othello was revived at Bury in October after twenty years, with the following cast: Othello—Peterson, Iago—Sanders, Roderigo—Crouse, Cassio—Maclellan, Duke—Hinde, Brabantio—Pearson, Lodovico—Bawtree, Gratiano—Hicks, Montano—W. Hinde, Emilia—Mrs Sanders, Desdemona —Mrs Pearson. This is the first we hear of Maclellan, who had been with the York Company,[1] and who probably replaced Moody. Morris, a dancer, was another newcomer. Yarrow's afterpiece *Trick upon Trick*[2] was produced at Bury, followed by an epilogue of thanks from Miss Hinde; *Barbarossa* was graced with an original humorous prologue and epilogue spoken respectively by Crouse and Peterson.

Mendez's *The Double Disappointment* was brought out at Ipswich under the title of *The Fortune Hunter; or Phelim o'Blunder*. Another new afterpiece, called *The Plotting Lover*,[3] saw the light at Yarmouth during the winter season.

Maclellan's first appearance on the Norwich stage was as Lycon in a revival of *Phaedra and Hippolytus* in February 1756; later he played Faulconbridge in *King John* and spoke 'a new occasional Prologue in which will be consider'd The Rise, Progress and Grand Use of the Stage' to *Barbarossa*. He specialised in speaking prologues and epilogues among which was a prologue in the character of the recruiting officer 'calculated to the present Crisis'. New entertainments were Murphy's *The Apprentice, Harlequin Captive; or the Humours of May-Day*, and *The Happy Captive; or the Loves of Harlequin and Columbine*.

At Dereham Master Hinde, aged five, assumed his sister's former role of Tom Thumb. *Henry IV* and *The Merry Wives* were both new to this town.

A great event took place at Bungay, when a performance

---

[1] See *post*, p. 142.   [2] See *post*, p. 131.
[3] Possibly Charles Shadwell's *The Plotting Lovers*, printed in *Five New Plays*, 1720.

was given by desire of the Beccles masons. The *Norwich Gazette* for July 31, 1756 pictures the scene for us:

They set out from their Lodge at Beccles, accompanied with a Number of the Fair-Sex by Water, and were saluted at their Landing in Bungay, with firing of Guns and ringing of Bells; after Dinner they proceeded to proper Business in the Lodge, and were usher'd to the Playhouse with Musick preceding, amidst a numerous Throng of People. The Play of A Wonder! a Woman keeps a Secret; was play'd for their Entertainment, which was universally approved of; and every Thing carried on with Great Decorum. The Night concluded with a cheerful Glass, and firing of Guns.

Foote's *The Englishman in Paris* was the new farce given in August in Ipswich and during Norwich Assize week. Mrs Chalmers made her début in Norwich as Juliet. At Bury *The Merry Wives* was advertised as 'With the Characters dress'd in the Old English Taste'. When *All for Love* was revived this year at Ipswich for the benefit of Mrs Bowman, Mrs Chalmers played Cleopatra, Peterson Anthony, and Maclellan Ventidius. Though James Chalmers[1] had probably joined the company at the same time as his wife, he is first mentioned as Sir Francis Gripe in *The Busy Body* at Norwich on February 1, 1757. Crofts, for long a member of the York Company, also made his appearance as Whisper on the same night. A dancer of the name of Gosnold is a third addition. During this season, too, Mattocks from Drury Lane acted with the company, playing Macheath, Sir John Loverule in *The Devil to Pay*, in which part he sang The Early Horn, and Quaver in *The Old Man Taught Wisdom*. For his benefit, which he shared with Mrs Freeman, he repeated his performance as Macheath. William Hinde had deserted the legitimate stage for puppets and was exhibiting artificial comedians at the Red Lion.

[1] He was long with the company. An engraving of him as Midas, by Watson after a painting by Wm. Williams, shows him as a stumpy little man, with a coarse face.

An otherwise unknown farce called *The Privateer; or Love with Honour* was brought out this season. On June 4 a news item reads: 'On Thursday Mr. Crouse paid into the Hands of the Mayor 30*l*. being the whole Money collected at a Play acted on Wednesday Night for the Benefit of the Poor in this City.' The old custom of a tax for the poor on the players thus persisted. The paragraph leads us to assume that Crouse was the manager, or at least the treasurer, of the company at this time, and it also shows how comparatively small were the takings of the house.[1] On June 11 the *Gazette* printed 'An Occasional Prologue, wrote and spoke by Mr. Maclellan, on Wednesday the First Inst. (at the Play of Romeo and Juliet, for the Benefit of the Poor of this City) which met with more than expected Applause, from a very Genteel and Polite Audience, assembled upon that Occasion.' The prologue's opening couplet runs

> Of all the social Virtues Men esteem,
> Sure Heav'n-born-Charity's the worthy'st Theme—

the rest can well be left to the imagination. In this *Romeo and Juliet*, Moody no doubt played the hero and Mrs Chalmers the heroine, as they did a fortnight afterwards at Aylsham. Aylsham was honoured by the opening production of Home's *Douglas*, 'As lately acted at Edinburgh' and at Covent Garden, 'with all decorations proper to the play'. At Ipswich this tragedy was followed by Smollett's comedy *The Reprisal*, as performed at Drury Lane for twenty nights, with a humorous epilogue 'Address'd unto Every-Body, not aim'd at Any-Body, to be spoke by Some-Body, in the Character of No-Body'. At Walsingham the epilogue was given 'With some few additional Lines annex'd as a Return of Thanks for Favours conferr'd; address'd to the Ladies and Gentlemen of the Town of Walsingham; together with all its several most worthy Environs: by H. Maclellan.' The

---

[1] At King's Lynn in May Herbert's Company had made £74 for the masters and seamen who were prisoners of war.

gallery of the playhouse was enlarged 'for ease and coolness' for this occasion. During Norwich Assize week Stebbing made his début as Henry V.

Among those commanding performances at Bury the Duchess of Grafton was one, the family thus keeping their long connection with the Norwich Company.

The Crouses for their benefit in Ipswich put on *Œdipus* 'With Alterations by Sherridan': and with 'The Scenes, Machines, Prodigies, Flyings, Sinkings, and other Decorations proper to the conducting the whole, entirely new', including the public entry of Œdipus into Thebes, Purcell's original music, and a humorous epilogue! I have not seen it elsewhere stated that Thomas Sheridan tampered with *Œdipus*. In Yarmouth the company produced a couple of new afterpieces, *The Comical Reconcilement* and *The Humorist; or The Miser Reform'd*, both of which are otherwise unknown.

Whilst the company was still acting in Ipswich, the first notice about the new theatre building in Norwich appeared in the *Gazette*:

To all Gentlemen and Ladies. The Proprietor of the New-Theatre, humbly Requests that no Gentlemen or Ladies would desire Admittance till the same is quite finished; as the Business they are now engaged in there, will receive great injury and be much incommoded thereby; and as he has given this publick Notice, hope no Gentlemen or Ladies will give themselves the Trouble of going for the Purpose till the House is opened, or take it amiss in case of Refusal of Admittance.

This request of December 17 seems to have been ineffective, for on January 14, 1758, it was reinforced by another:

Gentlemen and Ladies 'Tis humbly beg'd by the Proprietor of the new Theatre, that no Gentlemen or Ladies will ask for admittance after this 14th of January as the House is proposed to be entirely shut up for the better conveniency of finishing the same, till it is opened, which will be on Thursday the 31st Inst. with Romeo and Juliet. The grand Procession with all other suitable Decorations, a complete band of Musick, &c.

The *Gazette* of January 28 blazes into laudatory description:

The Grand and Magnificent THEATRE in this City, which is now finish'd, and to be open'd on Tuesday the 31st of this Instant January,—is allow'd by all Connoisseurs and Judges to be the most perfect and compleat Structure of the kind in this Kingdom. It is most admirably constructed for seeing and hearing; —the Stage is large and lofty;—and the Scenes so highly finish'd and executed, by the late ingenious Mr. COLLINS, that they are accounted far superior to any of the kind.

The Satisfaction the Structure and Decorations hath given, has induc'd the Gentlemen who are Subscribers, to desire the Receipts of the First Night may be solely appropriated to the Use of the Proprietor, . . . a compleat and regular Band of Musick is provided —and the greatest Care has been taken to air the House, by keeping constant Fires, so that we can assure the Ladies, Gentlemen, &c. that there is not the least Damp throughout the whole Building.

Romeo and Juliet was replaced by *The Way of the World* and *The Mock Doctor*: 'on Account of the Processions not being compleated, nor the Musick properly adapted—the Proprietor and Company being resolved to entertain the City in the most correct Manner, and with the Elegance the Structure requires.'

The prices were, boxes 3s., green boxes 2s. 6d., pit 2s., first gallery and slips 1s., upper gallery 6d. Places were to be taken for the boxes at the theatre from ten to twelve in the morning, and servants were to be sent to keep those places at 4 p.m. Thomas Ivory's theatre opened its doors on January 31: 'when the Elegance of the Structure, and the easy manner of conducting the appertaining Materials (a choice Band of Music &c) gave great Pleasure and solid Satisfaction to a very numerous, genteel, and polite Audience; consisting of more than a Thousand Spectators.'

The other side of the picture is to be found in an entry in Faculty Book 3 of the Diocese of Norwich[1] under the date

---

[1] See *East Anglian Notes and Queries*, New Series, vol. II, p. 408.

March 31, 1758, which records the grant of an Episcopal Licence or Certificate for a body of Protestant Dissenters to meet for religious worship in the old White Swan Playhouse.

On October 22, 1758, Joseph Peterson, aged forty, died in the arms of Moody, whilst playing the Duke in *Measure for Measure* at Bury, and was buried on October 24 in St James's Church there.[1] The *Biographia Dramatica* says that he had 'great versatility of talent', and cites Moody that 'he looked the perfect gentleman on the stage, fenced and danced elegantly, excelled in the parts of Sciolto [*Fair Penitent*] and Sir Charles Raymond [*Foundling*] and was also a very good harlequin'.[2] In character he is said to have been 'a gentlemanly, affable, and good-natured man, and much beloved'.

One or two matters remain for consideration. The prices generally advertised at Norwich during these years were boxes 3s. or 2s. 6d., upper boxes 2s. or 1s. 6d., pit 2s. 6d. or 2s., first gallery 1s., upper gallery 6d. As both scales of prices are in most cases quoted for special occasions, such as opening nights of the season, one cannot be sure whether the lesser of them represented normal prices which sometimes also obtained on special occasions (though usually the higher range of boxes 3s., upper boxes 2s., pit 2s. 6d. was charged for first and last nights, benefits and new plays); or whether both scales represented prices which had been raised above the ordinary. Prices were not always augmented for a new play, for when *Edward the Black Prince* and *The Lover's Opera* were first presented it was 'at common prices'. In Bury the prices were stage and boxes 3s. or 2s. 6d., pit 2s. 6d. or 2s., gallery 1s. 6d. or 1s., upper gallery 1s. or 6d.; in Colchester the stage is quoted at 2s. 6d. or 2s., boxes 2s. 6d., pit 2s., gallery 1s.; in Ipswich, at the first night of *Merope*, the boxes

[1] Bury St Edmunds, St James's Parish Registers, xvii.
[2] We find him playing this role to the Columbine of Mrs Freeman and the Clown of Crouse in *The Intrigues of Harlequin*.

and stage were 2s. 6d., pit and side balconies 2s., gallery 1s. These were probably all advanced prices. Yarmouth had pit and boxes at 2s., gallery 1s., upper gallery 6d., but raised the pit and boxes to 2s. 6d. on a last night. Twice for perform- ances there by desire of the Gregorians, the pit and 'twelve- penny' gallery were laid together, and the upper gallery raised to 1s. The charges usually quoted at the smaller towns were pit 2s. 6d., gallery 1s. At North Walsham the stage and pit were 2s. 6d. for the Petersons' benefit, and, for the opening of *Merope*, the boxes and pit were laid together at 2s. 6d. But at Lynn, when the boxes and pit were laid to- gether at 2s. 6d. an apology was made, as we have seen, for raising the prices, which leads us to surmise that normal charges were less and that prices were only mentioned at all when they were higher than usual.

Times of starting ranged from six to seven, according to the time of year, getting later as the days lengthened.

Benefits were usually given on last nights and never more than one in any town but Norwich, where there was always a series of four or five at the end of the spring season. Some actors had one, some two, and some three benefits a year. These seem to have varied in different years, though in the absence of complete information we cannot definitely say that this was so. They certainly did not keep to the same towns for their benefits. Thus the Petersons had benefits in Lynn and Harleston in 1750, in Ipswich, Norwich and Walsingham in 1751, and in Norwich, Bungay and Ipswich in 1752. Sometimes husbands had more benefits in the year than their wives, sometimes wives than their husbands, depending, no doubt, on their importance in the company.

Of the twelve Shakespeare plays or adaptations[1] given during these years on the whole circuit, *Romeo and Juliet* in its new version is far the most advertised with eighteen per- formances. The others are *All's Well*, *Hamlet* and *King John*,

[1] I have not counted Hill's *Henry V* or *The Universal Passion* in this list, as they were more the adapter's than Shakespeare's.

nine; *Richard III*, eight; *The Merry Wives* and *Henry IV*, seven; *King Lear*, six; *The Merchant of Venice* and *Othello*, five; *Measure for Measure*, four; *Macbeth*, three. The only other Elizabethan play given was *A New Way to Pay Old Debts*.

Twenty-four Restoration plays were performed of which the following lead in number of performances advertised: *The Committee*, fourteen; *Sawney the Scot*, twelve; *The Cheats of Scapin*, *The Provok'd Wife*, ten; *The Beaux Stratagem*, *Love for Love*, *Oroonoko*, *The Orphan*, *The Way of the World*, nine; *The Old Batchelor*, *The Relapse*, *The Squire of Alsatia*, *Œdipus*, six; *The Rival Queens*, *Love's Last Shift*, *The Constant Couple*, five.

Forty-eight full-length eighteenth-century plays were in the repertoire, the most often performed being: *The Beggar's Opera*, twenty-six; *The Conscious Lovers*, twenty-three; *Love Makes a Man*, eighteen; *The Suspicious Husband*, seventeen; *The Provok'd Husband*, fifteen; *Merope*, *Barbarossa*, fourteen; *The Roman Father*, *The Foundling*, thirteen; *The Careless Husband*, *The Fair Quaker*, *The Gamester*, twelve; *The Earl of Essex*, eleven.

Of the fifty-six afterpieces Garrick's *Lethe* takes the lead with forty performances, followed by *The Devil to Pay*, thirty; *Miss in her Teens*, twenty-five; *The Lying Valet*, twenty-three; *The Mock Doctor*, *A Lover's Resolution*, twenty; *The Intrigues of Harlequin and Columbine*, *Pygmalion*, *The Double Disappointment*, nineteen; *The King and the Miller of Mansfield*, eighteen; *The Honest Yorkshireman*, *Damon and Phillida*, seventeen; and *The Pleasures of the Town* and *The Merry Counterfeit*, fifteen.

Rival entertainments in Norwich included the diversions of the 'celebrated Mr Cooke' and 'the famous African prince' on the slack wire, followed by tricks by a trained dog and Foote's new entertainment with an additional scene, in January 1753, at the Red Lion; the feats of the famous Maddox on the slack wire at the White Swan in November 1754, and Mrs Midnight's concert and oratory performances of pieces such as *The Beggar's Opera* for a winter season in 1755 at the White Swan.

Other companies visited Norfolk towns. Thus we find a company, possibly the Huntingdon one, at Swaffham at the Crown Inn playhouse three evenings a week from December 2 to January 3, 1754–5. We learn that 'The Place of Performance is warm and Commodious, and the utmost Care will be taken to render the whole agreeable.' *Theodosius* was performed with 'all the Paintings and Illuminations proper to the Play'. When the Huntingdon Company was at the Red Lion Inn, Fakenham, January to February 1755, they advertised this same play as 'with Dresses, Paintings, Illuminations, and every Decoration proper to the Play, Likewise a grand Altar-Piece, and a New Transparent Scene'. After a few days' stay they announced that 'Proper Musick will be provided for the Future', and that they would perform only on Mondays and Thursdays.

Of the activities of Herbert's Company, the only trace is the benefit performance, referred to above,[1] of *The Fair Penitent* at King's Lynn.

[1] P. 89, n. 1.

Chapter V

A NOTE ON THE PLAYERS IN
IPSWICH 1728–1750

The theatrical history of Ipswich in the eighteenth century is, as we have seen, largely bound up with that of the Norwich Company. However, in addition to the information given here and there in the preceding chapters, something remains to be said of the early visits of the Norwich Company, of the visits of other companies, and of the city's theatres. These matters have only been partially dealt with by H. R. Lingwood, in his *Ipswich Playhouses*, 1936.[1]

We first hear of the Norwich Company in Ipswich in November 1727, though no doubt many previous visits had been paid. The company played in the Shire Hall which had been erected in 1699 for the Quarter Sessions. Two engraved views of the exterior of this hall, long since demolished, can be seen in the Ipswich Public Library, but unfortunately no print of the interior has come to light.

It was at this time that the Norwich Company was split into two factions, and that known as the old company of comedians appeared in Ipswich in February 1728. They produced Welstead's *The Dissembled Wanton* and Lee's *Mithridates* 'Drest'd in Cloaths entirely new, with a new Set of Scenes from London'. *Hamlet* was given with the following cast: Hamlet—Frisby, Polonius—Paul, Horatio—Morris, Queen —Mrs Paul, Ophelia—Mrs Frisby. In the first performance here of *Henry IV* the cast was: K. Henry—James, P. of Wales —Frisby, Hotspur—Marshall, Falstaff—Paul, Bardolph—

---

[1] A series of articles reprinted from *The East Anglian Times*.

Milward, Lady Percy—Mrs Buck, Mrs Quickly—Mrs Plomer. The season lasted until the beginning of April.

The reunited company returned in November and stayed until December 14. They performed at six o'clock 'by Order of their Worships the Bailliffs'. A yearly benefit 'and positively the only one in Town' was accorded to Plat, Mrs Buck and Mrs Pearson.

Unfortunately, no advertisements are available for 1729, and we do not know where the company played that year. That disaster overcame them is evidenced by a paragraph in a pamphlet entitled *A Prelude to the Plays*, 1729, by a follower of Collier's, which cites the falling down of the Ipswich play-house, 'to the Hurt of many, and the fright of many more', as a divine rebuke.

At the usual winter season in 1730 lasting from November 18 to December 21, the Norwich Company was again at the Shire Hall. *Julius Caesar* was presented for the first time in the city. When *Damon and Phillida* was played, the book was to be obtained at the printing office, and at the playhouse, for 1s. We next trace the comedians to Ipswich in the winter of 1733. They acted there in a playhouse in St Nicholas Street, all traces of which have disappeared. They gave Steele's *The Tender Husband* and Hawker's *The Wedding* for the first time, and a performance of *King Lear* with the following cast: Lear —Pitt, Edgar—Bowman, Bastard—Woodward, Kent—Paul, Cordelia—Mrs Buck, Goneril—Mrs Bowman, Regan—Mrs Plomer.

In November 1734 the famous tight-rope walker, Madame Violante, appeared at the Great Booth in Griffin Yard, near Cornhill. In July 1735, John Child's puppets performed a whole play entitled *The Inconstant Lover* at the Cock and Pye Tavern.

The playhouse in the yard of the Griffin Inn was used by Dymer's Company of Comedians[1] in November 1735, who

---

[1] This was the Kentish Company whose usual circuit was Canterbury, Maidstone, Dover, etc. See *post*, pp. 218 *et seq.*

seem to have taken the place of the Norwich Company this winter. His actors were Dymer, Scudamore, Giles, Bawtree, Paddick, Jones (the dancing master), Osmond, Maxfield, Tenoe, Master Dymer, Mrs Paddick, Mrs St Nicholas, Mrs Scudamore, Mrs Northey and Mrs Adams, many of whom afterwards joined the Norwich Company. *The Beggar's Opera* was performed with the men playing the women's parts and the women the men's. On December 6-13, the *Ipswich Journal* hears that 'Mr Dymer's Company intends to perform three times a Week, during their stay in this Town, except a Play be desir'd on any particular Night'. The following pieces were given: *The Provok'd Husband, The Miser, The Mock Doctor, Tunbridge Walks, Damon and Phillida, The Inconstant, Flora,* and *Love for Love,* at which Giles spoke Haines's famous epilogue riding on an ass. On the production of this last play it was announced 'particular care will be taken that every Part shall be performed as above'; on another night, that 'particular care will be taken to keep the House warm'. The company stayed until January 13, and launched four benefits. The season is said to have met with the 'general applause of the Auditors'. The Duke of Grafton's Servants still made use of the Griffin Yard Playhouse when they visited Ipswich in June 1736. They played three times a week, and on account of the races started at the late hour of 8 p.m. *The Jew of Venice* was acted with a cast as follows: Antonio —Woodward, Bassanio—Buck, Shylock—Pitt, Gratiano— Platt, Lorenzo—Upton, Duke—Giles, Salerio—Bawtree, Portia—Mrs Plomer, Nerissa—Mrs Buck, Jessica—Mrs Jackson. *Love Triumphant, The Honest Yorkshireman, A Wife Well Managed* and *Pasquin,* in which the parts were 'to be perform'd in the exactest and most modern Manner', were all new to the town.

In this year Sir Anthony Wingfield's house in Tacket or Tankard Street, as it was then called, was bought by Henry Betts and converted into the Tankard Inn. And next door to the inn arose a new theatre which was to have a long history.

THEATRE IN TANKARD STREET IPSWICH WHERE GARRICK MADE HIS FIRST PUBLIC APPEARANCE, 21st JULY 1741.
IT WAS STANDING TILL ABOUT 1600 WHEN THE PRESENT THEATRE WAS BUILT UPON THE SAME SITE.

Engraved from a Drawing in the Possession of James Winston Esq.

The Shire Hall, the Griffin in Westgate Street, and the play-house in Tacket Street are all marked in John Pennington's map of Ipswich in 1778. An engraving of the Tacket Street Theatre, showing the exterior of the theatre as it appeared in 1800,[1] is reproduced opposite p. 98. We first hear of it in use, described as the New Theatre in 'Tankard Street', by Shepphard's puppets in November 1736. At the end of their season Shepphard gave a benefit performance of *Dido and Æneas* for Betts the builder, for which he charged 1s., 6d. and 3d.

The Norwich Company were at the Tankard Street Theatre in July 1739: 'The Company will begin at 7 o'Clock exactly, during this Season, which will be no longer than One Week after the Races.'

King John was first given in Ipswich at common prices, as follows: John—Drury, Prince Arthur—Mrs Jackson, Queen Eleanor—Mrs Plomer, Faulconbridge—Pitt. The actors were followed by a medley from Bury Fair in October, which consisted of a 'machine clock', puppets, sleight of hand, dancing and pantomime. For these performances side boxes were 1s. 6d., pit 1s., middle gallery 6d., upper gallery 3d.

The Norwich Company had evidently not yet made a regular practice of including both a summer and winter visit to Ipswich in its annual itinerary. In January 1741 a company, which included the Daniels, Cuthberts, Hasleups, Whitakers and Freeman, was at Tankard Street, acting Mondays, Wednesdays and Fridays only, unless desired, for a month. Among the plays they gave were: *The Busy Body, The Lover His Own Rival, The Jew of Venice, Chrononhotonthologos, The Spanish Fryar, Britons Strike Home, Tunbridge Walks, A Bold Stroke for a Wife, Hob in the Well, Love Makes a Man, The Devil to Pay.*

But the great event of the year 1741 was the arrival in June of a company from London, under the direction of Giffard

---

[1] It was pulled down soon afterwards and a Salvation Army building now stands on the site.

and Dunstall, in which David Garrick made his stage début
under the pseudonym of Lyddall. In the company were also
Yates, Paget, Crofts, Vaughan, Julian, Marr, Dunstall,
Giffard, Harrington, Mrs Dunstall, Mrs Yates and Miss
Hippisley. The principals had their names distinguished by
capitals in the advertisements. *The Beaux Stratagem* was given
with Giffard as Archer, Harrington as Aimwell, Yates as
Scrub, Mrs Dunstall as Mrs Sullen, Miss Hippisley as Cherry.
The cast for *Henry IV* was: Prince of Wales—Giffard,
Hotspur—Paget, Falstaff—Dunstall, Hostess—Yates, Kate
[Lady Percy]—Miss Hippisley.

Tom Davies[1] tells the story of Garrick's début:

The first effort of his theatrical talents was exerted in Aboan, in
the play of Oroonoko, a part in which his features could not easily
be discerned; under the disguise of a black countenance, he hoped
to escape being known, should it be his misfortune not to please.
...Our young player's applause was equal to his most sanguine
desires. Under the assumed name of Lyddal, he not only acted a
variety of characters in plays, particularly Chamont in the Orphan,
Captain Brazen in the Recruiting Officer, and Sir Harry Wildair;
but he likewise attempted the active feats of the Harlequin. In
every essay he gave such delight to the audience, that they gratified him with constant and loud proofs of their approbation. The
town of Ipswich will long boast of having first seen and encouraged so great a genius as Mr. Garrick.

Of the plays mentioned only *The Orphan* appears in the
newspaper advertisements, but this does not prove anything,
since there are gaps in the available issues; though the
company played every Monday, Wednesday and Friday, we
have, for instance, only the plays for Monday, June 1,
Monday 8, Wednesday 10, Friday 12, Monday 22, Wednesday 24, Friday 26, Monday July 6, Wednesday 8, Friday 10,
Tuesday 21. It was on this last date that Lyddall's name is
first mentioned as Duretete in *The Inconstant* with Giffard as
Young Mirabel and Miss Hippisley as Bisane. In his own
farce of *Lethe* he played Ventrebleu and Sir Roger Rakeit.

[1] *The Life of David Garrick*, 1780, vol. I, p. 17.

Lethe was first given on June 20 and repeated on July 21. It is curious that in the announcement of *The Merry Wives* the only casting mentioned is that of Lyddall as Caius.

The company announced that 'Being particularly desir'd we are resolved to begin, for the future, punctually at Seven o'Clock; wherefore we hope those Ladies and Gentlemen that intend to favour us with their Company, will be so kind as to come at that Time'; a very gentle hint to late-comers. During race week the company performed every day, and three benefits were given in all. Paget chose *The Merry Wives* and it was probably then that he spoke one of his two prologues in praise of commerce and in honour of Admiral Vernon and his victory at Portobello, which are incorporated in his *A Voyage to Ipswich* (1741).[1]

Garrick was borne back by Giffard to his London triumphs, and at the beginning of December Yeates's Company from the New Sadler's Wells arrived with a repertoire of farces and pantomimes. They played every evening at six o'clock until December 17 and opened with *The Mock Doctor* and a new pantomime called *The Rival Highlanders*, which was cast as follows: Harlequin—Rosoman, Highlander—Yeates, Father to Columbine—Parker, Pierrot—Waters, Gubby the Clown—Warner, Columbine—Mrs Warner. 'All the Scenes and Tricks' were 'entirely new', and it was announced that 'For the better Reception of Gentlemen and Ladies there is a Fire in the Pit on purpose to keep the House warm'. The boxes were 2*s*., pit 1*s*. 6*d*., first gallery 1*s*., upper gallery 6*d*.

In June 1742 Giffard's Company returned to Ipswich but without Garrick, who had migrated to Drury Lane. They opened with *Richard III* with the following cast: Richard—Peterson, Henry VI—Giffard, Prince Edward—Miss Hippisley, Duke of York—Miss Naylor, Richmond—Yates, Buckingham—Taswell, Stanley—Vaughan, Catesby—Marr,

---

[1] Advertised in the *Ipswich Journal*, August 29, as 'Now in the Press And will speedily be publish'd by Subscription, at 2*s*. 6*d*. each'.

Tressel—Dighton, Oxford—Naylor, Mayor—Dunstall, Queen Elizabeth—Mrs Giffard, Lady Anne—Mrs Dunstall, Duchess of York—Mrs Yates. Peterson later became the leading actor in the Norwich Company. *Richard III* was followed by *The Lying Valet*, advertised as having been written by Garrick and performed upwards of thirty nights successively at Goodman's Fields. *Othello* was chosen for the Giffards' benefit on August 17, Giffard playing Othello, Peterson Iago, Yates Roderigo, Mrs Yates Emilia and Mrs Giffard Desdemona.

The Norwich Company were in Ipswich in December 1743, and from that time onwards gave two regular seasons at the Tankard. They advised their patrons that 'particular Care will be taken that their Performances shall be conducted with the utmost Decency and Regularity'. *Pygmalion* with *The Marriage of Harlequin and Columbine* was brought out with 'Musick, Songs and Dances proper to same', and with Cartwright as Harlequin, Mrs Schoolding as Columbine, Crouse as Pierrot and Stone as Pygmalion. When *Pygmalion* was given the second time it was followed by a Lilliputian epilogue in the character of a Recruiting Sergeant by Miss Frisby. Bespeaks were given by Lady Barker and Philip Broke, and performances were held every night but Saturday, nothing under full price being taken. During the summer season *The Provok'd Wife* was done with 'All the characters New-dress'd', Stevens playing Sir John Brute, Mrs Bowman Lady Brute, and Mrs Crouse Belinda.

During their month's stay in December 1744, Cale made his first appearance as Scrub in *The Beaux Stratagem*, and Beaufort his in *The Roman Maid*. Cale also played Harlequin to Mrs Freeman's Columbine. In the summer of 1745 the company chose Ipswich in which to bring out *As You Like It* with the following cast: Duke Senior—Freeman, Duke Frederick—Allen, Amiens—Miller, Jaques—Beaufort, Oliver—Crouse, Orlando—Bawtree, Adam—Upton, Touchstone—Pearce, Le Beau—Mrs Marshall, Silvius—Mrs

Allen, William—J. Girling, Rosalind—Mrs Bowman, Celia
—Mrs Freeman, Phebe—Mrs Crouse, Audrey—Mrs Plomer.
It is to be noted that two of the men's parts were taken
by women.[1] *Macbeth* was put on the following summer,
Mrs Pearson making her first appearance here as Lady
Macbeth and Mrs Hill as Hecate. The former was gradually
to take the lead from Mrs Bowman, and the latter was for
some time the company's singer. Peterson came back to
Ipswich with the Norwich Company in June 1747, playing
Sir Courtly Nice and Alexander in *The Rival Queens*, to the
Statira of Mrs Pearson and the Roxana of Mrs Bowman. By
Philip Broke's desire in July 1748, *Measure for Measure* was
revived, after five years, with the following cast: Duke—
Peterson, Angelo—Pearson, Escalus—Hicks, Claudio—Baw-
tree, Lucio—Freeman, Provost—Mrs Sunderland, Fryar
Peter—Massey, Pompey—Holland, Barnardine—Crouse,
Isabella—Mrs Bowman, Mariana—Mrs Pearson, Juliet—Mrs
Hill, Francisca—Mrs Freeman, Mrs Overdone—Mrs Plomer.
The last night of this season Hughes's *The Siege of Damascus*
was produced for the benefit of the Freemans and the Pearsons
with Peterson as Caled, Mrs Pearson as Eudocia, Pearson as
Eumenes, 'The Saracens and Christians in proper Habits. . . .
The Grand Meeting of the Two Nations before the Walls
of the City, will be adorn'd,' continues the advertisement,
'with all the Magnificence and Splendour suitable to so grand
an Occasion.' When this play was later given at Colchester,
it was foretold that 'the Justness of the Drama. . .Delicacy of
Language and Elegance of Stile, will, we presume, recommend it to all that have a Taste of Theatrical Performances,
not only as it is wrote with the true Spirit of English Poetry,
but wholly intended to inspire the most noble Sentiments,
and inculcate the strict and laudable Rules of Virtue'.
    At the end of 1748, Cunningham made his first appearance

[1] Though advertised as the first time by the company a version had
been played at Woodbridge in 1742 with Silvius—Mrs Schoolding, Le
Beau—Coyle.

in Ipswich as a singer, and took the part of Macheath with Mrs Hill as Polly. *A New Way to Pay Old Debts* was produced on the last night for the benefit of Peterson and Mrs Hill, with this cast: Overreach—Peterson, Lovell—Pearson, Welborn—Bawtree, Order—Mrs Sunderland, Amble— Miss Frisby, Farnase—Hicks, Walthall—Girling, Will-do— Cunningham, Tapwell—Hicks, Greedy—Crouse, Alworth —Mrs Freeman, Marrall—Freeman, Margaret—Mrs Pearson, Mrs Froth—Mrs Plomer, Lady Alworth—Mrs Bowman. Mrs Freeman did not usually take men's roles and it looks as though the Company was short on the male side. For this performance the stage was 2s. 6d., pit 2s., galleries 1s., presumably an advance on the normal prices.

Romeo and Juliet, in the new Garrick version, was revived in the summer season of 1749: Romeo—Peterson, Paris— Mrs Sunderland, Peter—Miss Frisby, Mercutio—Freeman, Nurse—Mrs Plomer, Juliet—Mrs Pearson, Escalus, Prince of Verona—Bawtree, Tybalt—Morgan. The boxes were 2s. 6d., pit and balconies over box 2s. Prices for the last night of the winter season of 1749-50, when Steele's *The Lying Lover* and Henry Ward's *The Widow's Wish* were given, are quoted as boxes 2s. 6d., pit and balconies 2s., gallery 1s. One surmises that the balconies, which were also called side balconies, took the place in this theatre of upper boxes.

Thereafter for several years the theatrical history of Ipswich is just a part of that of the Norwich Company. They continued to visit the town regularly for a summer and winter season, except in 1755 when the summer season was omitted. The Tankard Street Theatre was remodelled in 1754 and the announcement of the 'opening of the New Theatre' for the benefit of the builder of the house was made in the *Ipswich Journal* for November 23. The opening took place on November 29, and tickets were to be had from Mr Betts near the theatre, Betts being almost certainly the builder in question. Two years later, on October 30, 1756, an advertisement appeared 'To be Lett immediately A

Publick-House known by the Name of the Tankard situate in Tankard-Street, the greatest Thoroughfare in Ipswich; to which is annex'd, the Playhouse....For further particulars enquire of Sarah Ward at the said House; Mr Edward Betts, Common-Brewer in Ipswich; or of James Pollard, Shopkeeper in Claydon.'

Whether the theatre passed out of the hands of the Betts we do not know, but it continued to be used by the Norwich Company until 1802.

Chapter VI

THE YORK COMPANY, 1705–1744

York follows naturally upon Norwich since, as we have noted, the two cities were closely connected theatrically in the early part of the eighteenth century.

Our main sources of information about the York players are the minute books of the Merchant Taylors' Hall,[1] the contemporary issues of the *York Courant*[2] and the *Leeds Mercury and Intelligencer*,[3] and the plays and poems written by various members of the company. The Corporation House Books have only one mention of the players; and licence to act is not recorded in them.

In two ways York differs considerably from the other towns dealt with in this book. First, the season in York was organised, at any rate from 1732 onwards, on a subscription basis, though since there were not enough subscribers to fill the theatre, seats for individual performances were available. This system affected the payment of the actors who, as a result of it, were early put on a salaried instead of a sharing footing. Secondly, York is unique in producing its own dramatists. Arthur, Yarrow, Peterson, Ward, all members of the company, produced comedies, many of which were also acted outside York. In addition, one, John Maxwell, a blind poet, wrote several verse tragedies which were probably not produced at all. That other centres did not create

---

[1] Kindly examined and transcribed for me by Mr B. P. Johnson.

[2] The *York Herald* office has a good series from 1733 onwards, which I have been allowed to examine. There are, however, many years completely wanting and several with large gaps.

[3] Extracts from Leeds papers quoted from Thoresby Society Publications.

any drama of their own is in fact a curious feature of provincial theatrical activity. Even in York the local comedies do not seem to have been revived, and are none of them mentioned in newspaper advertisements.

We first hear of the players in York from a memorandum in the minute books of the Merchant Taylors, dated February 23, 1705:[1]

It was then Ordered and Agreed the Day and year above written by us whose names are here unto Sett, at The Court then Assembled the said day, That Mr. Gilbert and his Company shall have the use and bennifitt of the Hall to play in and shall pay for the same to the p'sent Master Mr. Jñ Riveley, for the use of the Company the Sume of Twenty Shillings weekly And it is further Covenanted and Agreed that Jñ Jackson the Printer and Jñ Gilbertson Joyner shall Give bond that none of the Sealing or fflower in the said Hall shall in any ways be Damnifyed but shall make good and leave the same in as good order as they now find it; and shall now begin to pay weekly or enter to pay untill Thursday next be the 29th of Instant.

The next entry concerning the players is dated July 10, 1711: 'Agreed then with Mr Ager for the use of the Hall with the p'sent Master Mr Geo. Barnatt and he the said Mr Ager is to pay unto the Said Master £1. 1s. 6d. Weekly and is to Enter on tuesday the 16th of this Instant July./10th August.' 'Mr Ager' was without doubt the 'Thomas Aiger' who succeeded Doggett as manager of the Duke of Norfolk's Servants and whom we have met acting in Norwich in 1707.[2] For, in 1713, there was printed a blank verse tragedy entitled 'The Fall of Tarquin. A Tragedy. By W. H. Gent', which, the Biographia Dramatica[3] tells us, was acted by the Duke of Norfolk's Servants at the Merchant Taylors' Hall, and was

---

[1] About 1682 Sir Thomas Player wrote to Sir Henry Thompson and Sir John Hewly to ask them to encourage Elkanah Settle, who designed to carry down Coysh (see ante, pp. 38 et seq.) and others to act plays or drolls in York. We do not know if the plan was ever carried out (Cal. S.P. Dom. 1682, p. 536).

[2] See ante, p. 46.   [3] Vol. II, p. 217.

never acted or printed anywhere but in York. The dedication
to Madame Bethel of Ryse confirms that 'the drama had
never presum'd beyond a Northern Theatre', and it may be
assumed that Ager acted it either in 1711 or on an unrecorded
return visit in 1712 or 1713. Gent informs us that the author
was William Hunt, 'a gentleman adorned with great learning
and humanity, who had been near twenty years before his
death composing a book of Geography', that he was a
collector of excise at York, and that he died in 1714.[1] The
verdict of the *Biographia Britannica* that the tragedy is 'a most
wretched performance' can only be endorsed. It is an old-
fashioned, blank verse play, a poor remnant of heroic tragedy
tradition; the scenes are mere episodic snatches which do not
build up to a whole. It is full of bombastic blood and fury of
this kind:

> 'Twas Hero like, to have a ravish'd Crown
> Streaming with Blood, and gorgeously beset
> With Royal Deaths

to which we might well reply with Clelia the heroine:

> Oh dont I pray, do not thus wildly rave,
> 'Tis useless all, indeed 'tis all in vain.

This kind of ineptitude perilously reminds us of Pyramus and
Thisbe. The prologue and epilogue were written by Dr
Towne.[2]

A scurrilous satire entitled *The Northern Atlantis; or the
York Spy*, which appeared in print in 1713, after giving an
unpleasant description of the odours in the crowded playhouse continues:

We sat not long before the Musick entertain'd us with a
Flourish, the Curtain was Drawn, and the strutting Actors
Commenc'd their Foolery. I was extremely satisfy'd with their
Performances; for every Thing was Acted to such a perfection

---

[1] *Historia Compendiosa Anglicana*, 1741, pref. p. viii.
[2] According to a note in MS. in the British Museum copy.

of Uncouthness, that had so many Dicks and Dolls, as are sold in the French Shop i' th' Minster Yard, been Cloth'd and qualified with Speech, we cou'd not have Laught more heartily at their preposterous, awkward Imitation; every one looking, notwithstanding his Garb, like what he really was, and not what he represented.

But we must remember that this description, in a coarse and satirical pamphlet, does not necessarily convey a true picture of theatre-going in York.

On September 5, 1715, another Memorandum records an agreement:

that Mr. Ager is to have and Enjoy the Hall…Six Weeks at Lent Assize and Six Weeks at Lammas Assize, he paying to the Said Company fforty shillings in each Assize being in part of Six Pounds then payable, And he the Said Mr. Ager is to give the Said Company One Month's Notice before Either of the Said Assizes shall happen to begin or doe fall. And upon failure of the Said Notice to be Given to the Said Company by the Said Mr. Ager then the Said Company shall be ffree to let the Said Hall to whom they please and the fforty shillings…to be fforfeited by the said Mr. Tho: Ager in his not Coming or Giveing notice as aforesaid,

signed by Thomas Ager and John Lupton.

Thus were inaugurated the two York seasons, the first a spring one, the second covering the August race week.

On August 29, 1716, Ager secured a lease of the Hall for seven years, for which he was to pay £12, whether he came or no. If he exceeded the six weeks assigned him at Lent and Lammas, he was to pay £1 a week for every extra week, 'provided the Right Honourable the Lord Mayor of this City Give him Liberty to Act. And further it is Agreed that the Master, Wardens, and Assistants shall Call a Court in time within the said six weeks without any Disturbance or Molestacon of the said Mr Ager.'

The Merchant Taylors' Hall was not, however, the only place of acting about this time, since Mary Davys's *The Northern Heiress: Or, The Humours of York* was presented at the Market House in the Thursday Market, now St Sampson's Square.[1] Francis Drake[2] says that this 'beautiful and useful structure', which was completed in 1705 'for the shelter of market people in bad weather', stood on the west side of the square; the engraving of the exterior in his volume shows the upper room where plays were acted, and the steps leading up to it.[3] According to the *Biographia Dramatica*, Mary Davys was born in Ireland, was a correspondent of Dean Swift's, married a clergyman and, after his death, kept a coffee house in Cambridge. She, however, alludes to herself in the prologue to the comedy as 'A Female Muse from Northern Clime'. In her preface she relates 'how industrious some of the York Gentlemen were to damn this Play', yet how on the first night the result was but two hisses. This comedy contains some satire at the expense of York society: 'we have abundance of People, but little Company; much Ceremony, but little Manners; many Folks with Titles, but few of Quality', the usual flock of coxcombs and country boors, and the ubiquitous quartette of lovers. The situations and intrigue lack inventive power; the style, which is windy and heavy, is completely devoid of wit.

The next we hear of the players is in 1720, when the Merchant Taylors' minute book records that it is 'ordered by the General Consent of this Court that whatsoever of the Sealing, fflower or Glass Windows which is or Doth in any way appear to be Damnifyed or Broke by the players, the Said Master is to Gett them repaired and that the players shall make Satisfaction for the same before they be Admitted to have the Benefitt or use of the Said Hall'.

By 1721 the company had been taken over by Thomas Keregan, whom we have already met acting with the Duke of Norfolk's Servants as early as 1710.[4] He continued for a

[1] The comedy was given at Lincoln's Inn Fields, April 1716. The York production must have been earlier in the year or possibly in 1715.

[2] *Eboracum*, 1736, p. 324.

[3] It was later used as a school, and demolished in 1815.

[4] See p. 49.

while to keep his connection with Norwich, and, as we have seen, his company appeared there in 1723, 1724 and 1725. He is said to have visited Leicester and Nottingham during the races, and, in 1721, The Moot Hall, Castle Garth, Newcastle, was let to him for six weeks from June 5. During Race Week there he played: Monday, *Twin Rivals*; Tuesday, *Country Lasses*; Wednesday, *Man's Bewitch'd*; Thursday, *Woman is a Riddle*; Friday, *Fair Example*; Saturday, *Inconstant*; Monday, *The Unhappy Favourite*; and on Monday, July 3, *The Island Princess*, 'with a sea-scene wherein Neptune, tritons and mermaids, are floating on the waves'; when, 'notwithstanding the vast charge, we shall play at common prices, although at other places, the prices were doubled'. On another Monday *Sophonisba* was given.[1] On June 3, 1722, Ralph Thoresby noted in his Diary that a 'Vicar in Leeds' particularly inveighed against plays, which reproof was the more necessary, because 'we have had in town a company of players six or eight weeks, which has seduced many, and got abundance of silver'.[2] Keregan's Company was probably the cause of this outbreak. He revisited Newcastle in 1723 and acted *The Conscious Lovers* at the Moot Hall on June 10.

We first positively hear of him in York on March 19, 1724, when, Ager's contract having expired in 1723, he obtained a renewal from the Merchant Taylors:

At a Court of Assistants by Speciall Warning Given, it was agreed upon that a Lease of the Hall be Granted to Mr. Thomas Kerigan for the terme of ten Years to enjoy the Same twelve Weeks in each Year vizt: Six Weeks about Lent Assizes and Six Weeks about Lammas Assizes to commence from the building of the stage at each of the same times which shall not exceed a Week in building. It was then also agreed that if three Sufficient Workmen do agree that in Case a Sellar be Sunk in the Hall for the More Conveniency of the acting to no disadvantage to the Hall that leave be Given to Mr. Kerigan to Sink one at his Own expense, he paying half of the Charge of the Workmen's View.

[1] *Archaeologia Aeliana,* 2nd series, vol. IV, p. 235.
[2] *Diary of Ralph Thoresby,* ed. Rev. Joseph Hunt, 1830, vol. II, p. 341.

After 1725 Keregan abandoned Norwich to his rivals; in 1726 he was in Canterbury for Easter, but thereafter seems to have concentrated on the north.

For some reason during the summer season of 1727 Keregan did not act at the Merchant Taylors and on August 14, 1727: 'It was unanimously agreed that Mr Kerrigans rent due, in the Months of July and August, 1727 Shall be remitted him.' He played instead at Banks's Cock-Pit without Bootham Bar, as is proved by a playbill reproduced by Tate Wilkinson.[1] This bill, though dated only T. 15, is safely assigned to this year, since the performance advertised includes a Congratulatory Poem on the Accession of King George[2] written, and to be spoken, by Orfeur. Since the 15th fell on a Tuesday in August, during the race week season, we are able to date the bill precisely. The play performed was *The Mourning Bride* and it was for the benefit of Orfeur: 'Who is debarr'd the Liberty of paying his Respects, and making his Interest on the Account of an Action in the Power of Mr Huddy from one at London.'[3] The cast list enables us for the first time to know the names of some of the actors and actresses in the company: King—Orfeur, Gonsalez—Woodward,[4] Garcia—Theo. Lacy, Perez—Goodfellow, Alonzo—Gibbs, Osmyn—Keregan, Hely—Miller, Selim—Fuller, Almeria—Mrs Glassington, Zara—Mrs Keregan, Leonora—Mrs Goodshaw. Dancing and dialogues, set to music by Purcell, filled out the entertainment, which started at 6 p.m.

On October 2, 1727, Keregan was cited, together with one Joseph Simpson, for not paying church assessment, and was indemnified at the Merchant Taylors' charge. A year later, on September 17, 1728: 'At a Court of Assistance it was Ordered that in case the Overseers of the poor of St Cuthbert

---

[1] *Wandering Patentee*, 1795, vol. II, p. 202.

[2] George II acceded to the throne on June 11, 1727.

[3] Orfeur was acting in Richmond in 1724, see *post*, p. 284.

[4] Probably the actor who joined the Norwich Company in 1730. See p. 56, n. 4.

in York do distreyn of Mr Kerrigan for the Poor's Tax for the Hall that the Company will vindicate him for not paying the said tax & that Mr Jenkinson, the Master, Two Wardens and two Assistants have Power to get Councell about the Same at the Company's Charge.'

In the same year, 1728, he played against Herbert's Company in Newcastle. Herbert having secured the Moot Hall, Keregan performed in the Great Booth in Usher's Timber Yard. The companies gave rival productions of *The Beggar's Opera*, Keregan advertising Hulett as the original Macheath from London,[1] and Herbert having Woodward 'who lately performed it at York, in Mr Keregan's Company'.[2] On May 27, 1730 Keregan performed in Newcastle *The Committee* and 'Hob's Opera' at a Freemason's bespeak, with a special prologue and epilogue, and the Freemason's song, with the result that 'Never such an appearance of ladies and gentlemen were ever seen together in this place'.

Keregan extended his season in York in 1731, as we find by an entry in the minute books under October 5: 'it was unanimously agreed that Mr Kerrigan shall have the use of the Hall from the day of the date hereof till Candlemas day [February 2nd] next comeing at the rate of ten shillings per Week during the said terme.'

A spirited epilogue spoken by Mr and Mrs Keregan in York at the end of this winter season, 1731–2, is printed in *The Gentleman's Magazine* for July 1732:[3]

Wife. Hold Consort—Where's this Epilogue I pray?
   You know was promis'd in the Bills to Day.
Hus. Our Poet has deceiv'd us,—and what then?—
   D—n his dull Head, and split his venal Pen;
   The Price I offer'd might have spurr'd his Wit—

---

[1] Walker was the original Macheath, but Charles Hulett is said to have excelled him in the part. See Genest. Herbert visited Leeds in 1729 and played Coffey's *Beggar's Wedding*. *Leeds Mercury*, Nov. 4–11.
[2] *Archaeologia Aeliana*, 2nd series, vol. IV, p. 236.
[3] P. 871.

Wife. Rail not on him, 'tis you yourself is bit.
    Poor man, I'm sure, he labour'd Day and Night,
    And work'd his Brain some mighty thing to write,
    'Till tir'd, at last, this Truth he came to know,
    No Words can paint the Gratitude we owe.
Hus. But something must be said; *W.* Why, yes, 'tis true;
    H. And must be spoke by, either me or you.
Wife. Come on then Sir, clear up your cloudy Face,
    A Look like that wou'd the best Words disgrace!
    We're us'd t'harangue in Verse, faith e'en let's try
    Who best can chant Heroicks, you or I.
    What! marching—stop for shame, and turn again:
    You shall address the Ladies,—I the men.
Hus. Well, since it must be so,—I'll do my best;—
    Ladies!—see here a truly grateful Breast,
    Which labours now and heaves to think which way
    To ease a Debt, it never can repay.
    Your favour to our late Subscription shown,
    An Obligation we shall ever own
    Has rais'd us from the Depth of black Despair,
    And made the Winter, as the Summer, clear.
    What Choice of Blessings ever wait the Dead,
    Who cloath the Naked, and the Hungry feed;
    Behold these Objects—those your Kindness warms,

                   (pointing to his Actors)

    Secur'd by you from Winter's fierce Alarms;
    Whilst Days and Nights pass cheerfully away,
    Pray for their Benefactors—when they pray.
    How oft within these Walls has Hamlet dy'd,
    With not a cross his Fun'rals to provide?
    Mark Anthony has drop'd so very poor,
    His Chandler's Bill has took up all his Store.
    Nay, the great Cato, we've been forc'd to show
    T'an Audience, as his little Senate, few.
    But now—this charming Pit and glorious Stage,
    So cheers my Heart, as warms me into Rage.
    Let Rich and Cibber boast their crouded Seats,
    Half fill'd with painted Whores, and Bawds, and Cheats;
    Here sit the Northern Stars, and shine so clear
    T'out-rival all within the Hemisphere.

Whose darling Beauty strikes the strongest Light,
With sterling Virtue join'd—makes all divinely bright.
Oh may your Influence another Day,
(For this, alas, is but a parting Ray,)
When next we court your favour, kindly shine,⎫
And our best Services, we'll not repine,   ⎬
But offer 'em humbly up at beauty's Shrine.   ⎭
Wife. Well off indeed!—now Gentlemen for you,
To whom an equal Share of Thanks is due,
But don't expect it in his high flown Lays,
Pick'd out from Ends of Verse and Scraps of Plays.
A plain and humble Muse shall speak my Mind,
I'll call you Mortals,—but of gen'rous Kind;
Whose Goodness, to our Company express'd,
Shall dwell for ever in my Grateful Breast.—
But now, to end this Struggle for the Bayes,
How shall I gain your Hands t'applaud my Lays?
My Spouse has plac'd your Ladies in the Sky, ⎫
Pray where must I put you? above 'em—'fy!   ⎬
Why then, e'en pluck 'em down again, you cry;⎭
For, after so extravagant a Sketch,
They seem as gone as ever,—from your Reach.
Such strange Poetick Flights will never bear;   ⎫
How bright soe'er he's made his Stars appear,   ⎬
Believe me, they'd look dull enough—were you not⎭
    here.

From this epilogue we learn that the season was now run
on the subscription system, possibly for the first time, and
that it had proved a success, and had rescued the company
from the poverty to which empty benches had reduced them.

The following September Keregan again extended his
winter season, being granted 'liberty to act in the Hall from
Martinmas next [November 11] to May day following after
at the rate of ten shillings per Week exclusive of the terme
limited for Lent Assizes in his Articles'.

As the interval between his winter and summer seasons
was now only from May to July, he left his stage standing,
whereupon an order went forth on June 20, 1733, 'that from

the 12th instant So long as the Stage Stands till Mr Kerrigan's time of acting by vertue of his Lease that the sd Mr Kerrigan shall pay Weekly five shillings for His Stage Standing & at every time he shall leave the Hall the Windows and Wainscot shall be in repair'.

Keregan's two-year lease of the Merchant Taylors' Hall was due to expire at the end of 1733, and in January 1733 he applied to the Mayor's Court for permission to build a play-house. The Court's judgment, given in the House Books[1] dated January 29, 1733, was as follows:

Mr Thomas Keregan haveing remonstrated to this House that for the Conveniency of the Gentry resorting to this City he purposes to build a playhouse and requesting that some order might be made in his favour. This House being of opinion That the having a commodious playhouse in this City may very much conduce to the Entertainment of the Nobility and Gentry resorting to this City and incourageing them to spend their Winter Seasons here and Mr Keregan having always behaved himself very well in this City. This House dothe approve of the said proposal and resolve to give Mr Keregan all proper Encourage-ment therein and do hereby recommend it to the present and future Magistracy of this City to prohibit all other Companys of Comedians from playing in this City.

Keregan was fortunate in finding so progressive and far-seeing a corporation.

The company spent the three months between the two York seasons at Scarborough and Newcastle. The *York Courant* for May 8, 1733, reports: 'We hear that Mr Keregan was last Week at Scarborough, where he obtained Leave of the Worshipful the Bailiffs, for his Company of Comedians to perform the ensuing Season; upon which he has taken a Piece of Ground to build a large Booth on, by the Sign of the Crown and Scepter in the Horse-Fair, near the Market Place, very convenient for Coaches &c.' Thenceforward

[1] Vol. XLII, p. 161, quoted by kind permission of the Corporation of York.

Scarborough became a regular port of call. The author of *A Journey from London to Scarborough in Several Letters*[1] writes to his friend:

> In the Afternoon are Plays acted, to which most of the Gentry in Town resort; Kerregan from the Theatre at York, is here every Season with his Company; and allowing for Scenes and Decorations here, they perform several Plays very well. After the Play is over it is customary to go to the Long-Room again, where the Gentlemen and Ladies dance or play 'till about Nine, and then sup in Companies'.

On May 1, 1733, Keregan advertised his return to Newcastle in the *York Courant*:

> Mr Keregan's Company of Comedians, which play'd last Year in the Moot Hall in Newcastle upon Tyne, will, in the Time of the next Horse Races there, which begins the 21st of May Instant, perform in the Great Booth in Mr Usher's Timber-Yard, near the Black Gate, which is the Enterance into the Castle-garth; and hopes for a favourable Encouragement from the Quality and Gentry, being at a great Expence in Building, and bringing down the fullest and best Company he ever yet had there.

Keregan's new theatre in Minster Yard, York, was not ready until October 1734. It was situated in Lord Irwin's Yard where the Residentiary now stands, a position too near the Minster to be altogether tactful. In the *York Courant* of September 17, a reward of 5s. is offered to anyone 'who shall write the best Prologue or Epilogue, for the opening of Mr Keregan's New Theatre in this City: And, that the ingenious Mr Maxwell, the celebrated Mr Lashley, and a Reverend Clergyman in the Country have already sent in their Performances.' The authors were to have the privilege of speaking their verses should they wish to do so. On September 24, the newspaper announces: 'that on Tuesday next [October 1] will be open'd Mr Keregan's fine new Theatre, with a Prologue and Epilogue suitable to the Occasion. It is to be

[1] [1736] 2nd ed. p. 42.

hoped that the Gentry and others of this City will consider the great Charge he has been at for their Diversion, and let him taste a little of their Bounty before the Subscription Plays begin.'

Wilkinson[1] reproduces the playbill for this occasion, at which *Henry IV* was given for Keregan's own benefit: 'it being the only night he desires' of the ladies and gentlemen 'before subscription time, notwithstanding his great Charge for their Reception'. Charges were boxes and stage 3s., pit 2s., middle gallery 1s. The playbill continues:

The Play will be all new dress'd with New Scenes, from London, suitable to his House: With a Prologue and Epilogue. The Musick consists of Overtures, Concertos, Sonatos, and Solos. Three Pieces will be perform'd before the Play begins: The first at five o'Clock, the second at half an hour after five, and the third at six; at the end of which, the Curtain wil' be drawn up.

It adds that, on Thursday, October 3:

Will begin a Subscription for Twenty-six Plays at Two per Week, Box and Stage Tickets a Guinea and a Half each; A Ticket for the Pit One Guinea. Tickets may be transferr'd. Those who don't subscribe, are liable to the above-mention'd Price. As there is no difference made of the Boxes, those who bespeak them first, sending their Names to the Box-Keepers, will have 'em kept for them. N.B. No Servants will be admitted to any part of the House with a Subscription Ticket.

The subscription for twenty-six plays allows for a thirteen weeks' season which in future years was to start at the beginning of January. Saturdays were usually devoted to benefits which were not, of course, included in the subscription series. The *York Courant* of October 8, speaking of the opening night, relates that 'a vast Concourse of Gentry, &c. appeared; and were exceedingly well pleased with the Elegance of the Scenes, and the Performance of the Actors'. The prologue, which was written by Maxwell and spoken

[1] *Wandering Patentee,* vol. II, p. 203.

by Keregan, is the customary well-worn defence of the stage by classic example:

When Athens flourish'd, and the Grecian State,
Submissive, on its great Decrees did wait,
Over their Manners then the Stage did rule,
Approv'd with Wit, condemn'd by Ridicule,
Each virtuous Mind, by just Example form'd;
And show'd how Vice and Folly shou'd be scorn'd.
In Public, Kings, disdain'd not then to shew
Favour to Poets, and to Actors too.
So much they esteem'd all those who did excel,
Either in Writing, or in Speaking well.
Augustus in the Zenith of his Fame, ⎫
When suppliant Kings in Adoration came, ⎬
Preferr'd a Poet's to a Monarch's Name. ⎭
In Public wou'd his Tragedies rehearse,
And dwell with Pleasure on the Charms of Verse.
This shew'd how much Antiquity approv'd
The Buskin'd Muse, how well the Comic lov'd.
While Sophocles, by Turns the Soul alarm'd, ⎫
Now chil'd with Terror, now with Pity warm'd, ⎬
And polish'd Terence every Audience charm'd ⎭
The British Muse disdains to stoop her Wing,
No higher soars, but does as sweetly sing.
Whether in Love's delightful Scenes she strays,
Or to severer Virtue points the Ways;
Harmoniously, her numerous Beauties shine,
As if Apollo dictated each Line.
Studious to please, we'll rifle all her Store,
And to Delight unusual Paths explore;
But if the modish Taste so far prevail
That our Attempts to please in this shou'd fail,
Then we'll engage Attention by Surprize, ⎫
Make Witches Ghosts, and frolick Devils rise, ⎬
And dance to the hoarse Music of the Skies, ⎭
All Ways we'll prove, your Favour to obtain;
Than your Applause, we wish no other Fame.
If You, ye Fair, approve of our Design,
And in this Galaxy vouchsafe to shine?
The Men, compell'd, your Motions will obey,
They must attend, where Beauty leads the Way.

The Epilogue, spoken by Mrs Keregan, was in lighter vein:

I Think, I've somewhere read in antient Stories,
Of strange Philosophers call'd Pytha-gories.
I'm sure 'tis some such Latin Name they give 'em,
And I, who know no better, must believe 'em.
To these same Men, they say, such Souls were given,
That after Death ne'er went to Hell, nor Heaven,
But liv'd, I know not how, in Beasts, and then
When many Years were past, in Man again.
Methinks, we Play'rs resemble such a Soul,
That, does from Bodies, we from Houses strole,
That Aristotle's Soul, of old that was,
May now be damn'd to animate an Ass;
Or in this very House, for ought we know,
Is doing painful Penance in some Beau.
Our Fate, to whom we've often been a Sport,
At length has toss'd us to a Tennis Court.
These Walls have, some time since, been fill'd with Noise
Of roaring Gamesters, and your Damn-me-Boys.
Then bounding Balls and Rackets they encompass'd;
And now they're fill'd with Jests, and Flights, and Bombast:
But I vow I don't much like this Transmigration; ⎫
Grant Heaven we don't return to our first Station, ⎬
Strolling, from Place to Place, about the Nation. ⎭
I know not what he thinks, but, for my Part,
I can't reflect, without an aking heart,
How we shou'd end in our Original—a Cart.
But Providence, we hope, design'd this Place
To be the Players Refuge in Distress;
That, when the Winter comes, we may all flock hither,
As to a Shed, to shield us from the Weather.
For, like Noah's Dove, the Water's yet afloat,
We must return from whence we first set out.
And now we're thus set up, pray don't leave us;
We cannot fear, when you're so good to save us.
For from the past, we hope for future Grace,
I beg it—
And some here know I have a begging Face.
Then pray continue this your kind Behaviour,
For a clear Stage won't do—without your Favour.

It is of interest to note that, as so often, the theatre was an adapted tennis court.[1]

There is an unfortunate gap in the newspapers from 1735 to 1738, so that we know but little about these years. A playbill in the Minster Library[2] can, however, be dated January 1736. A mention of King Charles's martyrdom gives us the month, and, since the bill is marked Tuesday the 27th, the year must have been 1736, when January 27 fell on a Tuesday. It is reproduced opposite p. 122.

A few words about one or two of the actors who figure on the bill.

Chetwood[3] tells us that Mrs Furnival, having acted several capital parts in York, was sent for by the manager of Drury Lane, on the recommendation of a person of high birth. She must have left the York Company early in 1737, as she made what Genest considers may have been her first appearance in London on March 17.

The Copens had previously been in the Bath Company.[4]

Crisp, who had but a minor part in *Timon*, was later to become the leading actor in the company, and to retain that position until ousted from it by Frodsham. He was a relation of Keregan's and had previously played at Goodman's Fields. He is said to have been well made but awkward. His acting was of the strutting, bouncing variety, and he was always at the top of his voice. His fellow-actor Robertson satirically writes of him:

> Lo! Nature's direst foe, King Crisp appears,
> And with discordance vile torments our ears;
> The signal cue when giv'n, the machine moves,
> It strikes the same whether it chides or loves;
> An octave higher always than the rest;

[1] The tennis court is marked on *A New and Exact Plan of the City of York*, Haynes, 1748.
[2] In a volume *York Playbills Printed by Thomas Gent.*
[3] *General History of the Stage*, 1749, p. 157.
[4] See *post*, p. 173.

Sweet harmony ne'er touch'd that callous breast
A wooden poor Automaton at best:
With toes turn'd in, thumbs cock'd, and bellman's cant,
It scolds, nay whispers always in a rant:
Ended the speech, fix'd to the spot it stands,
Till cue-struck, once again it lifts its hands.

He married Miss Tollett, who had been an actress at Drury
Lane, who dressed neatly and was a genteel person, but who
as a tragedian quavered in imitation of Mrs Porter. She
played the young girl too long and brought upon herself the
scorn of Robertson, who writes of her:

'that wither'd, antique dame,
Murders the youthful parts; oh, shame! shame! shame!
Patches and paint in vain their aid supply.
The old crack'd wall tho' varnish'd o'er we spy.'

The Crisps were held in high esteem in York. Crisp died in
February 1768, Mrs Crisp in 1782.[1]

John Arthur had recently joined the company in which he
was to remain but a short while before he was engaged at
Covent Garden for the 1737-8 season. Of his acting Tom
Davies[2] tells us that he was 'a very good copier of nature in
some particularities of humour. His Periwinkle, in the Bold
Stroke, was diverting; and his Don Manuel, in She Wou'd
and She Wou'd Not, critically just.' He was a diverting
clown and was also famous in old men's parts. He was of a
mechanical turn of mind, and a man of understanding and
good observation. He later became manager of the playhouse
in Bath until his death in 1772. Gent printed his opera, *The
Lucky Discovery: or, The Tanner of York*, in 1737, as it was
acted at the theatre there.[3] Arthur, in his preface to the
gentlemen and ladies of York, tells us how, after finishing

---

[1] Tate Wilkinson, *Wandering Patentee*, vol. I, pp. 29-31.
[2] *Memoirs of the Life of David Garrick*, 1780, vol. I, p. 36.
[3] It was given at Covent Garden April 1738.

By SUBSCRIPTION.
Not PLAY'D Here, thefe Sixteen Years,
At the NEW THEATRE in the Lord IRWIN's Yard.

THIS prefent *Tuefday* being the 27th of this Inft.
will be prefented, *The Hiftory of*

TIMON of Athens :

O R,

The Man Hater.

Written originally by *Shakefpear*, and fince alter'd by Mr. *Shadwell.*

Timon,			Mr. KEREGAN,
Alcibiades,			Mr. EMMETT.
Apemantus,			Mr. FURNIVAL.
Nicias,			Mr. COPEN.
Phœax,	Senators.	By	Mr. ARTHUR.
Ælius,			Mr. SMITH.
Cleon,			Mr. EVANS.
Demetrius,			Mr. CRISPE.
Diphilus,			Mr. HALLAM.
Poet,			Mr. MARSHAL.
Evandra,			Mrs. KEREGAN.
Meliffa,			Mrs. FURNIVAL.
Chloe,		By	Mrs. EMMETT.
Thais,			Mrs. MARSHAL.
Phrinias,			Mrs. COPEN.

Beginning exactly at Six o'Clock.

N. B. The CONCERT being on *Thurfday* (by Reafon of K. CHARLES's
Martyrdom) the SUBSCRIPTION PLAY will be on *Wednefday.*
And, on *Saturday* next, being for the Benefit of Mr. *KEREGAN,*
will be Acted a Comedy, call'd, *Rule a Wife and have a Wife.*
Never Perform'd Here.

Nightly TICKETS to be had at Mr. KEREGAN's, at the *Theatre.*

YORK : Printed by THOMAS GENT in *Coffee-Yard,* near *Stonegate.*

AN EARLY YORK PLAYBILL

the opera, he successfully 'waited on several Gentlemen for their Approbation', and expresses his obligations to the town for the kind reception the performance was given, as well as for 'their Indulgence shewn me, in making my Benefit so considerable'. Nevertheless, Arthur had met with some trouble in the form of accusations that he had levelled ridicule at particular people and families, which he strenuously denies. He however suffered some disadvantage on account of these misconstructions. The cast was as follows: Modish—Ware, Bark the Tanner—Marten, Simon—Arthur, Mrs Modish—Mrs Keregan, Mrs Bark—Mrs Emmett. This piece, which deals with the plot of Mrs Bark and Mrs Modish to reform their husbands and how it went agley, owing to the antics of Simon the drunken serving man, has a certain liveliness, especially in the cut and thrust dialogue of its opening scene. The hesitations of Mrs Modish before she plays the trick on her husband are witness to how far we have travelled from the Restoration comedy, where no heroine would have dreamt of indulging in such scruples.

The following year another comedian, Joseph Yarrow, published *A Choice Collection of Poetry*, including many prologues and epilogues which had been spoken by himself or others at Lincoln, Derby, Spalding and elsewhere. Among those certainly appertaining to the York Company are three epilogues delivered by Mrs Furnival: one to Cibber's *The Careless Husband*, which commences 'York, fam'd for virtuous Wives, and modest Maids', a second to *Julius Caesar* when her husband played Mark Anthony for his benefit, and a third in the character of Mrs Clerimont in Steele's *The Tender Husband*; besides an epilogue spoken by Miss Copen in the character of Dicky in Farquhar's *The Constant Couple*. From these we obtain a glimpse of the plays performed.

Keregan was soon compelled to reduce his pit subscription. Drake,[1] writing in 1736, says that the comedians acted twice a week and were 'allowed to be the best strollers in the

[1] *Op. cit.* vol. 1, p. 240.

kingdom', and puts the play subscription at 15s. instead of the original guinea. Just about this time, then, must be dated Keregan's illuminating complaint, which has been preserved to us in the pages of Tate Wilkinson,[1] and which tells its own sad story. In it the organisation and financial workings of the company are set out, and one cannot but quote in full so valuable and unique a document.

The Case of Thomas Keregan Proprietor of the Theatre, Humbly addressed to the Quality, Gentry and Citizens of York.

Having suffered very much of late in my business, and, as I apprehend, by an ill opinion conceived of me for keeping up my subscription tickets at the price they were first given out after the erecting of my new theatre, it having been suggested that they might be afforded at a lower price, but an unreasonable desire of gain to myself had made me reject the advice of my friends in that respect; I thought it my duty, as well as interest, to give the inhabitants of this ancient city the best satisfaction I was able in this affair, by voluntarily laying before them the state of my last quarter's accounts; whereby it will appear, that I was near one hundred pounds a looser by the last quarter's subscription only: And as I never did desire any thing more than a reasonable maintenance for myself and family, I humbly hope, after the great expence I have been at, that I shall not be compelled to remove my Company to some other place for want of encouragement here: I beg leave further to inform the public that notwithstanding I have lowered the pit tickets to sixteen shillings, the advantage I have received by it hath been very small, viz. only the addition of fourteen subscribers, notwithstanding it reduces the pit to *sevenpence halfpenny a night*, which is less than half the price paid to the meanest company of Players in the kingdom. Before I conclude this short representation of my case, I cannot but take notice, that it hath been insinuated very much to my prejudice, *That neither myself, nor my wife, have been sufficiently thankful for the favours which have been done us in coming to our benefits*: Whereas I can say, with great truth, that no one was ever more sensible of (and thankful for) such favours than we both have always been; however we may have failed in any acknowledgments from the

---

[1] *Wandering Patentee*, vol. II, p. 204.

stage; a thing never practised in any theatre but this, it being contrary to the rules of the stage: But as we are now sensible it is expected from us, we shall take care for the future, to the best of our knowledge, to do nothing which may give offence to any of our friends and benefactors.

Money received last Quarter.

	l.	s.	d.
47 Box tickets, at one guinea and a half each	74	0	6
34 Pit, at one guinea each	35	14	0
The half of five benefit plays	53	9	9
Chance money taken in time of the subscription	125	9	0

Money paid last Quarter.

	l.	s.	d.
To sixteen actors and actresses at 12s. and a pit ticket per week	145	12	0
To Mrs. Evans, and Mrs. Copen's children	1	10	0
For the use of clothes, scenes, properties, &c. four shares or salaries, allowed by the meanest companies abroad	72	16	0
Getting up two entertainments, with new scenes and clothes &c.	30	0	0
To charges of new people coming from London	10	10	0
31 nights charge, at 4l. per night, viz. 5 benefits, and 26 subscription nights	124	0	0
Sum total of expences	384	8	0
Of receipts	288	13	3
Lost last quarter	95	14	9

The persons who take my money, and deliver out all the subscription-tickets, have set their hands to this account; and, if occasion be, are ready to make oath of the same.

William Green
John Emmett.

For a more particular satisfaction, the following account *of the* nightly charges *of* acting, *exclusive of* salaries, *&c.*

	l.	s.	d.
Music	0	10	6
Office keeper	0	2	6
Wardrobe keeper	0	2	6
Clerk and numberer	0	3	0
Door keepers	0	6	6
Stage keeper	0	3	6
Coals	0	2	0
Tallow, oil, cotton, and candles	0	12	6
Bills one day with another	0	6	0
Incidents one night with another	0	1	0
Rent of the house as now built up	0	1	0
Mr. Chock	0	2	6
Drink to the Doorkeepers	0	0	6
	2	14	0

Besides play books, writing of plays out, and odd parts; for writing out music for entertainments; drink for the music at practice; letters from several players; carpenters and smiths; jobs, often for particular plays; glasses, frequently broke; washing the stock linen; cards, wax, and the printing subscriptions tickets; and many other little articles that are impossible to remember, which exceed four pounds *per* night.

Tickets delivered for the present quarter are, 32 box tickets at 1*l.* 11*s.* 6*d.* each, is fifteen pence a night. 31 pit tickets, at 16*s.* each, is sevenpence halfpenny a night; both which in the whole, pay me no more than two pounds sixteen shillings and fivepence a night, for acting, or five pounds twelve shillings and tenpence *per* week: So that I am obliged to stand the favour of the town for 16*l.* 7*s.* per week.

N.B. All those, who are willing to encourage the present box subscription, shall be allowed in proportion for the PLAYS that are past.

The following points may especially be noted. The members of the company were each paid 12*s.* a week and a pit ticket. Thus the equality of the sharing system was preserved. Half their benefits were handed over to Keregan, who, as usual, also took four shares or salaries a week for expenses with regard to scenes and clothes. Money taken nightly, outside the subscription, was not shared among the company, necessarily, since their salaries exceeded what was taken in subscriptions. These chance sales brought in more money than the subscription tickets. Fares of new actors from London were paid by the management. The cost of putting on two entertainments was high (£30), and the nightly charges outside salaries averaged £4. 0s. 0d. The rent worked out at only 1s. a night. 'As now built up' evidently refers to the Minster Yard theatre as it was changed from the tennis court.

The passing of the Licensing Act in 1737 probably caused further embarrassment to the company, and it is possible that, on account of it, the authorities refused to allow them to continue to act in the Minster Yard. Though this is mere conjecture, the company certainly did not perform there after 1739, when they were back at the Merchant Taylors' Hall. There is a playbill in the Minster Library for Saturday April 7, 1739, for a performance of *The Twin Rivals* at the Merchant Taylors for the benefit of Craig. The cast is: Elder Woudbe—Baker, Young Woudbe—Peterson, Richmore—Yarrow, Trueman—Crisp, Subtleman—Norris, Balderdan—Pearson, Clearaccount—Burt, Teague—Smith, Constance—Mrs Pearson, Amelia—Mrs Crisp, Midnight—Mrs Yarrow, Steward's Wife—Mrs Peterson. Entertainments of singing and dancing between the acts were given by Craig, Baker and Smith. The afterpiece was *Flora*: Sir Thos. Testy—Norris, Friendly—Craig, Hob—Baker.

It will be noted that the company had almost completely changed since 1736; the two bills have only the name of Crisp in common. A few words must be said about the more important newcomers. Joseph Baker, of whom we first hear in this bill, was to succeed to the management of the company, and, in his turn, to hand it on to Tate Wilkinson.

Joseph Peterson, who joined the Norwich Company in 1746, was the author of an opera called *The Raree Show, or*

The Fox Trapt, printed by Gent in 1739. Whether or not it was acted in York is doubtful, as Peterson gives only a designed cast:[1] Graspall—Norris, Timothy—Baker, Manly —Yarrow, Belamour—Craig, Sir Fopling Conceit—Peterson, Smart—Pearson, Jack—Smith, Belinda—Miss Hughes, Corinna—Mrs Burt, Betty—Miss Ardington. The prologue and epilogue were to have been spoken by Mr and Mrs Peterson. There is, in addition, an epilogue spoken by Peterson at his benefit; but, although this would point to the play having been acted, it is possible that the epilogue was intended for an ordinary benefit night, not necessarily for the third night of the play. *The Raree Show* is a poor piece, without originality. The usual quartette of lovers, churlish guardian, hunting squire, coxcomb and servant appear yet again. The contrivance of shutting the obstructive guardian in a raree show box, and one passable song are about all the 'opera' has to offer.

Henry Norris, who had adapted *The Royal Merchant* in 1706, published at Hull in 1740 *Poems upon Various Subjects*. Among the subscribers was one P. Keregan, who was probably the son of Thomas Keregan.[2] Norris was the son of the actor known as Jubilee Dicky. He acted in London and Dublin, only coming to York late in life. Chetwood says he resembled his father only in stature.[3]

Another comedian who must have joined the company about this time was James Robertson. In the baptismal register of Holy Trinity, Goodramgate,[4] we find an entry under February 7, 1739: 'Ann, Daughter of Mr James Robertson, player, by his wife Frances.' Robertson was born in Ireland in 1714, and was for a while with the company at Smock Alley, Dublin. He had a long career with the York

---

[1] The 2nd edition, 1740, omits the cast list.
[2] He was probably the Keregan who owned the Billiard Table Inn in Stonegate, which he advertises in the *York Courant*, July 30, 1731.
[3] *Op. cit.* p. 196; see also *Biographia Dramatica*.
[4] Ed. R. B. Cook, 1911.

Company, retired from the stage in 1779, and died in York sixteen years later. He published *Poems on Several Occasions* in 1773, reprinted with additions and alterations in 1780 and 1787. He has given us a picture of himself in a satire he wrote in 1764 on the members of the York Company:[1]

> See Robertson's poor Merry-Andrew mien,
> The footman's Zany—mar the comic scene;
> He squints, distorts, and aims the scurvy jest;
> An actor he! A mere buffoon at best.

Tate Wilkinson says he was a comedian of true merit[2] and a great favourite. His popularity was in fact such that an etching was made of him in 1798.

We do not definitely hear of Keregan after 1736, and he must have died between then and 1741. On January 13, 1741, the *York Courant* advertises the sale of the brewing vessels, coppers and malt belonging to the late Mr Keregan, who was probably Thomas's son, and was doubtless the man who owned the Billiard Table Inn. Inquiries were to be made 'of Mrs Keregan on the Lord Irvine's Walk'. Soon after John Arthur issued from London his proposals for a new theatre in which he mentioned the death of Keregan and his son. These proposals are preserved in Wilkinson's *Wandering Patentee* and are worth quoting in full:

To the Gentlemen and Ladies of the City of York.

Gentlemen and Ladies,

The present indifferent situation of the PLAY-HOUSE at YORK, and your great disposition to promote Theatrical Diversions, encourag'd me, since the death of Mr. *Keregan* and his son, to undertake the regulation and improvement of that STAGE: Upon which I apply'd in person to Mrs. *Keregan*, thinking I might, upon reasonable terms, enter upon the management, both with your and her approbation, but to my surprise, instead of meeting

---

[1] I have been unable to trace a copy of this fragment, but passages from it are quoted by Tate Wilkinson, *Wandering Patentee*, vol. I.

[2] *Memoirs*, vol. IV, p. 19.

with the civility I imagin'd my proposals deserv'd, she treated me in a manner I as little merited as expected. However, finding this usage from Mrs. *Keregan*, I made my design known to some gentlemen of this city, who were pleased to promise me all the encouragement they seemed to think such an undertaking deserved, and persuaded me to publish my Proposals for a Subscription, not doubting, as I had the good fortune formerly to meet with tolerable success in my theatrical capacity, I should not now fail of it in my present undertaking.

PROPOSALS

I purpose to have a new and commodious Theatre (to be situated in some convenient part of the city) the model of those in *London*. There shall be several complete sets of new Scenes, painted by the best masters in London, with all such properties and machines as are required as well for ornament as use.

The *Orchestra* shall consist of a proper number of hands, to make a complete Band of Music, that may correspond with the rest.

A Wardrobe of such clothes as shall no ways be inferior in shape or trim to those on any stage, the quantity excepted.

The Company shall be made up of several persons from London, the rest to be collected from travelling companies; in which particular care shall be had to their private life, that they may be as social off the stage as entertaining on it. And that I may be enabled to procure such people, I will make an addition to the salary before given, and by that means make up a better company than has been in any city but London.

Every season there shall be got up such Plays, Operas, Farces, and Pantomimical Entertainments as are done with any reputation in London, and with the utmost expedition.

There shall be a Quarterly Subscription for the Boxes and Pit, as before has been practised, and at the usual rates, that is to say, One Guinea and an Half the Boxes, and the Pit One Guinea.

Mr. *Keregan*, for several quarters last past, made an abatement in the Subscription, which I believe was occasioned through the barrenness of his diversions, rather than a desire in the Subscribers to reduce the price, I therefore hope it will not be considered as an imposition if I restore the Subscription to what it was, since my expence both as to house and performers will be more considerable, and consequently more agreeable.

The Gentlemen and Ladies who are willing to encourage this undertaking, I hope will excuse my personal application, my business obliging me to attend the theatre in London till the latter end of May; and am

Their most obedient humble servant

JOHN ARTHUR

LONDON, *April 5*
1741.

These rather grandiose schemes came to nothing, and Mrs Keregan continued to conduct the company without the help of Arthur.

In 1742 Yarrow published three plays. *Love at First Sight; or The Wit of a Woman* was a worthless ballad opera dedicated to the ladies and gentlemen of Hull and Newcastle. In the British Museum copy the designed cast is added in MS.: Boastwit—Yarrow, Gayford—Baker, Flush—Achurch, Aurelia—[Mrs?] Wheeler, Liddy—[Mrs?] Vandersluys. This piece was printed by subscription. *Trick upon Trick; or the Vintner in the Suds* is not original at all but merely derived, like another version, *The Bilker Bilk'd*,[1] through Bullock's *Woman's Revenge*, from Betterton's *Vintner Outwitt'd; or a Match in Newgate*, which in turn was taken from Marston's *The Dutch Curtezan*. This piece, which is little more than a droll, was performed by the York Company with the following cast: Freeman—Crofts, Mixum—Yarrow, Vizard —Ward, Solomon Smack—Robertson, Fidler—Smith, Sam —Cunningham, Mrs Mixum—Mrs Yarrow. I have been unable to trace a copy of the third piece—the musical interlude *Nancy*.

Our information about the movements of the company in 1743 is rather fuller. On April 12, the *Leeds Mercury* reports: 'We hear that a Company of Comedians from York will be

---

[1] See *The Stroler's Pacquet open'd*, 1742.

at this Town the beginning of next Month'; and on August 30 the *Hull Courant*[1] announces:

We hear that the York Company of Comedians will very shortly be at this Place, (they having got already to Beverley) and design to entertain the Town with some Grand Tragedies, never perform'd here, which they have got up on purpose to please the Gentry &c. And we are also inform'd that they intend to decorate the Stage, much Superior to any in the Country, having already, for that Purpose order'd New Scenes &c. to be got ready with the utmost speed; resolving to have every Thing brought in with the utmost Regularity and Decorum.

On September 27 there is a further advice that 'To-morrow the York Company of Comedians will perform at the New-Theatre in Lowgate, Hull a grand Tragedy call'd Julius Caesar', and on October 4 a notice that Mr Smith, Comedian, teaches dancing. It has not hitherto been known that the theatre in Lowgate was functioning as early as this.[2] It was built in George Yard on a site now occupied by the Queen's Hall.

By the end of December Mrs Keregan was back in York and opened, as was hereafter customary, with a benefit for the County Hospital on December 27 at the Merchant Taylors' Hall. The play was Ambrose Philips's *The Distress'd Mother*, with a new prologue and epilogue suitable to the occasion. Box and pit tickets were 2s. 6d., gallery 1s., and no one was to be admitted without a ticket. On December 27 the advertisement adds: 'And To-morrow will be deliver'd out Tickets for Mrs Kerregan's Subscription; which will be Open'd on Thursday Evening with a Concert of Musick:

[1] An odd volume seen by kind permission of the Hull Literary and Philosophical Society.

[2] Henry Ward's *The Petticoat Plotter*, 1746, has a prologue 'spoke at the Opening of the New Theatre in Hull' which must, I think, refer to the opening of the Lowgate Theatre. That Hull had performances of some kind long before this is proved by the existence of a Prologue to *The London Cuckolds*, acted at Hull, November 1683, in *Poems on Several Occasions*, by W. C. 1684.

Between the Two Parts of the Concert will be perform'd (Gratis) a Comedy, call'd Love Makes a Man...with an Entertainment, as will be express'd in the Bills of the Day.'

We hear nothing further of the company until June 20, 1744, when they opened a short season in Leeds to 'exhibit the best and newest Plays Extant, or any other at the Request of the Gentlemen and Ladies'. Thence they went on to York for race week where their new theatre was awaiting them.

Chapter VII

THE YORK COMPANY, 1744-1765

Unfortunately most of the newspapers for 1744 are missing, but the Minster Library possesses a playbill dated Thursday, August 2, which can only belong to that year. It advertises the first performance we know of 'At the New Theatre in the Mint Yard'. This must have been opened by Mrs Keregan, either in the middle or at the end of the winter season, or at the beginning of the race week season. It was built over part of the cloisters of the united Hospitals of St Leonard and St Peter; *A New and Exact Plan of the City of York* (Haynes, 1748) shows it, marked as 'New Theatre', standing among trees. It was practically on the same site as the present Theatre Royal in which one may still see the vaulted remains of the cloisters.

To return to the playbill—it announces the usual concert of vocal and instrumental music with, in between the two parts of the concert, gratis, the Shakespeare-Hill *Henry V*, never before performed in York, 'With proper Decorations and an Entire New Set of Scenes not inferior to any in England'. The new prologue was to be spoken by Mrs Keregan, the epilogue by Crisp, and the parts were filled as follows: K. Henry—Crisp, Dauphin—Stone,[1] King of France—Yarrow, Exeter—Achurch, Bourbon—Ward, Orleans—Oram, Scroope—Crofts, York—Norris, Gray—Robertson, Harriet—Mrs Robertson, Charlot—Mrs Crofts, Princess Catherine—Mrs Crisp. *The Devil to Pay* was the afterpiece. Boxes were 2s. 6d., pit 2s. and gallery 1s., charges that were to remain constant for the rest of the period, and

[1] Stone had previously belonged to the Norwich Company. See *ante*, p. 60.

'As the House is made so Complete and Large, no Person is to be admitted on the Stage'. The concert began at 6.30.

Soon after Henry Ward left the company and joined the one in Edinburgh. Advertising the coming publication by subscription of his comedies, in the *Hull Courant* of August 21, 1744, he says: 'As I have left Mrs Keregan, I shall very soon make my personal Application. The Gentlemen and Ladies &c. of York, Doncaster, Leeds, and Wakefield, have generously encouraged this Undertaking beyond Expectation.' The volume of Ward's *Works* was printed and went into a third edition in 1746; it contains a ballad farce *The Happy Lovers*, and two farces *The Petticoat Plotter* and *The Widow's Wish*. All these were performed at York and Ward gives the following casts:

(1) *The Happy Lovers*:[1] Careful—Norris, Modish—Ward, Constant—Crofts, Friendly—Stone, Jeremy—Oram, Charles —Smith, Celia—Mrs Crofts, Betty—Mrs Ward.

(2) *The Petticoat Plotter*: Thrifty—Yarrow, Scrape-all— Norris, Truelove—Crofts, Plotwell—Ward, Shortgrace— Oram, Ananias—Stone, Nincompoop—Robertson, Cabbage —Smith, Snip—Evans, Isabella—Mrs Ward.

(3) *The Widow's Wish*: Bellair—Crofts, Fluellin—Norris, Culverin—Achurch, Pinchgut—Heron, Loadham—Yarrow, Sharp—Ward, Meagre—Robertson, Widow Rich—Mrs Yarrow, Belinda—Mrs Crofts, Charlotte—Mrs Ward, Jenny —Mrs Achurch.

In September 1744 the Company revisited Hull and performed *The Distress'd Mother* for the benefit of the new workhouse on Thursday 27th with: Pyrrhus—Yarrow, Orestes—Crisp, Phoenix—Oram, Pylades—Achurch, Andromache—Mrs Keregan, Cephisba—Mrs Achurch, Cleone— Mrs Cross, Hermione—Mrs Crisp. An epilogue suitable to the occasion was spoken by Achurch, and the afterpiece was Chetwood's *The Lover's Opera*. Box, pit and gallery tickets were to be had of Mrs Keregan. 'The House being made

---

[1] Also performed at Lincoln's Inn Fields and printed in 1736.

much larger and very Commodious', continues the advertisement, 'no Gentleman will be admitted to Stand upon the Stage.' Further, a subscription of twenty-five plays is announced with box tickets at £1. 5s. and pit at £1. 1s. to start on October 1, the tickets to be 'deliver'd out by Mrs Keregan from Friday Morning till Monday Evening, and no longer'. This meant that playing twice a week the company would make a stay of nearly three months in Hull which would bring them to the opening of the winter season in York.

Baker's name had not appeared for some time, but he had not necessarily left the company. Some time between October and December 1744, Mrs Keregan must have died or retired. Baker had taken over the management when the company opened in York on December 26 with *Macbeth*, 'With new Cloaths, Scenes, Machines and other Decorations proper for this Play and never used before', for the benefit and towards the furnishing of the New County Hospital. As a result of this benefit, at which the city waits and others performed gratis, Mr and Mrs Baker handed 'upwards of £55' to the hospital.

The subscription was for twenty-six plays, box tickets £1. 5s., pit tickets 18s. Henceforward regular advertisements for the Saturday night benefits appear in the *York Courant*, though subscription nights are rarely announced. No advertisements occur for the summer seasons, which covered August race week, probably because no benefits were given. The rarity of command or bespeak performances is remarkable, but may be due to the subscription system. Masons and other fraternities and societies do not seem to have patronised the theatre in York as elsewhere. During the 1745 season we hear of the production of several pieces new to York: Hughes's *The Siege of Damascus*, Otway's *The Cheats of Scapin*, Ambrose Philips's *The Briton*, Edward Philips's *Britons Strike Home*, and Thomson's *Tancred and Sigismunda*. This last, for the benefit of the Giffards, was played as follows: Tancred (new dress'd)—Giffard, Siffredi —Achurch, Rodolpho—Stone, Osmond—Crisp, Laura— Mrs Crofts, Sigismunda—Mrs Giffard.

It was followed by a new pantomime called *Harlequin Restor'd*, 'Containing the Imprisonment, Release, Adventures and Death of Harlequin. The whole concluding with the Grand Scene of his Monument and Restoration to Life by the Power of Magick': Harlequin—Crofts, Pantaloon— Robertson, Pierrot—Cartwright, Hecatissa—Miss Pearson, Columbine—Mrs Crofts. A notice was appended: 'As there are a Number of new Deceptions in the Entertainment, and their Performance so greatly depends on the Stage being kept intirely clear, 'tis hoped no Gentlemen will insist upon coming behind the Scenes.'

The Briton was given a local flavour as containing 'the Overthrow of the Romans in three successive Battles near the River Ouze'. It, too, was followed by a new pantomime called *Pygmalion; or Harlequin Triumphant.* A playbill is extant in the Minster Library for April 6 of this year announcing a revival of *The Beggar's Opera* for the benefit of Cartwright with the following cast: Macheath—Cartwright, Peachum—Achurch, Lockit—Yarrow, Mat o' the Mint— Crofts, Ben Budge—Oram, Wat Weary—Stone, Robin of Bagshot—Norris, Polly—Mrs Robertson, Lucy—Miss Yarrow, Jenny Diver—Mrs Crofts, Sukey—Mrs Achurch, Mrs Coaxer—Mrs Giffard, Doll Trull—Mrs Yarrow, Mrs Slamakin—Robertson, Diana Trapes—Stone, Mrs Peachum —Mrs Crisp. The opera was followed by *Pygmalion* with Cartwright as Harlequin and Mrs Giffard as Columbine.

The Mourning Bride was presented 'With a new magnificent Scene of the Tomb of Anselmo'. This tomb scenery was to do service in many plays, as was likewise an altar scene which was in constant use, and, later, a banquet scene. In York the company advertised every time a character was newly dressed. At the production of *Tancred and Sigismunda*, for instance, only the hero was thus honoured, the rest of the characters having to make shift with stock costumes from other plays. There was one command performance this season by Lord Kingsland for the benefit of Miss Yarrow, and the play chosen was *The Distress'd Mother*. We hear of no further performances after this one on May 4, and the company then went to Leeds, where they held out the promise of 'the newest and best Plays, Entertainments, &c. The Scenes and Cloathes most of them new.'[1]

For the season of 1746 there is only one advertisement available, and this gives notice of a benefit for Mr and Mrs Crisp on April 12, at which two pieces never played in York before, Dryden's *Don Sebastian* and Dodsley's *The Blind Beggar of Bethnal Green*, were to be given. Baker protected himself against the penalties of the Licensing Act not only by sandwiching the play as a free entertainment between two parts of a concert, but by frequently stating that it was acted by people for their own diversion! At the same time he announced on one occasion that: 'The first Part of the Concert will be over exactly at Half an Hour after Six', thus giving his patrons the cue as to when the play would start. The Mint Yard Theatre is for the ensuing few years known alternatively as the 'new' or 'late' theatre.

In the winter of 1746–7 the theatre reopened with the customary hospital benefit, the play being the Shakespeare-Tate *King Lear and his Three Daughters*, 'With Scenes, Machines and other Decorations proper for the Occasion'. Of this season also little is known, as most of the newspapers are missing. A stray number for January 13 advertises, for the benefit of Crisp, Rowe's *The Ambitious Stepmother* and *Merlin*, neither of which had been previously played in York. Giffard's *Merlin; or the British Enchanter* was an ambitious effort: 'With great Variety of Scenes, Machines, Musick, Dances, and other Decorations; all entirely new, and proper to the Entertainment. With the Statues of Queen Elizabeth, Minerva, British Druid, and Nurse, being the exact Repre-

[1] *Leeds Mercury*, April 2, 1745.

sentation of those admir'd Statues in Merlin's Cave, in Richmond Gardens'; 'No Expence', it was declared, 'has been wanting to make this the most grand and perfect Entertainment of the kind ever yet seen in the Country.' Gentlemen were not to be admitted behind the scenes on account of 'the great number of Deceptions' which could not otherwise be performed 'with due Decorum'. Frequent revivals of this entertainment are proof of its long popularity. In 1747 and succeeding years the York Company held a regular summer season in Newcastle[1] instead of in Leeds.

When the company returned to York in 1748 we find one or two new names: Jones and Waker, who contributed to the singing and dancing between the acts, and Mr and Mrs Wignell.[2] We now first hear of a second charity benefit, which always henceforth followed the one given for the hospital, for the two charity schools, the blue-coat boys and the grey-coat girls. New pieces this season were Mallett's *Mustapha* and Moore's *The Foundling*. The management was careful to make the best of both worlds by assuring 'the Public that the Foundling is a Comedy where the Rules of Virtue and Decency are so strictly observed that the most scrupulous must approve it; and yet so diverting, and abounding in such a Variety of new Characters and pleasing Incidents, that it must be equally agreeable; as well as in-structive, to the gay Part of the World'. The cast was as follows: Sir Charles Raymond—Crisp, Belmont—Oram, Young Belmont—Crofts, Col. Raymond—Wignell, Faddle—Achurch, Villiard—Stone, Rosetta—Mrs Crisp, Fidelia—Mrs Robertson. This production, for the benefit of Mrs Crisp, was supposed to close the season on April 16, but a further performance was given on the 23rd for the benefit of Norris, who excused himself from personal attendance as he was dangerously ill from the gout.

Bullock's *Woman is a Riddle* was revived after eight years

[1] See *post*, pp. 163–7.   [2] See *ante*, p. 80.

with 'a new beautiful fram'd Scene made on Purpose for this Play', and Hill's *Alzira* after three years, with Alzira new dressed. Shakespeare is represented by *Macbeth* and *Hamlet* with Wignell as Hamlet. Meanwhile the Merchant Taylors' Hall was rented to rope dancers and tumblers, among whom were Mrs Garman, Pedro and Dominique, the last-named performing the feat of beating a drum on a stiff rope. These exertions were followed by *The Force of Magick; or the Birth of Harlequin*. Twice weekly performances were given at six; the doors opened at five, and the charges were pit 2*s*., middle gallery 1*s*., upper gallery 6*d*.

For his 1748-9 season Baker announced that he had engaged some new actors from London, though the only new name that is to be found is that of Conyers who played Harlequin in *Merlin* and Loverule in *The Devil to Pay*. His subscription for twenty-six plays was at the rate of boxes £1. 5*s*., pit £1. 1*s*., the tickets being transferable. The benefit for the County Hospital only fetched upwards of £25, a considerable drop from the £55 of 1744. Baker had moved into a house in Blake Street adjacent to the theatre. He was an artist as well as an actor, and the *Protestant York Courant* of November 6 advertises two engravings from his drawings of York and Lincoln Cathedrals.

The only new pieces we hear of this season were Cunningham's *Love in a Mist*, as performed in Dublin the previous winter, and Garrick's *Lethe*. There were several revivals, among which were *Caius Marius*, after ten years, as it was being acted at Drury Lane, *The Committee* after five years, and *The Tempest* with the *Masque of Neptune and Amphitrite*, and entirely new scenery and machinery. The women's characters in *The Foundling* were new dressed.

The season of 1749-50 opened with a performance of Otway's *The Orphan* for the benefit of the hospital, with the following cast: Chamont—Davies from Covent Garden, Acasto—Achurch, Castalio—Wignell, Polydore—Crofts, Page—Miss Pearson, Chaplain—Oram, Ernesto—Adams,

Serina—Miss Yarrow, Florella—Mrs Achurch, Orphan—
Mrs Robertson. As a result of the benefit £22 and upwards
was handed to the hospital. Davies was none other than
Tom Davies, later the famous bookseller, who was an un-
successful actor at Covent Garden. He married Miss
Yarrow in December 1749 or January 1750, performed in
Edinburgh in 1753, and was engaged with his wife for a
while at Drury Lane. Nichols says her 'beauty was not
more remarkable than her private character was ever unsullied
and irreproachable'.[1] The subscription this year was for
thirty-three plays, boxes £1. 13s., pit £1. 6s.

The tomb scene once again came in handy for the production of the Voltaire-Hill *Merope*, which had been brought
out nine months previously at Drury Lane, and which was
graced in York by 'new Dresses and all other Decorations'.
The other new production was that of *Henry VIII* with the
coronation of Anne Bullen and the christening of Elizabeth.
Lee's *Theodosius* had 'a new grand Altar Scene, representing
the Cross that appear'd to Constantine the Great', and Davies
as Varanes wore a new costume. Davies also played Hamlet
to the Ophelia of Mrs Robertson, and King Henry in
Richard III with Adams as Richard and Mrs Crisp as Queen
Elizabeth.

Among the revivals were *Tamerlane the Great*: Tamerlane
—Crisp, Bajazet—Davies, Moneses—Wignell, Selima—Mrs
Robertson, Arpasia—Mrs Crisp; Coffey's *The Boarding School
Romp*, and *Phebe* with Haughton (a new name) as Harry
Hunter.

Robertson spoke Jo. Haines's celebrated epilogue riding
on an ass, and thereafter became popular as a speaker of prologues and epilogues in all kinds of characters.

The Merchant Taylors' minutes record a letting of the Hall
to Dominique the rope dancer on July 20 for £1 a week,
but no advertisement of his performances appears. In Leeds,
the company had been replaced by Whitely's Company of

[1] *Literary Anecdotes*, 1812, vol. VI, p. 421.

Comedians, who not only had given successful perform-ances, but whose private and public behaviour was especially commended.[1]

Considerable additions to the company mark the 1750-1 season.[2] Sherriffe and Morgan made their first appearances as Dorilas and Ismene in *Merope* for the benefit of the hospital on December 27, 1751; the same evening Mrs Wheeler first performed here as Nell in *The Devil to Pay* and provided the singing between the acts. Morgan took over Harlequin in *Pygmalion; or Harlequin's Escape into a Quart Bottle*, Maclellan, Pearce and Miss Pearce appeared as Mirabel, Sir Wilful and Betty in *The Way of the World*. In addition an under actor named Daly, and Master Morgan are mentioned. In *Richard III* Adams now played Richard, Sherriffe, King Henry, Mrs Crofts, Lady Anne, and Mrs Crisp, Queen Elizabeth. *Macbeth* was cast as follows: Macbeth—Crisp, Macduff—Sherriffe, Banquo—Achurch, Lady Macduff—Mrs Crofts, Lady Macbeth—Mrs Crisp. In *The Beggar's Opera* Haughton played Macheath to the Polly of Mrs Wheeler. Whitehead's *The Roman Father* was given its first presentation in York cast as follows: Horatius—Crisp, Hostilius—Wignell, P. Horatius—Crofts, Valerius—Adams, Valeria—Mrs Crofts, Horatia—Mrs Crisp, and was followed by the ever-popular *Merlin*, adorned with 'Scenes, Machines, Music, Dances, and other Decorations' and a new, additional scene. York first saw this year also Bullock's *The Cobler of Preston*, adapted from *The Taming of the Shrew*.

In 1752 the company was further strengthened by the accession of Mr and Mrs Dancer, Hopkins, Younger, Smith, Haddlesey and last but not least, Bridge Frodsham. The Wignells had joined the Norwich Company in 1751 and

---

[1] See Mr A. Mattison's Lecture to the Thoresby Society on the Leeds Theatre, MS. Leeds Public Library. He quotes from the *Leeds Intelligencer*.

[2] Information for this season mostly from a volume of the *Protestant York Courant* in the York Public Library.

Adams too had left. Frodsham was to become the idol of York and to be known as 'The York Garrick'. He was born in 1734 of an ancient Cheshire family which hailed from the town of Frodsham.[1] He was a scholar at Westminster School from which he twice ran away. The second time he attached himself to a troupe of players in Leicester and thus began his theatrical career.[2] He was only eighteen years of age when he joined the York Company, and he was to die in his thirty-fifth year at Hull on October 21, 1768.[3] Wilkinson tells us that he was by nature a great actor who possessed 'a quick genius, aided by a liberal education...but his mind, his understanding, and superabundant good qualities were all warped and undermined by nocturnal habits' with the result that he became 'enfeebled, disordered, mad, dropsical'. The brandy bottle was 'his fatal and false friend'. As an actor he was awkward, merely from want of good training, and he never attained elegance, but he had strong feelings, a melo-dious voice and the capacity of tears at will. His Hamlet and Jaffeir, Wilkinson judges to have been surpassed only by those of Garrick and Barry. Unfortunately, 'The public were so infatuated (and indeed he was so superior) that he cast all others at a distance in his York situation; and the audience too blindly and too partially (for his good) approved all he did beyond comparison.' He had little opportunity for observation or improvement. Primarily a tragedian, Frod-sham also acted the young sparks of comedy and made a 'decent Macheath', as he sang tolerably well. A deal of Frodsham's conceit and independent spirit is manifest in Wilkinson's anecdote[4] of how he visited Garrick during a fortnight's holiday in London. He left a card inscribed

[1] Wilkinson, *Memoirs*, vol. IV, p. 36.
[2] Welch, *Alumni Westmonasterienses*, 1852.
[3] *York Courant*, October 28, 1768. The date is usually wrongly given as October 26. The burial register of St Mary, Sculcoates, gives the date of his burial as October 25. This information was kindly supplied by the Vicar, the Rev. W. Coggill.
[4] *Memoirs*, vol. IV, p. 37.

'Mr Frodsham of York' on the great man, who struck by its simple title decided to interview his caller. Garrick was surprised at the freedom with which Frodsham spoke, especially on the subject of Shakespeare. Frodsham did not hesitate to tell Garrick that he thought his Hamlet clever in parts but that he was unimpressed with his interpretation as a whole. Garrick, used to flattery, was amazed at his audacity, but gave him an order for the pit to see his Sir John Brute and an invitation to breakfast the following morning. After expressing delight at Garrick's rendering of Brute, Frodsham without fear or hesitation spoke, at Garrick's request, Hamlet's first soliloquy. Garrick offered him a London job and was astonished to find that he had not come a-begging but merely because he adjudged it his duty to wait on a brother genius. One would give a lot to have been present at the interview between the two men. Robertson in his satire on his fellow-actors has given us another picture of Frodsham's conceit and avidity for praise:

> Lo! Frodsham roars or whispers through the scene;
> He rants, he splits the tasteless groundling's ear,
> And Herod's self, out heroded appears,
> Quaintly ridiculous his starts, his throes,
> His attitudes, his sing-song ahs! and ohs!
> Nor like a man pours he his plaintive strains,
> But blubbers, school-boy-like, his love-sick pains....
> His robe with air affected he infolds,
> And like a bear his dulcinea holds...
> Above mankind in his own mind he soars,
> Himself the idol he himself adores.
> Of coarse-spun flattery proud, we oft may view,
> Frodsham amid a low-liv'd servile crew;
> Creatures who, spaniel-like his footsteps tend,
> And to Sir Oracle with rev'rence bend:
> Among whom enthron'd he wields his critic rod,
> While gaping fools admire their wooden-god:
> Hence on the stage, spite of much grandeur's scene
> A taste indelicate, and manners mean;
> Those who with lepers herd, are seldom clean.

MR FRODSHAM

JAMES ROBERTSON,
Comedian.

Born at Dublin 1714, Died at York 1795

London, Published 11 October 1812 by Rob.t Wilkinson, N.º 58 Cornhill.

Frodsham gradually took over the leading parts from Crisp and attained a salary of a guinea a week. But Crisp was tenacious, and it was long before he would give up Hamlet to Frodsham and be relegated to the role of the Ghost. At first Crisp acted Richard to Frodsham's Richmond and Sir John Brute to Frodsham's Col. Bully, then they took these parts alternately.

The first performance in which I can trace Frodsham is one of *King Lear* for the benefit of Mr and Mrs Dancer on February 28, when he acted Edgar with the following cast: Lear—Dancer, Gloster—Achurch, Kent—Oram, Bastard—Younger, Albany—Hopkins, Cornwall—Smith, Burgundy —Jones, Goneril—Mrs Achurch, Regan—Mrs Morgan, Aranthe—Miss Pearce, Cordelia—Mrs Dancer. Mrs Dancer, who afterwards became Mrs Barry and then Mrs Crawford, must also have added considerably to the company's prestige. Genest[1] says of her that 'she was graceful, genteel, spirited and feeling—she had a certain modest gaiety in her manner and address,...in her figure she was just above the middle size', of fair complexion and light auburn hair. She was well made and her features were regular. She played tragedy to please the town and comedy to please herself. Five advertisements of this season are extant. *The Roman Father* was given for the second time and *The Pleasures of the Town* revived with Robertson as Jack Pudding; after which Master Morgan spoke an epilogue to the ladies and gentlemen, which was printed and delivered free of charge, in the theatre, at the end of the third act.

Owing to gaps in the newspaper our information for 1753 is even more scanty. Mr and Mrs Vandersluys[2] and Fisher had joined the company. Fisher played Valerius in *The Roman Father*, Vandersluys danced between the acts and played Harlequin in a revised edition of *Merlin*, and Mrs

[1] Vol. VII, p. 353. For Dancer's career in Bath, see *post*, pp. 189, 191, *et passim*.
[2] But see p. 131 for Mrs Vandersluys.

Vandersluys was responsible with Mrs Wheeler for the entr'acte singing. The Dancers had returned to Bath. The newspaper series is almost complete for 1754. Frodsham was already playing most of the leads and we find him as Jaffeir in *Venice Preserv'd* to the Pierre of Crisp and the Belvidera of Mrs Robertson, Varanes in *Theodosius*, Osmyn, for his own benefit, in *The Mourning Bride*, Don Carlos in *Alzira* for the first time, Aribert in *The Royal Convert*, Tancred in *Tancred and Sigismunda*, Scapin in *The Cheats of Scapin*, Macheath, Demetrius in *The Brothers*, and Nerestan in *Zara*. A Mrs Frodsham was now a member of the company and Hughes's *The Siege of Damascus* was revived for her benefit. New plays were Jones's *The Earl of Essex*, which had been brought out at Covent Garden a year previously, with Frodsham as Southampton; Foote's *The Englishman in Paris*; Mrs Clive's *The Rehearsal: or Bayes in Petticoats*; *The Birth of Harlequin; or the Burgomaster Trick'd* with Vandersluys as Harlequin; and Glover's *Boadicia* with Frodsham as Dumnorix, Crisp as Ænobarbus, Mrs Crisp as Boadicia and Mrs Robertson as Venusia. Master Morgan, besides speaking an epilogue mimicking a diversity of characters, took part in the entertainments between the acts. Master James Morgan played Tom Thumb for the first time, and Master Wheeler jun. performed Loverule.

Baker was no longer living at his house near the theatre and his address is given in Stonegate.[1] He played Perseus in Young's *The Brothers* and Puff in Foote's *Taste* at his benefit.

Romeo and Juliet was chosen to open the following season, 1754-5, for the benefit of the hospital. This was probably Garrick's version. No admission was possible behind the scenes owing to the funeral procession. The cast was as follows: Romeo—Frodsham, Capulet—Crisp, Laurence—Oram, Mercutio—Achurch, Apothecary—Robertson, Lady Capulet—Mrs Achurch, Nurse—Mrs Crisp, Juliet—Mrs Robertson. This benefit fetched £26. 17s. 5d.; that for the

[1] He had, however, a house next to the theatre the following season.

schools, at which *The Royal Convert* and *Flora* were played, only £19. 4*s*. 6*d*. The subscription season was for thirty-three plays at £1. 13*s*. the boxes, and £1. 6*s*. the pit. A Mrs Hopkins now shared some of the leading women's parts with Mrs Morgan, Mrs Robertson, and Mrs Crisp. A benefit was given for the Yarrows who must have been growing old and whose names do not appear often in the cast lists after 1751. It is remarkable how long actors stayed in the York Company; Oram, the Crisps and the Achurchs, for example, were to remain with them for years. Frodsham's parts this season include Dorilas in *Merope*, Damon in *The Chaplet* for the first time, Campley in *The Funeral*, Moore in *The Dragon of Wantley*, Ventidius in *All for Love* with Crisp as Anthony and Mrs Morgan as Cleopatra, Orestes in *The Distress'd Mother*, Courtwell in *Woman is a Riddle*, Aboan in *Oroonoko* and Dumont in *Jane Shore*. Many new plays and afterpieces were produced. Brown's *Barbarossa* was on the York boards one and a half months after its production at Drury Lane, with the principal characters new dressed and Frodsham as Achmet, Mrs Hopkins as Irene and Mrs Crisp as Zaphira. The Morgans were going to repeat the tragedy for their benefit two weeks later, but, on the advice of friends, altered it to *The Mourning Bride* with Mrs Morgan in the title role. Whitehead's *Creusa* was given for Mrs Crisp's benefit with a grand new scene of the Temple at Delphos and the following cast: Aletes—Crisp, Ilyssus—Frodsham, Phorbas—Achurch, Xuthus—Oram, Pythia—Mrs Robertson, Lycea—Mrs Hopkins, Creusa—Mrs Crisp. New afterpieces were *Harlequin's Vagaries; or The Power of Witchcraft*, 'The Plan, Deceptions, Chorus's and other Decorations entirely new', in which Frodsham played Harlequin; a farce, otherwise unknown, called *The Cornish Knights*; Woodward's alteration of Mrs Centlivre's *Marplot in Lisbon*; Carey's *The Press-Gang*; and *Harlequin Statue; or The Sheep-Shearers Joy* with 'Musick and Songs compos'd and set by the Society of the Temple of Apollo' and a new Harlequin in the person of Reed. In addition *The Birth of Harlequin* was put on with alterations and additions and music from Woodward's *Queen Mab*, and *Merlin's Cave* was presented with 'all the Machinery, etc. new painted'.

Master Morgan continued to speak new epilogues, one of which, written by a local man, was distributed free at the end of the second act. This child shared his benefit with Miss Achurch who was now old enough to make her appearance.

Barbarossa opened the 1755–6 season and obtained £20 for the hospital. *Henry V* was given for the schools and fetched £19. 10s. 6d. A number of Shakespeare plays and adaptations were given this year: *Hamlet* with Hamlet—Frodsham, Ghost—Crisp, King—Achurch, Ophelia—Mrs Robertson, Grave-Diggers—Robertson and Morgan; *Romeo and Juliet* in which the altar scene was utilised, with Mrs Hopkins as Juliet for the first time and Capulet—Achurch, Mercutio— Dancer, otherwise the cast as in 1754–5;[1] *The Merchant; or, The Jew of Venice* 'With a grand Buffet Scene, Caskets, Musick, and all other Decorations proper to the Play', with Shylock —Achurch, Antonio—Crisp, Bassanio—Frodsham, Gobbo —Robertson, Gratiano—Dancer, Jessica with a new song in character—Mrs Dancer, Portia—Mrs Morgan; *King Lear* with cast as before,[2] and a further performance of *Romeo and Juliet* with Mrs Dancer as Juliet. The Dancers, it will be noted, had returned after a two years' sojourn in Bath. Mrs Dancer also played Calista in *The Fair Penitent*, Elizabeth in *The Earl of Essex*, Cleopatra in *All For Love* and Zara in *The Mourning Bride*. Frodsham repeated his performance of Harlequin in *Harlequin's Vagaries*, with alterations and additions 'as performed last Season at the Theatre at Hull, several Nights, with great Applause'. New afterpieces were Thomas Sheridan's *The Brave Irishman*, with Robertson as Captain O'Blunder, and Foote's *The Englishman Return'd from Paris*. Dancer also presented 'the Ladies with A Dish of Mr Foote's Tea', an entertainment advertised as performed at the Hay-

[1] See p. 146.   [2] See p. 145.

market for forty-two successive mornings. The entertainment was repeated two weeks later; a point to be noted since Wilkinson was to have such a failure with this piece.

In August the famous rope dancer Maddox performed at the Merchant Adventurers' Hall every night and, during race week, every morning at 10.30.

The 1756–7 season opened with *King Lear*. A further gap in the newspapers up to 1760 leaves us without much information for succeeding years. Sometime during 1758, Baker paid a visit to London to find a successor to Mrs Dancer, 'the York Heroine' who, with Dancer, had decamped to Barry's new Dublin Theatre.[1] He engaged 'the goblin Miss Roach, a horrid spectre'. According to Wilkinson she inveigled Baker into the belief that she was a great actress and a good woman, but York received her indifferently and she did not act three nights the whole season. However, she extorted a good benefit. 'She had much art, a cunning understanding, and a flow of spirits, yet affectation that would have been surfeiting in a beauty; but she flattered well.' Much more important than the engagement of Miss Roach was Baker's casual meeting with Wilkinson, which he was to remember and make use of five years later. Charles Lee Lewes[2] has an anecdote of Frodsham when he acted Richard III in Hull sometime in 1758. In the course of a speech he was interrupted by a loud Irish brogue from behind the scenes, shouting 'Arrah, Bell, what have you done with your husband's thirty shirt....' The convulsive laughter of the audience in all parts of the theatre threw the dismayed Richard into such an agony that he could not speak more of the soliloquy that night; so he quit the stage abruptly with a hearty curse on all Irish women. Frodsham evidently took his art with high seriousness.

In December 1758, Foote's *The Author* was stopped from performance in York as libellous.[3] The York ladies were

[1] Wilkinson, *Memoirs*, vol. II, p. 10.   [2] *Ibid.* vol. I, p. 74.
[3] *Ibid.* vol. IV, p. 13.

particular, and for long would not allow *The Provok'd Wife* to be presented on the score of its indecency.

It is probable, too, that there had been some trouble in Leeds. In a letter against cock-fighting, addressed to the *Leeds Mercury*, March 20, 1759, the writer praises the vigilance of the magistrates which 'secured the Town from the Danger of Raree-Shows, Puppet-Plays and Theatrical Entertainments'. A yearly subscription season continued to be given at Hull and the copy of a playbill[1] dated Wednesday, November 11, 1759, advertises the 22nd night of the subscription, at which *The Tempest* was performed at the New Theatre, Lowgate, with 'New Scenes, Machines and other Decorations proper to the Play' and the following cast: Prospero—Crisp, Ferdinand—Frodsham, Alonzo—Leng, Antonio—Maguire, Gonzalo—Hartley,[2] Stephano—Oram, Mustacho—Quin, Ventoso—Robertson, Trincalo—Achurch, Caliban and Sycorax—Binns, Pearce, Ariel—Miss Achurch, Miranda—Mrs Frodsham, Dorinda—Mrs Granger, Hippolito—Miss Helme, and in the Masque Neptune—Bellamy, Amphitrite—Mrs Quin. The performance began at 6 p.m. and tickets for non-subscribers were 2s. 6d., 2s. and 1s. as in York. On Friday, *Hamlet* with *Harlequin's Vagaries; or the Burgomaster Trick'd* was given for the benefit of Robertson. It will be noted that many changes had been made in the company, Leng, Maguire, Hartley, Quin, Binns, Bellamy, Mrs Granger, Miss Helme and Mrs Quin being new names. *Henry IV* was revived for the benefit of the charity schools of York in January 1760 with Hotspur—Crisp, King Henry—Achurch, Prince of Wales—Frodsham, Falstaff—Pearce, followed by *Lethe* with the additional scene of Lord Chalkstone, a part undertaken by Frodsham. The benefit only realised £13. 3s. 9½d. Other Shakespeare productions followed: Hawkins's alteration of *Cymbeline*; *Richard III* with

---

[1] MS. of Theatrical Memoirs in possession of Mr J. G. Sleight of Hull, which he kindly allowed me to examine.

[2] Prompter in 1760.

Frodsham in the title role for the first time supported by: King Henry—Achurch, Buckingham—Venables, Richmond—Leng, Prince Edward—Mrs Frodsham, Duke of York—Miss Achurch, Lady Anne—Mrs Robertson, Duchess of York—Mrs Rowley, Queen Elizabeth—Mrs Hibberton, and Hill's version of *Henry V* with Henry—Frodsham, Harriet—Mrs Granger, and a new patriotic prologue in honour of the British Militia spoken by Quin. Other interesting revivals were those of Jonson's *Every Man in his Humour* after six years, and Lee's *The Rival Queens* after fifteen years with several additions and alterations: Alexander—Frodsham first time, Roxana—Mrs Hibberton. Into the tragedy were introduced a grand procession to attend the entry of Alexander into Babylon, with a magnificent triumphal car drawn by four captive kings, a new choral ode composed for the occasion, a grand banquet scene adorned with several new dresses, and, in the fifth act, 'the last new Scene...to represent the Bower of Semiramis'. Finally, a new satirical epilogue written by Frodsham was spoken by Robertson in the dress and character of Asmodeus or the Devil upon Two Sticks.

New presentations were the Miller-Voltaire *Mahomet the Impostor*, 'With several new Dresses, new Scenes...particularly a grand new Scene of a Pagan Altar, with Images and Idols', doubtless adapted from all the other altar scenes, and *The Rehearsal* with Frodsham as Bayes and, 'In the 5th Act, a Dance of State and a Grand Battle: In which will be introduced an additional Reinforcement of Mr Bayes' new-raised Regiment of Horse; as also a wonderful Eclipse of the Sun, Moon, and Earth'. New afterpieces were Townley's *High Life Below Stairs*; a pantomime called *The Novelty* with an additional scene, Harlequin—Venables, Columbine—Mrs Granger; *Florizel and Perdita*, altered by Frodsham from *The Winter's Tale*,[1] with Frodsham and Mrs Granger as hero and

---

[1] Morgan's version had appeared in 1754 at Covent Garden but was not printed until 1767; Garrick's at Drury Lane in 1756, printed 1758.

heroine; and *Harlequin Magician* in which Granger first appeared as Harlequin.

There were two entertainments of special interest, the first a 'Grand Masque...in Honour of the Brave General Wolfe. The Representation will be heightened by a beautiful new Scene painted purposely for this Use' with Britannia—Mrs Robertson, Genius of Quebec—Mrs Quin, Genius of the Ocean—Frodsham; the second, on the same evening, a kind of mummer's play performed by a company of sword dancers, at which each performer, on his first appearance, was to repeat verses in which his character would be expressed. Other items this season are the first appearance of a Miss Carey as Lucy in *The Beggar's Opera*, and a bespeak by several officers of the militia.

For the benefit of the hospital at the opening of the 1760-1 season *Cymbeline* obtained £25. 9s. 4½d.; for the charity schools *The Earl of Essex* made £21. 6s. 8½d. It was announced that care would be taken to have the house very well aired. Mr and Mrs Fitzmaurice [1] and Mrs Maguire are additions to the company. Banks's *The Albion Queens* with Norfolk—Frodsham, Cecil—Achurch, Mary Queen of Scots —Mrs Robertson, Douglas—Mrs Frodsham, Queen Elizabeth—Mrs Venables, Ramsay's *The Gentle Shepherd* with Worthy—Oram, Mause—Mrs Fitzmaurice, Elspa—Mrs Quin, Madge—Robertson, and Shadwell's *The Fair Quaker of Deal*, with alterations and additions, and with Beau Mizen— Frodsham, Worthy—Leng, Rovewell—Venables, Flap— Fitzmaurice, Arabella—Mrs Frodsham, Belinda—Mrs Robertson, Dorcas Neal—Mrs Granger were the new productions. The new afterpieces were Colman's *Polly Honeycombe* with Miss Achurch in the title role; *Harlequin Salamander; or, The Jealous Shepherd* with Fitzmaurice as Harlequin, and Mrs Granger as Columbine; and *Harlequin's Adventures; or, The Farmer's Sheep-Shearing*, 'The Scenes, Machines, Music, Dresses, and other Decorations, entirely new.'

---

[1] Fitzmaurice had been in the Bath Company. See *post*, p. 191, *et passim*.

Among the revivals were Home's *Douglas*, after three years, Douglas—Frodsham, Old Shepherd—Crisp; *The Royal Convert*, Hengist—Frodsham, with music, dresses and a grand altar scene suitable to the occasion; Cibber's *The Refusal* with Frodsham as Witling; Rowe's *The Ambitious Stepmother*, with alterations and additions, Frodsham as Artaxerxes; and *The Beggar's Opera* with Miss Achurch playing Polly for the first time. The Frodshams chose *The Rival Queens* for their benefit with Mrs Frodsham as Statira. Frodsham wrote the words and Camidge the music for a new choral ode; a 'large Addition...both Vocal and Instrumental' was made on this occasion to the band 'by some of the best Performers in Town', and the banquet scene was introduced into the fourth act, 'the Feast, Music, and other Decorations quite new'. The augmented band enabled the grand chorus in Mendez's musical entertainment *The Chaplet* to be performed for the first time in York. Shakespeare was represented by *Othello*, Othello—Venables, Emilia—Mrs Venables, with a new prologue written and spoken by Venables in the character of Mercury and a new epilogue by Mrs Venables. Garrick's *Catherine and Petruchio* was given with Frodsham and Mrs Maguire in the title roles.

On Wednesday, January 18, a curious performance took place in the old Theatre in Thursday Market. The bookseller Thomas Gent, having fallen upon evil days, spoke a 'long and pathetick Prologue' on 'The contingencies, vicissitudes or changes of this transitory life'[1] for his benefit, 'at the deep Tragedy of the Beautiful, Eloquent, Tender-hearted, but Unfortunate Jane Shore', together with 'a Benedictive Epilogue of Thanks To the Worthy and Charitable Beholders'. That this magniloquently described performance was nothing but a puppet show is evident from two lines of the prologue:

> 'Twill be no Myst'ry I descend so low
> Here to harangue before a Puppet Show.

It was managed by one Clark. The entertainment included

[1] Printed under this title by Gent.

exhibitions of clockwork, waxworks and a view of the taking of Montreal.[1] The charges were pit 1s., middle gallery 6d., back seats 6d. The performance began between 6–7 and a good fire was promised. York rushed to see this pitiful spectacle so that many who had tickets could not find room in the theatre. In consequence a second performance was given on Friday with another play. Gent pays tribute to:

> Theatric Glory, Master Keregan:
> Dear Orator, adorning each lov'd Place
> With Cato's Virtues, and brave Caesar's Grace.

There were three newcomers when Baker's Company returned to York in the winter of 1761-2; they were Miss Oxnard, Owen and Buck. The benefits for the hospital and the schools fetched £19. 4s. and £24. 12s. 11d. respectively.

Whitehead's *The School for Lovers* was presented with the following cast: Dorilant—Frodsham, Modely—Leng, Belmour—Buck, Lady Beverley—Mrs Crisp, Caelia—Mrs Frodsham, Araminta—Mrs Granger. Murphy's *The Old Maid* is the one new afterpiece mentioned by name in advertisements. But there was a new pantomime introducing 'the Attitude Scene out of Queen Mab; the Additional Scene of Action out of Apollo and Daphne, occasioned by Cock-lane Ghost,...and the Taylor Scene out of Queen Mab'. It was a good year for Shakespeare. *As You Like It* was revived, after four years, as follows: Orlando—Frodsham, Adam—Granger, Oliver—Leng, Duke sen.—Crisp, Duke Frederick—Oram, Jaques—Achurch, Amiens—Fitzmaurice, Touchstone—Robertson, Celia—Mrs Robertson, Phebe—Miss Oxnard, Audrey—Mrs Quin, Rosalind—Mrs Granger. *Timon of Athens*, which had not been acted in York for twenty-six years, was revived with Timon—Frodsham, Alcibiades—Leng, Apemantus—Oram, Mellissa—Granger, Evandra—Mrs Robertson. In February Hawkins's version of

---

[1] Robert Davies, *A Memoir of the York Press*, 1868, p. 212.

Cymbeline was acted: Cloten—Owen, Leonatus—Leng, Philario—Achurch, Imogen—Mrs Frodsham, Bellarius and Cadwal—Oram, Granger, Palador with songs—Frodsham; in March *Richard III*, and *Romeo and Juliet* complete with funeral procession, dirge and grand altar scene: Romeo—Frodsham, Capulet—Achurch, Laurence—Oram, Mercutio —Granger, Apothecary—Robertson, Lady Capulet—Mrs Fitzmaurice, Nurse—Mrs Crisp, Juliet—Miss Achurch; in May *The Tempest* for the benefit of the prompter Bryan: Prospero—Crisp, Alonzo—Leng, Ferdinand—Frodsham, Ariel—Miss Achurch, Hippolito—Mrs Frodsham. On May 12 a benefit was given for a new actor 'that sweet Creature Mr Sweetman, but better known by the name of Sweetnam' at which Mrs Robertson played Roxana in *The Rival Queens* for the first time. Frodsham and Miss Achurch essayed on another night, also for the first time, the parts of Jack Stocks and Chloe in Fielding's *The Lottery*. Leng seems to have succeeded Robertson as prologue speaker in chief and delivered a patriotic prologue suitable to the times before *Alzira*, and a prologue on the Cock-lane Ghost, as spoken before *The Drummer*, at a revival of *The Siege of Damascus*. Another feature of this season was the introduction of comic interludes that had been performed at Drury Lane such as *Hearts of Oak* and *The Farmer's Return from London*.

Frodsham was now at the height of his popularity. He was a keen freemason and founded a lodge in February 1761. In February 1762 he became principal of the Grand Royal Arch Chapter.[1] In December 1762 he issued printed proposals for a course of lessons to be given by him on the art of reading and speaking publicly.[2] The scheme did not meet with much success, and Frodsham expressed his disappointment in a very interesting letter to a fellow-actor :[3]

---

[1] George Benson, *The Theatre Royal and Drama in York*, 1911.
[2] *York Courant*, December 14.
[3] In my possession. From Helen Faucit's collection.

Dear Aickin,[1]

I am heartily sorry for your Loss—let that suffice—I have been rather tedious in remitting the Farce to you—but I reflected that if it came time enough for your Benefit the Purpose intended wou'd be answer'd.

I have met with very ill Success here in regard to the Scheme I set about, owing chiefly to the damn'd Tribe of Levi—I gave a probationary Lecture to a numerous Audience—I read part of the Burial Service the 8th Cap. of Matt. & the Ode upon St. Cecilia's Day by Dryden after which I desir'd any Gentleman present to ask me any Questions concerning it—I was answer'd by a Clap of Applause—notwithstanding which their Pride is so very great that in short they will not submit to be taught by a *Player*—tho' I have made a Shift to pocket fifty Pieces since I saw you by those Means—News you know, is never stirring in this corner of the World—& for that very reason I cannot send you any—By the bye I have read the Discovery[2]—very elegant indeed —but as some of the Papers intimate it is rather upon the Richardsonian Stile—it is monstrously tedious, extremely affecting and I apprehend without good Acting in the *Country* will cut but an indifferent Figure.

For Heaven's Sake let me hear from you shortly if it is convenient to you—and believe me it is with Pleasure I subscribe myself

Y^r sincere Friend

BRIDGE FRODSHAM.

Here speaks the man who lectured Garrick about Shakespeare, and who was intensely interested in every branch of his profession. Though his lectures were a failure, he was so popular that on his benefit night, when he appeared only in the afterpiece, he had to insert a notice in the newspaper, 'As Mr Frodshams not appearing in the Tragedy may seem particular, he thinks it necessary to acquaint the Public, that it was absolutely impossible for him, in the Time, to make himself Master of both the Characters assigned to him in the

[1] An actor in the Edinburgh Company.
[2] Comedy by Frances Sheridan produced at Drury Lane, February 3, 1763.

Tragedy and Comedy; he therefore chose to give a Prefer-
ence to the latter'. On this occasion, too, he repeated his
recitation of Dryden's Ode on St Cecilia's Day. Two Miss
Frodshams also appeared that night in Mallet's new tragedy
Elvira; the new comedy was Murphy's *The Citizen*. The 1763
season was one in which many new plays were presented.
These include the Garrick version of *The Winter's Tale* with:
Leontes—Crisp, Old Shepherd—Oram, Clown—Robert-
son, Autolycus—Achurch, Florizel—Frodsham, Perdita—
Miss Achurch, Paulina—Mrs Fitzmaurice, Hermione—Mrs
Robertson; Shirley's *Edward the Black Prince* with Frodsham
in the title role; Murphy's *The Orphan of China*, Frodsham as
Zamti; Frances Sheridan's *The Discovery*, which Frodsham
had criticised so adversely and in which he played Branville;
Victor's version of *The Two Gentlemen of Verona* as it was being
performed at Drury Lane, with Thurio—Frodsham, Duke
—Crisp, Valentine—Leng, Proteus—Buck, Host—Oram,
Speed—Achurch, Launce—Robertson, Julia—Miss Achurch,
Lucetta—Mrs Fitzmaurice, Silvia—Miss Phillips, and the
following afterpieces; *The Spirit of Contradiction* (anon.),
Dell's *The Frenchified Lady Never in Paris*, and Reed's *The
Register Office*.

In addition Frodsham played Macbeth and Miss Phillips
Lady Macbeth for the first time and Frodsham took the part
of Parolles in a revival of *All's Well that Ends Well*, supported
by King of France—Crisp, Bertram—Leng, Lafeu—Oram,
Clown—Robertson, Interpreter—Achurch, Countess of
Rousillon—Mrs Robertson, Helena—Miss Phillips. The
woman's side of the company was strengthened by the
addition this year of Miss Phillips and Miss Grainsby. Miss
Phillips was the aunt of Mrs Jordan and is said to have been
greatly esteemed by the genteel families of York.[1] She played
besides the parts already mentioned, Merope, and Arpasia in
Tamerlane and spoke an epilogue on affectation. Miss
Grainsby afterwards married Leng. Besides the Frodsham

[1] Wilkinson, *Memoirs*, vol. III, p. 145.

children, a Miss H. Achurch makes her appearance as one of Alfred's children in the masque of *Alfred the Great* for which Arne wrote the music.

But perhaps the most important event of the year was the York début of Tate Wilkinson. It was the first time that Baker had attempted to cover the spring race week. He remembered his meeting with Wilkinson in London and engaged him to give a fillip to the last week of the season. Wilkinson arrived about April 22 or 23, for he tells us that he saw the bills plastered with the announcement of *Romeo and Juliet* and *The Frenchified Lady* for the benefit of Buck, a performance which took place on April 23. He lodged with Baker, who had taken a tremendous fancy to him and was to treat him rather as a son than a stranger. Wilkinson made his début in Foote's *The Minor* after a performance of *Richard III*. He states that he was 'well received by a very genteel house'.[1] He was impressed with the quality and behaviour of the audience, remarking how the ladies had 'a grace, a manner, a decorum not often met with outside London'. 'York', he continues, 'certainly boasts a pre-eminence when the boxes on public weeks are crowded, that dazzles the eye of a stranger.' But he elsewhere observes that 'The York audience then were particularly luke-warm as to applause, when compared to any other established theatre.'[2] Two humiliating customs then reigning he found particularly objectionable: one was that a man and his wife were required to return thanks on the stage after their benefit;[3] the other that a 'draggle-tailed Andromache in frost, rain, hail, and snow' had to go the rounds with the bill man, 'delivering her benefit play bills from door to door'. This latter custom was everywhere prevalent, but it pained Wilkinson to see 'Mr Frodsham, bred as a gentleman, with fine natural talents and esteemed in York as a Garrick, the Hamlet of the

---

[1] Wilkinson, *Memoirs*, vol. III, p. 135.   [2] *Ibid.* vol. IV, p. 24.
[3] Frodsham once contrived a comic epilogue carrying his wife on his back, since both were compelled to appear. *Ibid.* vol. III, p. 129.

age, running after, or stopping a gentleman on horseback to deliver his benefit bill, and beg half a crown'.

An advertisement for a repetition of Wilkinson's performance as Shift, Smirk and Mrs Cole in *The Minor* appears in the *York Courant* for May 3 to take place that day. It was announced as performed by him at the Theatre Royal in London; on this occasion no pit ticket was allowed to pass either 'into the boxes or on to the stage'. As Bayes in *The Rehearsal*, Wilkinson scored a triumph in a part in which Frodsham was esteemed capital. Wilkinson, however, considered that Frodsham was unsuited to the character and found in the applause he received in it another instance of the York public's undiscriminating hero worship. Wilkinson also played Cadwallader to the Mrs Cadwallader of Miss Phillips in Foote's *The Author* and on Wednesday, May 11, he attempted King Lear with Frodsham in his usual role of Edgar. 'My Lear', he tells us, 'was greatly received as it did not interfere with their darling Frodsham, and both being in the same play gave much satisfaction.' Frodsham was, in his opinion, the best actor he had seen in the mad scenes. On May 14 Wilkinson appeared as Horatio and Frodsham as Lothario in *The Fair Penitent*, after which *The Minor* was repeated. For his benefit on May 18,[1] Wilkinson played Oakley in *The Jealous Wife*, Trappolin in *A Duke and No Duke*, and revived the entertainment of *Tea*. He found 'a crowded audience, both before and behind the curtain; for the stage was filled with gentlemen', those frequenting the boxes being admitted behind the scenes. *Tea* was a failure, the satire and mimicry causing great disapproval, though, as we have seen, it had been played by Dancer without trouble.

York did not take kindly to strangers, and if they had any reputation they were not admitted to play either in York or Hull.[2] With the exception of Davies and Wilkinson, we find

---

[1] Wilkinson gives the date as May 17, the *York Courant* as 18th.
[2] *Memoirs*, vol. II, p. 10.

no actors brought from London to star for a week or a season to the disadvantage of the old favourites of the company.

Puppet shows and Italian operas compete in 1763 with the York Company. In Leeds during September there were Prussian Performers who had given 'general Satisfaction to the Duke of York, Marquis of Granby, and most of the Nobility and Gentry at Scarborough Spaw, and at York' and who were said to give performances such 'as can neither be conceived nor credited, but by ocular Demonstration'.[1] The Italian musicians were acting in the Mint Yard Theatre at York during October and met with approbation. The militia officers bespoke an evening. The pieces given were Rinaldo di Capua's *The Fortune Teller*; Pergolesi's *The Maid the Mistress*; *The Amorous Robber*, and *Harlequin's Happiness in Love*.

At the opening of the 1763-4 season *All's Well* brought in £15. 18s. 4d. for the hospital and *The Orphan of China* £15. 6s. 2d. for the schools. Thomas Powell and his wife had joined the company. Powell was an inhabitant of York who had married a lady of good Warwickshire family, by name Miss Steward, when he had been acting at Wolverhampton in 1763. His salary was 13s. 6d. a week and he remained with the company until 1775, later becoming the manager at Manchester.[2] Ryley says[3] he was 'a great favourite in Yorkshire', and that he was 'an actor of good conception and sound judgment, but his voice was inconceivably disgusting, a kind of speaking counter tenor, capable of little modulation'. He was a slow learner but never forgot a line. In Ryley's time he used to be in a constant state of intoxication. When Bickerstaffe's *Love in a Village* was given its first performance at York, Powell played Meadows to the Hawthorn of Frodsham. Mrs Powell acted Clarinda in a revival

[1] *Leeds Intelligencer*, September 27, 1763.
[2] *Wandering Patentee*, vol. I, p. 35.
[3] *Op. cit.* vol. I, p. 217.

of *Woman is a Riddle*. Other new productions of this enter-
prising season were Bickerstaffe's *Thomas and Sally*, with
Frodsham as Thomas; Mrs Centlivre's *The Man's Bewitch'd*,
Frodsham as Num; King's ballad opera *Love at First Sight*;
Brome's *The Jovial Crew*, Frodsham as Hearty and Mrs
Mytteer as Anne; Colman's alteration of *Philaster* which
Frodsham chose for his benefit, and in which he acted the
title role; Murphy's *What We Must All Come To*; Whincop's
Scanderbeg, with Frodsham as the hero; Colman's *The Deuce
is in him*, and Foote's *The Mayor of Garratt*.

Miss Phillips played Juliet, Audrey in *As You Like It*, and
Isabella in *Measure for Measure*. In the last named she was
supported as follows: Duke—Frodsham, Angelo—Crisp,
Escalus—Achurch, Claudio—Leng, Lucio—Owen, Clown
—Robertson, Abhorson—Fitzmaurice, Barnardine—Oram,
Mariana—Mrs Frodsham. In May, Mahon from Dublin
appears as a dancer. Wilkinson returned to the company for
the last fortnight of its stay in York. He appeared at the
Powells' first benefit at which Powell acted Gratiano and
Mrs Powell Portia in *The Merchant of Venice*. He then made
the great mistake of acting Othello on April 28. He was taken
ill during the performance, and the company was obliged to
dismiss. Wilkinson was thereafter abused for his rash attempt
to take over one of Frodsham's roles, and rumours were
maliciously circulated that he was either too afraid or too
drunk to make further appearances. On his playing Major
Sturgeon in *The Author* on May 1, he was greeted with hisses
and oranges, and told that Achurch could do better; but on
the following Saturday, when he acted Bajazet in *Tamerlane*
together with Foote's *The Orators* for the benefit of the actor
Tenoe, he met with neither applause nor hissing. In Murphy's
The Apprentice he was considered shockingly bad as Dick in
comparison with the beloved Frodsham, but was received
once more into favour when he ceased to challenge the
people's idol, and acted Kiteley in Ben Jonson's *Every Man
in his Humour* and Cadwallader in *The Author*. Col. Thornton

of the York militia bespoke his benefit and desired *The Mayor of Garratt* which was given with Steele's *The Funeral*. Wilkinson was gratified to see 'great boxes and a very genteel house', which brought the large sum of £50 in receipts.

Baker was at this time beginning to build his new theatre at a great, and his sole, expense. Wilkinson records that:[1] 'it was intended to be (as it now actually is) on a much more capacious scale than the old one, though nearly on the same spot, as he was then finishing the tail of the new, while the players were employed in the head of the old.' The real reason for Baker's rebuilding is to be found in the corporation records,[2] where a lease to him of a house in Blake Street with garden and appurtenances, 'besides the tenement used as a playhouse', was granted, from Christmas 1764 for twenty-one years at a rental of £20 a year, clear of all taxes, on condition that he spent £500 on the premises in lasting improvements, within two years from the beginning of the term.

The new theatre was ready for the commencement of the 1765 winter season, and was opened on January 3 with a performance of *The Provok'd Husband* and *The Lying Valet* for the benefit of Baker. The prologue was written by John Cunningham and spoken by Frodsham, the epilogue was written by Frodsham and spoken by Miss Phillips.[3]

'The Theatre', we read, 'is finished in an elegant Manner, and particular Care has been taken to have it well air'd.' In the *York Courant* of January 8 appears the following description:

This Theatre is by far the most spacious in Great Britain, Drury-lane and Covent Garden excepted, and for Convenience and Elegance it is thought to be equal, if not superior, to either of them.... As the Drama has, by all polite Nations, been allowed

---

[1] *Memoirs*, vol. III, p. 224.
[2] Proceedings of the Committee on Leases, 1704-1813.
[3] Printed respectively in *York Courants*, January 8 and 15.

to be the most rational and improving Entertainment, we beg leave to congratulate the Public on this accessional Ornament to the City.

Only two years later Wilkinson was to take over the ruling of the theatre and to find it 'in a very declining state, even to the disgrace of the city: dirty scenes, dirty clothes, all dark and dismal'. The opening of the new theatre and the appointment of Tate Wilkinson to the management ushered in a new era in the long theatrical history of York.

A few words remain to be added about the company's activities in Newcastle.[1] I have found no trace of Keregan visiting Newcastle after 1733, and, in 1739, a 'Newcastle Company' was in existence which also visited Edinburgh, and was renamed the Edinburgh Company in 1744. Baker renewed the York Company's connection with Newcastle on June 8, 1747 when he opened, at Mr Parker's Turk's Head Long Room in Big Market, with *The Suspicious Husband*, and announced his intention of continuing, during the races 'and as long after as their Season will permit, to divert the Gentlemen and Ladies with the newest and best Performances extant'. The last night was on August 10, when *The Ladies' Last Stake* was revived for Mrs Crisp's benefit, followed by entertainments and *The Devil of a Duke*. Plays were advertised as being given gratis between two parts of a concert, and charges were 2s. 6d. and 1s. Hereafter Baker ran a regular summer season in Newcastle from the middle or end of May until mid-August. In 1748 he put this season on a subscription basis, and twelve 'concerts' were given for 18s. for box, and 12s. for pit tickets. Race week was excluded from the subscription and prices were then raised. The company acted three times a week, and a series of benefits was given, outside the subscription, at the end of the season. The newest and best plays, together with a variety of entertainments and 'an entire new Set of Scenes, not inferior to any in Great Britain' were promised. The results of this season were

[1] See *Newcastle Journal*, Newcastle Public Library.

sufficiently encouraging for Baker to build a new playhouse. Under the date September 23, 1748, John Sykes notes, in his *Local Records*, that a new playhouse had been erected 'upon part of the walls of St Bartholomew's Hospital, near the Nun's Gate. The entrance to the play-house was from the Turk's Head yard'. The number of performances was increased in 1749 to eighteen, at the rate of £1. 7s. 0d. and 18s. for box and pit subscriptions respectively. For individual performances prices were boxes 2s. 6d., pit 2s., gallery 1s., except during race week when they rose to boxes 3s., pit 2s. 6d. In 1750 the subscription extended to twenty-one concerts at £1. 6s. 0d. for box, and £1. 1s. 0d. for pit, and 'the utmost Decorum and Regularity' were to be observed. No pit subscription ticket was valid for the boxes, even though a supplement should be paid.

Baker followed his York procedure, in 1751 and subsequent years, by devoting his first play to the benefit of the infirmary. For this he augmented his charges to boxes 3s., pit 2s. 6d., gallery 1s. 6d., later 1s., upper gallery 1s., later 6d. The receipts from these benefits show, as in York, a rapid decline: 1752 £48. 15s. 0d.; 1755 £30. 12s. 6d.; 1756 £43. 4s. 0d.; 1757 £34. 14s. 0d.; 1759 £25. 2s. 6d.; 1760 £19. 11s. 6d.; 1762 £14. 3s. 0d.; 1763 £17. 12s. 0d. The following plays were new to the town: 1748 *Debauchees*; 1749 *Merope, Henry VIII, Pleasures of the Town*; 1750 *Roman Father, Cobler of Preston*; 1752 *School for Wives, Double Disappointment*; 1753 *Gamester, Earl of Essex, Englishman in Paris*; 1754 *Virginia, Taste, Rehearsal or Bayes in Petticoats, Cornish Knights*; 1755 *Barbarossa, Press-Gang, Marplot in Lisbon*; 1756 *Athelstan, Novelty*; 1757 *Douglas, Reprisal, Catherine and Petruchio*; 1759 Hawkins's *Cymbeline, Cleone, Isabella, Harlequin's Vagaries*; 1760 *Mahomet the Impostor, Albion Queens, Way to Keep Him, Desert Island, High Life Below Stairs, Upholsterer*; 1761 *Fair Quaker of Deal, Jealous Wife, Harlequin Salamander, Harlequin's Adventures*; 1762 *School for Lovers, Polly Honeycombe, Merry*

Counterfeit, Old Maid, Alfred the Great; 1763 *Orphan of China, Edward the Black Prince, Discovery, Citizen, Scander-beg, Spirit of Contradiction, Frenchified Lady Never in Paris, Blind Beggar of Bethnal Green;* 1764 *Philaster, Love in a Village, Man's Bewitched, Marianne, Wife's Relief, Thomas and Sally, Love at First Sight, What We Must All Come To, Patron, Mayor of Garratt.* From this list it will be seen that the number of new productions increased towards the end of the period in what was probably an attempt to recapture lost patronage. Several of these plays were seen in Newcastle a few months after their appearance in London, and before their production in York.

In 1754 Mrs Davies, formerly Miss Yarrow, returned with her husband to play in Newcastle with the company; she performed Polly in *The Beggar's Opera* with universal applause, Calista to Davies's Horatio in *The Fair Penitent,* Queen in *The Spanish Fryar,* Indiana in *The Conscious Lovers,* Virginia in the play of that name to Davies's Virginius, Juliet and Cordelia to her husband's Romeo and Lear.

On May 26, 1755 Brown's *Barbarossa* was given 'To a numerous and polite Audience' and was honoured by the attendance of 'the Learned and Ingenious Author…who was pleased to express high Satisfaction with the Performers'.

Mrs Dancer, who was in the company 1756-7, played Thyra in *Athelstan,* and Cordelia, Ophelia, Lady Macbeth in 1756, and Lady Sadlife in *The Double Gallant,* Clarissa in *The Confederacy,* Hippolito in *The Tempest,* Cleopatra in *All for Love,* Mrs Riot in *Lethe,* Rosalind in *As You Like It,* and the Queen in *Richard III* in 1757. The Dancers were the only actors who succeeded in getting bespeaks for their benefits: in 1756 by desire of Francis B. Delaval, in 1757 by that of the Hon. Lady Blackett.

The box subscription for eighteen plays had been reduced by 1755 from £1. 7s. 0d. to £1. 2s. 6d. During the seasons 1757-9 the company probably went to Durham race week, as they advertised that they would play only one night in Newcastle owing to the Durham races.[1]

In 1759 Frodsham spoke a eulogium on Shakespeare 'in the proper Dress of the Times with a Curious Scene representing his Monument in Westminster Abbey', Hawkins's *Cymbeline* was presented with new habits, scenes and other decorations, and *Amphitryon* was revived with new dresses, paintings and other decorations. There was some trouble in connection with Frodsham's benefit in 1760, for with the second announcement of it on an altered date, the note was appended: 'The Disappointment Mr Frodsham met with in his Benefit when it was last proposed, he hopes will be no Objection to his Friends favouring him once more with their Company. He presumes the unavoidable Accident which then happened, is of itself sufficient Excuse for what followed. He flatters himself, therefore, that his Friends will not impute that to him as his Fault which was merely his Misfortune; but accept of his Invitation on Monday Evening, where every Thing, he hopes, will be conducted to their intire Satisfaction. Mr Frodsham, in this Place, cannot omit taking Notice of the many repeated Favours he has received from his Friends, and is proud of making this publick Acknowledgement'.

No mention is made of the subscription scheme in 1761 or thereafter, and the announcement that places for the boxes could be obtained of Mr Bearpark leads us to conjecture that Baker was running his season without a subscription. In August Frodsham made his first appearance as Macbeth to the Lady Macbeth of Mrs Venables.

When Garrick's adaptation of *The Winter's Tale* was brought out in 1762 it was carefully pointed out that this three-act version, with the statue scene and three principal characters restored, was not the same as the two-act comedy put forward by the rival Scotch company. Two years later

[1] The Edinburgh Company opened a new theatre in Durham in 1760.

another company, under Bates, engaged Baker's Theatre as soon as he had quitted it in August, but in spite of these competitors, Wilkinson, when he took over the management, continued to monopolise the Newcastle summer season until he abandoned the town in 1770, when the lease of the theatre fell in and Newcastle insisted on having only a winter season.

Chapter VIII

THE THEATRES OF BATH, 1705–1750

A history of the Bath theatres was written in 1892 by B. S. Penley in a book called *The Bath Stage*; but he has dealt somewhat summarily with the earlier years, and has concentrated on the Orchard Street and later theatres. A good deal of material is available for the first half of the eighteenth century that has so far been overlooked.

To prove that there were players in Bath during the second half of the seventeenth century, Penley quotes from the Chamberlain's Accounts for 1673 an item of a shilling given to 'the Playsters att the Towne Hall'. These are surely not players but plasterers who, on another occasion, we find were paid 9*d*. for their work. There seems indeed no proof positive that any company played in Bath during these decades, for even the laconic entry in the St Michael's Baptism Book under 1695, 'A players childe was born in July',[1] does not necessarily mean that a company was acting there.

Bath's days of glory opened at the beginning of the eighteenth century when Queen Anne and her consort visited the town in order to take the waters in 1702. In 1703 she repeated the visit, and Colley Cibber[2] relates that the Drury Lane Company went down to entertain her there. The occasion was memorable as giving Nance Oldfield her first chance. Mrs Verbruggen, having a mortal sickness upon her, was left behind in London, but in the 'female scramble'

[1] Noted in Lewis Melville, *Bath Under Beau Nash*, 1926, and kindly confirmed for me by the Rector.
[2] *An Apology for His Life*, Everyman ed., p. 157.

for her parts only that of Leonora in *Sir Courtly Nice* fell to
Mrs Oldfield. Cibber had but cold expectations of her and
gave her a perfunctory rehearsal; 'But when the play came
to be acted, she had a just occasion to triumph over the error
of my judgment...so forward and sudden a step into nature,
I had never seen; and what made her performance more
valuable, was that I knew it all proceeded from her own
understanding, untaught, and unassisted by any one more
experienc'd actor.' Mrs Oldfield was the first of a long line
of actors and actresses who were to make their name on the
Bath stage.

   Our only other scrap of information about this season is an
extract from *Heraclitus Ridens*, August 24–8, 1703, copied
by R. J. Smith in the fourth volume of his *Materials
Towards a History of the Stage*, which he opines refers to Tony
Aston:

Deserted from her Majesty's Company of Stage Players at
Bath with all his Cloaths and Accoutrements after having
receiv'd advanc'd Money: A Man that writes himself a *famous
Comedian*: Suppos'd to have enter'd himself among the Socks and
Buskins in Bartholomew Fair, and taken his journey through the
allurement of a thirty pound Bag. If he will return to his quarters
at the Bath in 14 days, he shall be kindly receiv'd: otherwise his
twelvepenny admirers will proceed against him with the utmost
severity, and have no more claps at his service, when the money
shall be spent, and he come upon the Stage again.

The whole tone of this paragraph, however, suggests that the
incident was some self-advertising escapade which should
not be taken too literally. The company stayed in Bath until
the end of September and are spoken of as having returned
thence in the *Daily Courant* of October 4.

   The first Bath theatre was built as early as 1705[1] by subscription which was supported 'by people of the highest

[1] *The Life of Richard Nash*, 1752. Rowland Mainwaring, *Annals of
Bath*, 1838, misreading a passage in F. Fleming's *The Life of Timothy
Ginnadrake*, mistakenly gives the date as 1730.

rank, who permitted their names to be engraven on the inside of the house as a public testimony of their liberality towards it'. The building, according to Wood, cost £1300.[1] It stood at the corner of the Borough Walls and Vicarage (now Parsonage) Lane, on the site of the east wing of the Mineral Water Hospital,[2] and was erected for the company of John Power, a former comedian of the King's Company in London. Power, despite the opposition of the Common Council, and the fulminations from pulpit and press of the Bristolian divine, the Rev. Arthur Bedford, had been active in Bristol in 1704 and 1705; but in August 1706 he was presented for the second time to the Grand Jury and suppressed. Either before or just after this disaster Power's Company, known as the Duke of Grafton's Servants,[3] appeared at the new Bath theatre in Mrs Centlivre's *Love at a Venture*. Mrs Centlivre, or Mrs Carol as she still was at that time, herself acted in the piece, and Miss Jacobella Power spoke the epilogue to it.[4]

It is recorded[5] that *The Recruiting Officer* was acted at Bath before the Duke and Duchess of Beaufort and other people of quality in September, on the auspicious day when news had been received of Prince Eugene's victory. Estcourt, who 'perform'd in honour of this great Success', added a topical verse to Kite's song in Act II, Sc. iii:

> The Noble Captain, Prince Eugene
> Has beat French, Orleans and Marsin,
> And march'd up and reliev'd Turin,
> Over the Hills and far away.

The presence of Richard Estcourt from Drury Lane may mean that he had temporarily joined Power's Company for

[1] *A Description of Bath*, 1747.
[2] See Stukeley's map, Itinerarium Curiosum, 1723; Strachey's Map of Somersetshire, 1732, and Wood's map, 1735.
[3] For his career in Norwich, see ante, pp. 45 *et seq.*
[4] Whincop, *op. cit.*; *Love at a Venture*, 1706.
[5] *Daily Courant*, September 24, 1706.

the summer, or that a London company was once again visiting Bath.

Of the next succeeding years little is known. A curious satire on Harley, Earl of Oxford, entitled *A Second Tale of a Tub: or, The History of Robert Powel the Puppet-Show-Man*, 1715, relates how Powell, acting as prompter in Bristol, was turned out of that city, and took refuge in Power's theatre; how he then set up a puppet theatre in opposition and 'was mightily frequented by all sorts of Quality, and Punch, with his Gang soon broke the Strolers, and enjoy'd the City of Bath by themselves'. Success enabled Powell to buy new sets of scenes for the dramas of his own composing, which included *Whittington and his Cat, Children in the Wood, Dr Faustus, Friar Bacon and Friar Bungay, Robin Hood, Mother Shipton, Mother Lowse*, together with the Pleasant and Comical *Humours of Valentini, Nicolini and King Bladud*. Powell is described as 'one of the most dexterous Managers of human Mechanism....His Wires are perfectly invisible, his Puppets are well jointed...and as for Punch, who used heretofore to be nothing but a roaring lewd, rakish, empty Fellow...he now speaks choice Apothegms and sterling Wit.'

The Tatler for May 14 and 17, 1709, makes capital of an incident, no doubt based on fact, arising from this rivalry between players and puppets and between two ladies of quality at Bath. One is said to have bespoken Alexander the Great from the company of strollers the other a puppet show. The puppet drummers beat up an audience and the lady enjoyed the tragedy alone. The next night the two rivals reversed their favours and it was the tragedy's turn to triumph. Embroidered with fancy though it be (Alexander the Great with its rival queens is almost too good a choice to be true), the passage reflects the way in which the ladies of fashion made use of the players for their own aggrandisement and in the cause of their petty jealousies.[1]

[1] Powell later drew the wrath of *The Tatler* upon him by making a prologue against Bickerstaff at Bath, July 19–21, 1709.

The story, indeed, is echoed in a letter from Dr William Stratford to Edward Harley nine years later:[1]

My Lady Harley's play last night was crowded more than any that has been acted this year, but discord and faction will break out in places dedicated to ease and diversion. Lady Katherine Edwin would not go to the play, nor let Lord Manchester's or her own daughter go, and was so well bred as to own her reason to be because it was bespoke by Lady Harley. But the ladies stand by us bravely, and have vowed revenge upon Dame Edwin, if she dares to bespeak a play this season.

Only through such frivolous episodes do we know that somehow Bath had its drama through these years. Except that in 1719 Henry Giffard, later proprietor of Goodman's Fields, 'entered himself among the Bath strolling Company of Comedians...whose Fortunes he followed two Years',[2] we know nothing of the players who entertained the growing crowds. That it was often a hard struggle is evident from a passage in the correspondence of Lady Bristol to her Lord in 1721.[3] The playhouse opened on the arrival of 'Governor Nash' on August 19 and Lady Drogheda bespoke a play on September 9. But on September 18 she writes, 'and for plays, there is hardly ever company to make it warm'. A doggerel poem on 'The Pleasures of Bath', 1721, repeats the tale of woe:

> Pray Madam bespeak,
> Or the Playhouse must break,
> We've had a bad Season,
> and hope for that Reason,
> You wont see three
> For a whole Company
>
> We'll strut you Cato,
> Or speeches of Plato,
> Farce, Comedy, Pastoral,
> we can master all;

[1] May 1, 1718, Hist. MSS. Com. Duke of Portland's MSS. VII, p. 237.
[2] Betterton's *History of the English Stage*, 1741.
[3] *Letter-Books of John Harvey*, 1894, vol. II, pp. 161, 188.

Pray let's weedle ye;
Damn the Medley,
Wou'd some-body poison him,
we'll raise lies on him;

Not only the medley but 'Punch shows at five', 'King
Edgar-Cocle' and 'puppet-show Powell' were rival attractions. Lady Harvey in 1723 mentions the puppet shows[1] in
Harrison's upper room and a play on May 22, bespoke by
the Duchess of Queensberry, which she was to attend in
company with the Duchess of Rutland and Lady B. Manners.
The Theatric Tourist, an unreliable source for both dates and
facts, asserts that one Watkins headed the strolling company
that visited Bath from 1720 onwards.

Defoe did not think highly of the Bath productions when
he visited the city on his tour through Britain in 1725: 'In
the afternoon there is generally a Play, tho' the Decorations
are mean, and the Performances accordingly; but it answers,
for the Company here (not the Actors) make the Play, to say
no more.'[2] And that, doubtless, was the blunt truth.

Puppet shows continued; the *Gloucester Journal* for
November 26, 1726, has mention of 'the so fam'd Entertainment, that has been this latter Season at Bath', which con-
sisted of plays performed by artificial actors five feet high,
a foretaste of the Über-marionette. In March 1727, the Bath
Company performed in Exeter and we get our first cast list:
'By the Bath Company of Comedians, Servants to His Grace
the Duke of Grafton, At the Seven Stars, at the Bridge Foot
in St Thomas's, on Monday next, being the 6th Inst. will be
Acted a Diverting COMEDY, call'd The Busie Body'; Airy—
Copen, Gripe—Howell, Traffic—Eldred, Charles—Agnew,
Marplot—Haynes, Whisper—Rous, Miranda—Mrs Howell,
Isabinda—Miss Power, Patch—Mrs Copen, Scentwell—Mrs
Rous; 'With a New PROLOGUE for the Opening, written by

[1] *Ibid.* May 1, 6.
[2] *A Tour Through the Whole Island of Great Britain*, ed. G. D. H. Cole,
1927, vol. II, 433.

A. Brice, and spoken by Mr Copen. Beginning exactly at 6 a-Clock.'[1] Andrew Brice was the owner of the newspaper. It is interesting to find that the company, though now known as that of Bath, continued under the patronage of the Duke of Grafton and that Miss Power still formed a link with past times.[2]

The year 1728 saw a turn in the players' fortunes, a miracle wrought for them by Gay and *The Beggar's Opera*. On May 16 Swift wrote: 'I have been at the Bath about ten days....The Beggars Opera is acted here; but our Polly has got no fame, though the actors have got money.'[3] The full accounts of their triumph in *Farley's Bristol News-Paper* and the *Gloucester Journal* are of much interest. On May 11 the *Bristol News* reports:

We hear from Bath, That last Week all the Quality were at the Playhouse, to hear the Rehearsal of the Beggars-Opera, collected a handsome Sum and presented the Actors with: And that on Monday and Wednesday last, notwithstanding the Pit and Boxes were laid together, they were so full, that they turn'd as many away as they took in: 'Tis evident, they were pleas'd with the Performance, because there was a Purse of Gold made up at the Pump-house, and presented to Lucy Locket, and Polly Peachum, to buy each of them a new Dress, in which they are each to perform their Part this Evening....We don't indeed much wonder at their performing of it well, when we hear, that Mr. GAY hath taken so much Pains to instruct them.

The tonic of Gay's instruction is commented upon by the *Gloucester Journal* for July 16, where it is said to have 'had so

---

[1] Brice's *Weekly Journal*, March 3, 1727.

[2] The *Gloucester Journal*, March 14, 1727 refers to the success of the Comedians from Bath acting there in a Medley: 'They are induc'd to play the Three Nights during our Assizes, and then they will go to another in the Neighbourhood' but I do not think that the Bath Company would descend to a despised medley and rather surmise that these were some other strollers who had visited Bath.

[3] *The Works of Jonathan Swift*, ed. Walter Scott, 1814, XVII, 221. *Notes and Queries*, May 13, 1905.

good an effect, that they not only gain'd a great deal of Money, but an universal Reputation'. On May 14 the Bath Company played to an audience of two hundred of the first rank, and the opera was bespoke for the following Tuesday with new dresses, including one for Mrs Peachum. Gay was to be present, and a dialogue of Henry Purcell's was to be sung by the girl who played Filch and her eight-year-old brother.[1] In June 'Princess Amelia, attended by the Dutchess of Marlborough, Dutchess of Ancaster, Lady Dalkeith, Countess of Pomfret and many other Persons of Quality, and Mr Gay...were agreeably entertained' by the performance. After about twenty performances the company moved to Bristol.[2] By August 24 they had played the opera forty-three times[3] and were engaged to give a further performance at Wells. In Bristol they acted it at the private houses of the nobility. Hippisley played Peachum, and others who took part were Haynes, Copen, Howell, Symmons, Hornby, Mrs Hornby, Mrs Copen, Mrs Howell and Miss Power.[4] This is the first we hear of Hornby. We learn from *The Life of Timothy Ginnadrake* that Power's widow still owned the Bath theatre in 1730 and that Hornby was then the manager. Another actor with a future, Charles Macklin, was in these years trying his strength with the company. He is said to have first played in Bristol in 1716 and then to have been engaged, together with a Miss Jackson, by Watkins, manager of the Bath and Bristol Company in 1720.[5] Kirkman,[6] who is unfortunately bare of dates, states that Macklin first joined an inferior band of players at Bristol, and strolled with them through the west of England and Wales. On returning to Bristol four years later, he joined a very respectable company

[1] *Bristol News*, May 18.   [2] *Gloucester Journal*, June 18.
[3] *Bristol News*, August 24.   [4] *Gloucester Journal*, July 16.
[5] Richard Smith, *Collections*, vol. 1. Bristol Reference Library. Smith adds that in 1731 he was engaged with Lady Hawley, manager of the Bristol and Bath Company, but it is unlikely that she had control before 1738.
[6] J. T. Kirkman, *Memoirs of the Life of Charles Macklin*, 1799.

of actors 'whose manager [possibly Watkins] was opulent, proud, critical, and cautious'. 'When the company moved to Bath, he there played the same distinguished part in the fives-court, and on the stage; and became no less a favourite there, than he was at Bristol. From thence he went, with the same company, to the various large towns in the western part of England; and played in all, with increasing success.' He contented himself with country playing until 1733, when he at last succeeded in getting a footing on the London stage. Though he still strolled in the summer, it is unlikely that he revisited Bath, whose season synchronised with the opening of the London theatres. Another actor who must have been playing about this time at Bath was William Mynitt who, after starting his career at the Haymarket, 'was solicited to add a promising Member to the Company of Bath, where there is a regular Theatre, and an audience as difficult to be pleas'd as that in London, being generally Persons of the highest Rank that frequent these Diversions in the Capital. He had the Fortune to give Satisfaction there, insomuch that several Persons of Distinction and Taste promised to recommend him to one of the established Theatres in London.'[1] We next hear of the company on their travels. On July 15, 1729, the *Gloucester Journal* announced: 'The Bath Company of Comedians are building a large commodious Booth in the White-Lyon Yard, near the Market-place, to entertain the Publick at the approaching Assizes, Races, and the Triennial Meeting of the Three Choirs: They have with them Mr Hippisley, and other Actors from both the Theatres in London; their Cloaths and Scenes far exceed any yet seen here. They will open the 28th Instant with The Beggars Opera, or Provok'd Husband.' The company in its summer progresses was evidently strengthened by recruits from London. We have seen how beginners like Macklin welcomed the opportunity of strolling in the dead months and

[1] They probably failed of their promises as he went instead to Ireland. Chetwood, *A General History of the Stage*, 1749, p. 194.

playing principal parts which they never had the chance of performing in the metropolis.

About this time the company performed John Hewitt's tragedy *The Fair Rivals*, which was printed at Bath in 1729.

The Bath Company spread wide its nets, and Devon, Gloucester, Wiltshire and Worcester were counties included in its itinerary. It visited quite small places as well as the larger towns, witness a paragraph in the *Gloucester Journal* of July 3, 1733: 'We hear from Bath, that the Bath Company of Comedians are upon their Progress to Wooton-under-Edge, Stroud, and Hampton, in order to perform there; their Cloaths and Scenes entirely new, and the richest that have been in the Country for many Years.' The same newspaper has a paragraph from Wells on July 24: 'A commodious Building is erecting in the Cannon Barn in this City, 44 Foot long and 22 Foot wide, in Order for Mrs Power's Comedians from the Bath to entertain the Publick at the approaching Assizes. They have with them Mr Jones, the eminent Dancer in the Footing Manner from the Covent-Garden Theatre, and a great Performer on the Violin.' The company also gave performances in some of the great houses, witness a letter from Mrs Delany, then Mrs Pendarves, addressed to her sister from Longleat on December 19, 1733: 'Whilst Lord and Lady Cartaret were here, Lord Weymouth sent for the players from Bath, and had scenes put up in the great parlour: they acted two plays very well. When they arrived with their baggage, Lady Weymouth says it was as entertaining a part as any, and put her in mind of Scarron's comical romance.'[1]

In Bath the following year we find the players again at the mercy of the cliques and caprices of fashionable society. Lord Chesterfield, in a journal letter to Lady Suffolk, records that, on October 31, 1734: 'The Countess of Burlington bespoke the play, as you may see by the enclosed original bill; the audience consisted of seventeen souls, of whom I

[1] *Autobiography and Correspondence of Mrs Delany*, 1861, vol. I, p. 424.

made one.' Two days later 'Mrs Hamilton bespoke the play at night, which we all interested ourselves so much to fill, that there were as many people turned back as let in; it was so hot that the Countess of Burlington could not stay it out.'[1]

Adversity outweighed prosperity until, according to Fleming:

> The company who then frequented Bath dedicated so great a part of their time to gaming, that the playhouse met with very bad encouragement for a succession of seasons, and the comedians in general were so much distressed as to be hardly able to support themselves:—Hornby accordingly applied to Lady Hawley, who kept the rooms, to take the property of the theatre into her hands, which was acceded to, but on conditions so much to her advantage, that the comedians received little relief from their former distress.

Lady Hawley, better known as Mrs Hayes, was the sister of Mrs Lindsay who owned the rival rooms opposite. Lord Hawley is said to have married her, sometime before 1718, for a maintenance when he was in reduced circumstances.[2] In 1737, on the death of Harrison, she took over the management of his Assembly Rooms. In the June of this year the Licensing Act, which suppressed by law all provincial playhouses, came into force.[3] This robbed Hornby of his theatre which was, on the passing of the Act, purchased by the Trustees of the Mineral Water Hospital and immediately demolished.[4] It was probably this final blow that drove Hornby to apply to Lady Hawley, who had just come into possession of the Assembly Rooms. The rooms, built in 1708 and subsequently enlarged, were situated on the east side of Terrace Walk towards the Orange Grove,[5] and there, under

---

[1] Quoted by Lewis Melville, *Lady Suffolk and her Circle*, 1924 from Add. MS. 22,626, f. 109.

[2] Mrs Delany, *op. cit.* vol. I, p. 64.   [3] See *ante*, p. 7.

[4] Wm. Baylis, *An Historical Account of the Rise, Progress and Management of the General Hospital*, 1757.

[5] A print of the Lower Rooms, as they were later called, was published by Barratt & Son, 1818, W. J. White sc., Neill del.

her ball-room, she offered the players an asylum, though on none too generous terms. These are set forth by Fleming, who also provides us with a description of the theatre:

> The seats were placed from the ground one above another, till they reached within four feet of the cieling; there was only one box, which held four persons, over the door; and what is very remarkable, the price was the same in every part of the house, half-a-crown each ticket. The house held thirty pounds compleatly; and Lady Hawley was entitled (according to agreement) to a full third of whatever money was taken, before any of the expences were paid for the use of her theatre, and one fourth of the nett profits for the use of her scenes and cloaths; as for example, supposing the receipt of the house to be 30*l.* her ladyship's share was 14*l.* the standing expence of the house was fifty shillings, for music, attendants, bills, candles, &c. and the remainder was divided among the performers, which were then about twelve in number.

If the house played to capacity each actor would receive about 27*s.* 6*d.*, but if half the benches were empty the actor would come but poorly off with 9*s.* or less.

How the company fared for the next few years under this system I have been unable to discover. In 1744 there is a glimpse of them in the *Bath Journal* for May 14: 'On Thursday last the Bath Company of Comedians perform'd the Comedy of the Conscious Lovers, for the Benefit of the Sufferers by Fire at Crediton in Devonshire. Sir Bouchier Wrey, Bart. and Samuel Strode Esq; collected the Money at the Doors, which amounted to near 60*l.*' On January 29, 1745, Lady Hawley died and the rooms came into the possession of one Simpson by whose name they were henceforward known.

From this time onwards the *Bath Journal* provides us with a good deal of information about the company's activities. On October 27, 1746, appeared a notice: 'Saturday last the Comedy of ALBUMAZAR (wrote above a Hundred Years ago) was perform'd here by the Bath Company of Comedians, at

the Desire of the Lady Smithson, with very great Applause.'
On December 22 it was announced that 'On Saturday next,
the COMEDY of the Conscious Lovers, will be perform'd at
Mr Simpson's, (unless any other is desir'd) for the Benefit of
Mr and Mrs Brookes; it being the last Benefit this Season.'
Garrick's *Miss in her Teens*, which had only seen the light at
Covent Garden on January 17, was performed at Bath on
February 2, 1747. After that the company moved: 'We
hear that the Bath Company of Comedians have taken the
Great-Room at the Globe, without West-Gate, which is
making very commodious; and that they intend to perform
on Monday next, The Tragedy of THEODOSIUS, or, The
Force of Love; with the Entertainment of Miss in her Teens
. . . The Prices 2*s.* 6*d.* and 1*s.* 6*d.*'[1] The Globe Inn, as indicated
by 'A New and Correct Plan of the City of Bath; Sold by
W. Frederick & W. Taylor', was in Kingsmead Square.
Also at the Globe were given Ambrose Philips's *The Distress'd
Mother* and *The Gardener's Wedding* on March 2 for the
benefit of Mr and Mrs Kennedy;[2] *Oroonoko* with *The Lying
Valet* on March 9 for the benefit of Fielding and Duncomb;
Jane Shore and *The Lottery* on March 16 for the benefit of Mr
and Mrs Brookes; *Tamerlane* and *An Old Man Taught Wisdom*
on March 23 for the benefit of Baker and Mrs Bishop; and
Othello and *The Honest Yorkshireman* on March 30 for the
benefit of Mrs Cox and Mrs Reed. In November the
company was in Bristol, where they revived *Albumazar* for
Hippisley's benefit at Jacob's Wells.[3] The first performance
we hear of at Bath that season is that of Mrs Centlivre's
The Gamester on December 3, at Simpson's Theatre for the
benefit of Cox and Mrs Reed, by the command of Lady
Fetherstone. Then again the company moved, this time to
a large room at the George Inn, near the Cross Bath, where

---

[1] *Bath Journal*, February 16, 1747.
[2] Kennedy was later manager of the Exeter, Plymouth, and Portsmouth
playhouses. See *Theatric Tourist*.
[3] *Bath Journal*, October 26.

prices remained the same as at the Globe. The following plays were given there:

February 15, 1748. *Cato, The Contrivances.*
February 22, 1748. *The Unhappy Favourite, The What D'ye Call It.* Benefit: Mr. and Mrs. Brookes.
March 7, 1748. *The London Merchant, The School Boy.* Benefit: Mr. Baker and Mrs. Bishop.
March 14, 1748. *The Jew of Venice, The Livery Rake.* Benefit: Mr. and Mrs. Martin.
March 21, 1748. *The Mourning Bride, The Gardener's Wedding.* Benefit: Mr. and Mrs. Cartwright.
April 4, 1748. *The Fair Penitent, Miss in her Teens.* Benefit: Mr. and Mrs. Kennedy.

Simpson's theatre was proving inadequate and it was during this season that John Hippisley, who ran the Jacob's Wells Theatre in Bristol, submitted a scheme for building a new theatre. 'The present Play-House or rather Playroom', he pointed out in his manifesto to the Nobility and Gentry at Bath,[1] 'is so small and incommodious, that 'tis almost impossible to have Things better done in it than they are. The Profits arising from the Performance, as now conducted, will not support a larger, or better, Company of Actors. And nothing can be more disagreeable, than for Persons of the first Quality, and those of the lowest Rank, to be seated on the same Bench together, which must be the Case here.' Naturally Hippisley met with strenuous opposition from Simpson but, such was the encouragement from 'People of Rank and Distinction'[2] that, although Hippisley died on February 12, 1748, his scheme was proceeded with. Meanwhile we hear of two further performances at Simpson's in 1748:

December 15. *The Double Gallant.* Benefit: Mr. and Mrs. Cartwright.
December 22. *The Constant Couple.* Benefit: Mr. and Mrs. Martin.

[1] *Bath Journal*, November 30, 1747. [2] Wood, *op. cit.* p. 166.

Another company, which was later to visit Bath, comes into view in an announcement in the *Bath Journal* for February 27, 1749: 'We hear that Mr Linnett's Company of Comedians open'd at Chippenham last Thursday with the Tragedy of Cato, to the general Satisfaction of the Audience, who allow'd the Performance surpass'd their Expectation; and that the Roman Habits were not inferior to those at the Theatres in London. They will continue acting three Times a week.' With Linnett's company about this time was Colley Cibber's notorious daughter Mrs Charke.[1]

In February 1750 the Bath Company was installed 'at the New Theatre' in Kingsmead Street. Penley[2] has an account of this theatre, probably from an eyewitness, since it was only pulled down about 1872. He tells us that it was situated behind what is now Fuller's garage, and that it consisted of a room measuring about 25 × 50 feet, with a gallery at the end opposite the stage. His conjecture that it was built about 1723 is mistaken as Mrs Charke, who was asked by Linnett to join his company there, calls it newly created in 1750. *The Theatric Tourist* gives the date as 1746 but is not a trustworthy authority. The charges were pit 1s. 6d., gallery 1s. The Bath Company's repertory was as follows:

February 19. *The Mourning Bride, The Lover's Opera.*
February 26. *Othello, The Contrivances.*
March 5. *The Revenge, Wit at a Pinch.*
March 26. *The Beggar's Opera, The Slip.*
April 2. *The Unhappy Favourite, The Lover's Opera* (last night).

The only new names in the benefit list are those of the Tuckers.

It was Linnett's company of which it was reported on

---

[1] *A Narrative of the Life of Mrs Charlotte Charke*, Constable's Miscellany, 1929, pp. 155–9. Lee Lewes refers to 'the veteran Linnett' playing at Hammersmith, 1760 and later to his being on an Oxford circuit, *op. cit.* vol. I, p. 16.
[2] *Op. cit.* p. 21.

June 4: 'This Evening the Tragedy of Cato will be performed at Calne, at the Desire of a Person of Distinction; and on Wednesday, King Richard the Third.' The company brought *Richard III* to Kingsmead Street Theatre on July 4 and during their two months' stay provided the following repertoire:

July 9. *The Inconstant, Tamerlane.*
July 12. *Tamerlane.* Command of the Lady Augusta. The Prince and Princess of Wales attended after drinking tea at Ralph Allen's.[1]
July 16. *Love for Love, The Honest Yorkshireman.*
July 19. *Oroonoko.*
July 23. *Hamlet, The King and the Miller of Mansfield.*
July 25. *The Orphan.*
July 27. *The London Merchant*, by particular desire.
July 31. *The Fair Penitent, Harlequin Skeleton.*
August 3. *The Spanish Fryar.*
August 7. *Henry IV, The Toy Shop.*
August 9. *Venice Preserv'd*, by particular desire.
August 13. *The Committee*, Teague—Barrington from London,[2] *Flora.*
August 20. *Jane Shore*, Mrs. Ward from Drury Lane in title role.[3] Dancing by Mrs. Baker, by particular desire.
August 28. *Othello*, Desdemona—Mrs. Ward.
      Damon and Phillida, by particular desire.

The visitors from London must have given tone to the company; in addition to them we get from the benefit list the names of Mr and Mrs Linnett, Mr and Mrs Carthy, Parsons, Mrs Clark. On September 24 an unnamed company performed *A Bold Stroke for a Wife*, and on 27 *Love Makes a Man* at the Kingsmead Street Theatre.

And now the new theatre in Orchard Street was ready and opened its doors on October 27 with *Henry IV* and a prologue

[1] *Bath Journal*, July 16, Bristol Ref. Lib.
[2] Barrington's first appearance at Covent Garden was on October 11, 1749. Tate Wilkinson considered him the best Teague he ever saw (*Memoirs*, 1790, vol. I, p. 123).
[3] Her first appearance at Drury Lane was as Cordelia to Garrick's Lear, October 13, 1749.

spoken by Watts who had been associated with Hippisley in the scheme. The theatre had been planned to replace Simpson's, but, in spite of an agreement to the contrary, Simpson not only continued to run his theatre in opposition, but obtained the services of the Bath Company to play in it.

The history of the Orchard Street theatre belongs to the later theatrical history of Bath, that of the remaining years of Simpson's theatre, years of struggle and rivalry, is matter for another chapter.

Chapter IX

SIMPSON'S THEATRE, BATH, 1750–1756

Did Simpson build a new theatre or did he merely renovate Lady Hawley's? Fleming tells us that Simpson 'built a theatre under the present large ballroom'.[1] *The Bath and Bristol Guide* [1760?], speaking of the two existing theatres, describes one as 'built by the late Mr Simpson, under his Long-Room'. Simpson certainly built a new room 90 × 30 feet, though curiously enough this is marked on a contemporary map simply as the new room, the old ballroom which only measured $61\frac{1}{2}$ × 29 feet being referred to as the long room.[2] Now either the map has gone astray in its references or *The Bath and Bristol Guide* is merely describing Lady Hawley's theatre under the old ballroom. It does, however, seem more likely that the new room, which was so much larger in proportion than the old, was known as the long room and that Fleming and the *Guide* are correct in their statements that Simpson built a new theatre under it. Additional evidence is provided by the newspaper advertisements which refer to it as Simpson's New Theatre, though they would probably have done this had it only been renovated. Opinions differ as to its comfort. In 1751 Pierre Clément described it as 'votre petit théâtre à quarante pieds sou terre; c'est une assez jolie catacombe, un peu écrasée comme de raison'.[3] Samuel Derrick[4] found it more capacious and convenient than that of Orchard Street, and *The Theatric Tourist* states that the stage and the lower part of the theatre

[1] *Op. cit.* vol. III, p. 34.
[2] *A New and Correct Plan of the City of Bath* [1750?].
[3] *Les Cinq Années Littéraires*, 1755, vol. II, p. 103.
[4] *Letters Written by Samuel Derrick*, 1767, vol. II, p. 69.

were on the model of Drury Lane only much larger. But
Richard Warner,[1] judging, perhaps, by standards of a later
day, only saw in the discarded room 'a proof that our
ancestors were not quite so studious of accommodations of
ease as their voluptuous descendants of these days'.

Whether his theatre was new or not, Simpson stole a
march on his rival and opened on October 22, 1750, with
a prologue spoken by Hallam to the Mayor and Corporation.
The prologue, which Penley gives in full, insists, in customary
fashion, on the moral purpose of the drama, extols the city,
flatters its Council and appeals for their support. I have
analysed the plays given during the season, which lasted until
June 17, under period headings, starring first performances
in Bath, and noting by a number in brackets if more than
one performance was given:

Elizabethan and Jacobean: *Romeo and Juliet* (3).
*King Lear, Richard III, *Volpone, Rule a Wife.*

Restoration: *Oroonoko, Venice Preserv'd, All for Love, The
Unhappy Favourite.*

Eighteenth century: *The Provok'd Husband* (2), *The Conscious Lovers* (2), *The Distress'd Mother, George Barnwell, The
Beggar's Opera, Miss in her Teens, The Busy Body.*

Afterpieces: *The Nuptials of Columbine* (5), *The Lying
Valet* (2), *Harlequin Fourbe-François, The Mock Doctor, An Old
Man Taught Wisdom.*

Both theatres gave annual performances in aid of the
General Hospital, *The Provok'd Husband* being the play
chosen by Simpson. 'A very numerous and brilliant
Audience attended' and £43. 8s. 6d.[2] was raised, the whole
takings, without deduction, being handed over to the
charity. For the production of *Oroonoko* we read 'that a
very elegant Dress, suitable to the Character, is just finish'd,

---

[1] *The History of Bath*, 1801, p. 363.
[2] This amount is not stated but we know Orchard Street made
£65. 4s. 0d. and both together £108. 12s. 6d., hence by simple
arithmetic.

in which the Royal Slave will then make his Appearance'. On another occasion a romantic attraction was provided by the singing of 'Mrs Hannah Snell who went by the Name of James Gray, serv'd his Majesty as a Marine several Years, behav'd with great Bravery, and receiv'd several Wounds at the Siege of Pondicherry in the East Indies'. Thus the theatre then absorbed the kind of entertainment now relegated to the music halls. The Bath Company was in Bristol on March 15, and back at Simpson's a month later.

Performances began at 6 or 6.30 and the charges were: boxes 3s., pit 2s., front gallery 1s. 6d., side galleries 1s., or on occasion both galleries were 1s. 6d. The company included:

Men	Women
Clough	Mrs. Cowper
Martin	Mrs. Martin
Cartwright	Mrs. Cartwright
Hayward	Mrs. Talbot
Julian	Mrs. Elrington
Smith	Mrs. Horton from Covent Garden
Richardson	Mrs. Richardson
Hallam	Mrs. Reed
Charles Jones[1]	Miss Baker
Griffith from Drury Lane	
Fielding	
Rigby	

The beautiful Christiana Horton had just retired from Covent Garden. She had been on the stage thirty-six years when 'Between Mrs Woffington and Mrs Pritchard she suffered shipwreck'. In Bath she played quite young heroines, Cleopatra in *All for Love* on April 8, 1751, Estiphania in *Rule a Wife* for her benefit on April 22, and the Queen in

---

[1] R. J. Smith, *op. cit.* has a cutting dated November 8, 1731 offering a £50 reward for the apprehension of Charles Jones 'a noted Gamester and Stage-Player in Bath' who is said to have been found guilty of the murder of one Basil Arden Prise and to have escaped from justice. He subsequently surrendered himself. *Gloucester Journal*, March 20, 1733.

Richard III on May 6. Mrs Cowper shared with her the principal women's roles. King came from Dublin and played Marplot in *The Busy Body* and the Lying Valet on June 18. Clough played Lear, Griffith George Barnwell, Hallam Mark Anthony in *All for Love*, and Rigby Richard III and Young Bevil. Pierre Clément has left for us his impressions:[1]

quand la scène vint à s'ouvrir & à vomir ces personnages, je crus voir arriver la bande de voleurs de la caverne de Gil Blas. Leur manière de représenter ne rompit point le drame, pas même la jeune Actrice qui parut en habit d'homme entre les deux pièces, pour nous réciter un compliment. On n'avoit point épargné le galon d'argent à son justaucorps gris, mais bien le satin à sa veste couleur de rose. Tou ce que l'affectation la plus grossière peut imaginer de grimaces déplaisantes, pour faire haïr une figure agréable, fut heureusement employé par la petite personne; jamais je ne fus plus choqué.

A very French point of view though hardly complimentary. Hayward and Cartwright from the Bath Company, and one Clark were in a company, probably Linnett's, that acted *Richard III* and *George Barnwell* at the Kingsmead theatre on August 19 and 26, 1751, respectively. The doors were opened at 5.30 for a 7 o'clock performance, and the charges were pit 1s. 6d., gallery 1s. When Simpson's reopened on September 23 it was under the management of one Henry Brown. When, in later years, Brown was manager of the Smock Alley Theatre, Dublin, Tate Wilkinson[2] acted under him and tells us that 'he had been in much esteem as an actor and a gentleman at Bath and Edinburgh...was a most pleasing well behaved companion, was very indolent, a second Digges for extravagance, was much in debt in England and in Dublin,...he was so well beloved that they never pressed him to any distress'. Were it not for this good character one would have judged Brown to have had a flair

---

[1] *Op. cit.* p. 103.   [2] *Memoirs*, vol. II, p. 161.

for quarrelling and self-advertisement;[1] in Bath at any rate he was not beloved by everyone.

Brown himself played most of the chief roles this season; his leading lady was Miss Ibbott and Pitt was his Harlequin. It was a very different company from that of the previous season:

Men	Women
Brown	Miss Ibbott
Layfield	Miss Lowe
Dancer	Mrs. Cowper
Pitt[2]	Miss Bradshaw
Griffith	Miss Hippisley
Singleton	Mrs. Pye
Lacey (joined 1752)	Mrs. Martin
Clough	Mdlle Huette
Martin	
Mons. Maltere	

Brown himself, Dancer and Lacey had deserted from Orchard Street. In fact the actors were always shifting from one theatre to the other, or to and from minor strolling companies, and it is difficult to keep track of their movements.

Macbeth was as usual advertised as 'With the Original Musick, Songs, and Dances'; *Merope* was given with 'Musick, Singing and Decorations proper to the Play' and, as Edward the Black Prince, Brown was 'now dress'd according to the Habit of that Time'. How near to historical accuracy he came who can now tell, but at least his attempt is an indication of a trend in production of his time. The greatest effort was reserved for the pantomime of *The Necromancer*: 'With the Original Musick, Songs and Dances; and The Scenes, Machines, Dresses, and other Decorations entirely New. As Mr Brown has been at a great Expence in

[1] For his troubles, which belong to the history of Orchard Street, see *Bath Advertiser*, November 27, *Bath Journal*, November 29, An Appeal to the Public by Signor Passerini bound with them in the B.M. copies, *Bath Advertiser*, April 23, 1757.

[2] Harlequin Pitt succeeded Kennedy as manager of the Exeter Theatre in 1758 (see *The Theatric Tourist*).

getting up this Entertainment, it is hoped the Town will not take it amiss that Nothing under full Price will be taken during the Run; and as the Success of it will depend upon the Stage being clear, it is hoped no Gentlemen will be offended if they are not admitted behind the Scenes.' On another occasion too Brown refused half-price terms to the audience.

Among those who bespoke performances were Beau Nash, the Duchess of Somerset, the Duchess of Queensberry, the Countesses of Northumberland, and of Hyndford and Nithsdale, Lady Betty Bathurst and Lady Throckmorton. £32. 11s. 6d. was raised for the General Hospital by a performance of *The Orphan*, preceded by a prologue by Brown of which the opening couplets will suffice:

> To raise the tender Passions, and impart
> The softest Anguish to the hardest Heart,
> For this the tragick Muse, melodious Queen
> Turns her soft lays, or swells the lofty Scene.

The first of Brown's quarrels arose in November when he accused the Orchard Street Company of intoxicating and inveigling away from him his carpenter and mechanist Thomas Smith. According to the Orchard Street affidavits, Smith complained of the bad treatment he had received from Brown, averring that he wanted his entertainments out before Smith could get them ready, and that he expected things to be done for 40s. or 50s. which would cost many pounds. What was the outcome of this theatrical storm in a tea-cup we do not know, but Brown seems to have had the last and best word when he got Smith to depose against the rival actors.

The following are the recorded performances for this season, 1751–2:

Shakespeare: *Romeo and Juliet* (4), *Richard III* (3), *Henry IV, Pt. I* (2), *Macbeth*, *The Merry Wives*.

Restoration: *Venice Preserv'd* (2), *The Constant Couple* (2), *The Orphan*, *The Anatomist*, *Love for Love*.

Eighteenth century: *The Beggar's Opera* (6), *The Busy Body* (2), *The Drummer* (2), *Zara* (2), *⋆The Twin Rivals, Edward the Black Prince, Love Makes a Man, Merope, The Fair Penitent, Cato, Jane Shore, The Distress'd Mother, The Recruiting Officer, Tamerlane, The Foundling*.

Afterpieces: *Harlequin Restor'd* (11), *Harlequin's Vagaries* (8), *The Lying Valet* (5), *Harlequin Mountebank* (2), *The Necromancer* (2), *The Chaplet, The Devil to Pay, Miss in her Teens*.

The pantomimes were continually being refurbished with new scenes, such as that from Covent Garden of Don Jumpedo in *Harlequin Jumping Down his own Throat* added to *Harlequin's Vagaries*. Indeed, various popular deceptions were easily introduced at will into any pantomime, the elastic structure of these entertainments being devised to accommodate all kinds of alterations and additions. The company again visited Bristol over Easter and played *Tamerlane* at Jacob's Wells for Mrs Hippisley's benefit.

The next season, 1752–3, the fickle Brown, together with Miss Ibbott, had reverted to Orchard Street; Dancer meanwhile had married a Bath belle, Miss Street, and had gone with her to York where she, too, became an actress, later celebrated both as Mrs Barry and Mrs Crawford.[1] The company at Simpson's was then:

Men	Women
Falkner from Dublin	Mrs. Cowper
Cooke	Mrs. Mozeen (from D.L. and Dublin)
Mason	Mrs. Wye
Philips	Miss Hippisley
Saunders	Mrs. Saunders
Martin	Mrs. Martin
Macgeorge	Miss Helme
Fawkes	Miss Fawkes
Jones	Miss Plym
Fitzmaurice from Dublin	
Harper	

[1] See *ante*, pp. 142, 145.

A lampoon, entitled *The Bath Comedians*, published in 1753, satirises the players of both houses. From it we learn that Philips had succeeded Brown as manager:

> He is a right good-natur'd Man;
> In comick Scenes he'll make you laugh
> In clownish Parts or in Falstaff.[1]

But he was useless in tragedy.

> And next to him I think is C[oo]k,
> Ugly his Person, mean his Look
> Yet of Admirers he's his Choice,
> Strong, clear and manly is his Voice,
> Of Judgement sound, good Education
> As any Players in the Nation.

This Cook was none other than Francis Gentleman of whom more later.[2] Falkner, the tragic hero, is said to want power yet:

> For comick Parts he is not fit
> He tragedises every Bit.

Jones is characterised as 'a Lanthorn-jaw'd long Bones', and Macgeorge is attacked as fit only for 'Harlequino's Running Footman'. Harper fares better:

> tho' bred an Apothecary
> Is capable to make me merry
>
> .   .   .   .   .   .
>
> He's a good Pierrot,[3] take my Word
> And Clown in Harlequin Restor'd.

'Old' Martin is described as the best pantaloon in Bath. Saunders as Teague in *The Committee* meets with scant

---

[1] He played Touchstone, Friar Laurence, Sancho in *Don Quixote*, King in *Tom Thumb*, Peachum.
[2] When Tate Wilkinson played with him in Portsmouth in 1759, he was 'very lame and in years' (*Memoirs*, vol. II, p. 92).
[3] He played Pierrot in *Harlequin's Vagaries*.

approval, and two new actors, Watts and Gates,[1] have 'heavy Heels and empty Pates'. Mrs Cowper 'plays fond Juliet excellently',

> In Athenais[2] she'll content ye;
> With graceful Person, Voice most clear,
> She'll please the Eye, and charm the Ear.

Though she is bad as Belvidera and she will not study anything new. Mrs Mozeen

> Whose Looks the most obdurate Heart
> Wou'd prepossess to take her Part;

sings with tuneful voice but cannot speak well. 'Little, neat Mrs Mozeen', Tate Wilkinson[3] calls her, and adds that she had 'a plurality of lovers'. Mrs Saunders suffers with her husband:

> With jaunting Mien, affected Air,
> I knew her at West Smithfield Fair
>
> .   .   .   .
>
> And she's the worst in all the Nation,
> She's so puff'd up with Affectation;
> She speaks nor well in Verse or Prose,
> But drowns her Language in her Nose.

Mrs Wye, the prompter, played Damon in *The Chaplet* better than Fitzmaurice played Palaemon. Mrs Martin 'is old and past her Day', and her best part is the Nurse in *Romeo and Juliet*. Mdlle Huette is complimented on her dancing and Miss Plym is 'a little Cherubim'.

Lastly, the lines about Miss Ibbott are of interest:

> faith she is a lovely Dame;
> They say her Voice can charm like Magick
> The Comick Scenes as well as Tragick;
> She acts well, and speaks well too.

---

[1] Wilkinson speaks of Gates as 'a very conceited actor' (*Memoirs*, vol. II, p. 197).

[2] In *Theodosius*.   [3] *Memoirs*, vol. III, pp. 144–5.

Of her also Mrs Charke said that she was

really deserving of Praise and Admiration, as all she does is from the Result of a very great and uncommon Genius. I own myself not very apt to be partial, but this Gentlewoman struck me into a most pleasing Astonishment, by her Performance of many Characters; but most particularly, in the Part of Isabella, in The Fatal Marriage. She not only drew the Audience into a most profound Attention, but absolutely into a general Flood of commiserating Tears; and blended Nature and Art so exquisitely well, that 'twas impossible not to feel her Sorrows, and bear the tenderest Part in her Affliction.

I must confess I never was more truly affected with a tragical Performance, and was rendered incapable of reading a single Syllable; but, luckily for Miss Ibbott, she is always so perfect, a Prompter is a useless Person while she is speaking.... And if she had the Advantage of seeing Mrs. Cibber, Mrs. Woffington, or Mrs. Pritchard, in their different Lights, it would make her as compleat an Actress as ever trod the English Stage.[1]

Tate Wilkinson, who acted with Miss Ibbott in Dublin in 1760, refers to her as 'a lady of merit in speaking blank verse'.[2]

We hear little this season of stage effects except for the ostrich introduced into Harlequin Restor'd: nearly ten feet high, it was

form'd and executed on the same Principles of Mechanism, as that introduced in the celebrated Entertainment of the SORCERER, perform'd at Covent-Garden Fifty Nights successively, with the greatest Applause. As Reviving the Play, and perfecting the Ostrich, will be attended with considerable Expence, 'tis humbly hoped that Ladies and Gentlemen will not take it ill, that Nothing under Full Price will be taken, during the whole Performance.

The Provok'd Wife and Tom Thumb were chosen for the hospital benefit and fetched £35. 10s. 6d. Philips spoke the prologue. The company probably played three times a week, and the season ended just after May 24. It is remarkable for

---

[1] Op. cit. pp. 197–8.
[2] Memoirs, vol. II, p. 181. For her later career in Norwich, see Bernard, op. cit. vol. I, p. 119, and in York, Wandering Patentee, vol. I, p. 65.

the many new plays that were staged. Of these Edward
Moore's *The Gamester*, brought out at Drury Lane on
February 7, was given in Bath on February 26 with Falkner
speaking Garrick's prologue, and Mrs Mozeen taking over
Mrs Pritchard's epilogue.

The analysis of advertised performances is as follows:

Elizabethan: *The Merchant of Venice* (2), *As You Like
It*, *Romeo and Juliet*, *A New Way to Pay Old Debts*.

Restoration: *Venice Preserv'd* (3), *Theodosius* (3), *The Provok'd Wife* (2), *Don Quixote*, *Mithridates*, *Love and a
Bottle*, *Love's Last Shift*, *The Constant Couple*.

Eighteenth century: *The Gamester* (3), *The Oracle* (2),
The Beggar's Opera (2), *The Inconstant* (2), *The Twin Rivals*,
The Conscious Lovers, *The Mistake*, *The Revenge*, *King
Charles I*, *The Double Gallant*.

Afterpieces: *Harlequin Restor'd* (7), *Harlequin's Vagaries*
(6), *Tom Thumb* (4), *Miss in her Teens* (3), *The Stage Coach*,
The King and the Miller of Mansfield, *The Chaplet*, *Chrononhotonthologos*, *The Devil to Pay*, *The Brave Irishman*.

Of the season 1753–4 we get an inside view from the pen
of Mrs Charke,[1] who was engaged by Simpson 'to prompt,
and undertake the Care of the Stage, incident to that Office'.
She fulfilled her duties from September to March though
'the Prompters of either Theatres in London have not Half
the Plague in six Months, that I have had in as many Days'.
She goes on to describe how Simpson's 'good nature and
Unwillingness to offend the most trifling Performer' prevented him from exerting due authority in the disputes that
arose among the actors. He gave most of his time to the
rooms, which left insufficient for the conduct of the theatre,
so that 'what ought to have been a regular Government, was
reduced to Anarchy and Uproar'. The poor prompter not
only had to arbitrate in the quarrels but to spend Sunday

---

[1] *Op. cit.* pp. 195–208. The year, though not given by Mrs Charke, is
settled by the fact that it is the only one before 1755 in which Maddox
appeared.

mornings rushing round to the printer, 'either for Alteration of Parts, or of Capital Distinctions in the Bills, without which very indifferent Actors would not otherwise go on'. Of these petty jealousies she pungently remarks: 'I think 'twould have been a greater Proof of Judgment to have distinguished themselves on the Stage, than up a Post or a Brick-wall.' When Miss Ibbott was not acting receipts fell, with the result that the rest of the company grew envious and would often, to their loss, give to others the leading parts. Nevertheless,

The Business in general was, according to all Accounts, that Season better than they had known it for many past, and was greatly heightened by the universal Admiration of the Performance of the justly-celebrated Mr. Maddox, who engaged with Mr. Simpson at a considerable Salary, though not more than he truly deserved.

I believe the Comedians found him worthy of his Fame, as he not only brought in what paid his Agreement, but more than doubled that Sum, which they shared among them; yet, to my certain Knowledge, there was private Murmuring, even in respect to him, though they profitted by his Success, and, in spite of their grudging Hearts, could not help being delighted at his surprizing Feats of Activity on the Wire.

Mrs Charke further tells how two members of the company interfered with her proposed performance as Lord Foppington in *The Careless Husband*. Falkner, of whom she says, 'I never heard him utter, or do a Thing, that was inconsistent with the true Character of a Gentleman', was ready to study the role of Lord Morelove, but Simpson gave way to her rivals and would not allow her to act. What finally decided Mrs Charke to leave Bath, however, was the shutting down of both playhouses consequent upon information lodged against them under the Licensing Act. Neither theatre had a legal right to exist, but both had so far been left undisturbed. Mrs Charke relates that a certain A— raised twenty guineas and bribed 'an old Scoundrel', to whom the good-hearted Simpson had been a liberal benefactor, to play informer. The theatre was, in consequence, shut down from March 25 for three weeks, and reopened as the Concert Room near the Parade on April 15. The law was evaded by the usual trick of sandwiching a play gratis between two sections of a concert. The *Bristol Journal* has the following account relating to the rival theatre on March 23–30, 1754:

Wednesday Information was made before our Magistrates against the Playhouse in Orchard Street, by a Gentleman who had been there the Night before, at the acting of *King Richard III*. And Yesterday the Company of the said House were summon'd to appear at the Guild Hall to answer such Information, when they were fined agreeable to Act of Parliament. Since which the said House has been entirely shut up.

Mrs Charke speaks of the exasperation and indignation of the people of quality at 'the Infringement upon their Liberty of Entertainment', and of how they 'interested themselves greatly in Behalf of each Theatre, and carried their Point against the insolent Invader of their Privileges'. Only the Bath chairmen exulted, inimical as they were to the 'show-folk' who interfered with their trade. It was the Methodist element, Mrs Charke hints, that had the playhouse doors shut and tried to keep them so. Further information about this period is to be found in the utterances of Francis Gentleman, alias Cook, actor and dramatist. When he joined the company in 1752–3, 'it was', he says,[1] 'under the gothic management of one Mr Phillips, an old theatrical coxcomb, vain of playing, and covetous of money'. The players he characterises as 'a very imperfect odd jumbled crew', though he admits that his own endeavours tended to make them even more ridiculous: 'being chiefly in a much varied capital line, I must necessarily have been often capitally wrong.' While studying a multiplicity of parts he yet found time to write *The Sultan* which was produced as *Osman*[2] and 'well

[1] Preface to *The Modish Wife* [1774].
[2] Whether *Osman* was first produced in the 1752–3 or 1753–4 seasons is a little uncertain. I incline to the former since Gentleman tells us that *Zaphira*, 1754–5, came out in his *second* season. But 1754–5 would have been his *third* season had he been in the company in 1753–4 as well as in 1752–3 when his name appears in the cast lists.

received, though weakly performed'. In the preface to the printed version he further states that it ran several nights and 'was indulged with singular Approbation from numerous and polite Audiences'. It drew a compliment from Quin, though that player described the actors as 'mere sprats of mussulmen'. Quin gave Gentleman two guineas for a ticket on his night and wished him better fortune than to be a Bath author or actor, since the people of fashion came but to tipple water and gamble, and the townspeople understood little but extortion. The 1753–4 season again saw a changed company; Miss Ibbott was back, but Brown remained at Orchard Street. There were:

Men	Women
Giffard from C.G.	Miss Ibbott
Falkner	Miss Hippisley
Pitt	Mrs Mozeen
Dancer	Mrs Fawkes
Fitzmaurice	Mrs Harvey
Wye	Mrs Wye
Jones	Mrs Martin
Mason	Miss Roche from Orchard St.
Longfield	
Fawkes	
Gates	
Martin	
Harper	
Morgan	
Costollo	

The system of denoting principal players by capital letters that caused Mrs Charke so much trouble was this season extended from the playbills to the newspaper advertisements. Miss Ibbott, Mrs Harvey on her first appearance as Lucy in *The Old Batchelor*, Falkner and Dancer are thus occasionally honoured.

An attempt was made to procure punctuality: 'As the complaint of not Beginning in Time, was last Season very general, the Company beg Leave to inform the Town, that for the Future the Curtain shall always be drawn up precisely at Six o'Clock.' Ladies and gentlemen, who had taken places for Maddox's benefit and last performance, were requested to send their servants by 4 o'clock. On another occasion when a new scene to *Harlequin's Vagaries* was promised the company was assured that they could depend upon not being disappointed. Probably in face of a poor attendance the curtain had on a previous occasion not been rung up.

When the concert system came into use prices of tickets were advertised as 3s., 2s., 1s. 6d.; no ticket could be taken after the concert was over nor could anyone be admitted without a ticket.

Hamlet secured £40. 4s. 6d. for the hospital, an interesting indication of its popularity. On the other hand, Dancer's benefit of *Love for Love* was so poor that he had to have another. A note in the *Journal* of October 15 reads: 'There is now in Rehearsal at Mr Simpson's Theatre, and will be reviv'd in a short Time, an old Comedy call'd Much Ado About Nothing written by Shakespear; for the Benefit of all the surviving Heirs, Male and Female, of that celebrated great Author.—The whole Receipt of the House will be apply'd to this Charity.' There is no record of the benefit taking place.

It was indeed Shakespeare's season, remarkable for the unusual number of his plays that were performed:

Shakespeare: *Othello* (3), *Henry IV, Pt. I* (2), *Hamlet* (2), *Romeo and Juliet* (2), *Richard III* (2), *Macbeth* (2), *As You Like It*.

Restoration: *Love for Love* (3), *The Orphan* (2), *The Constant Couple* (2), *The Old Batchelor*, *The Fatal Marriage*.

Eighteenth century: *The Conscious Lovers* (3), *The Busy Body* (2), *The Beggar's Opera*, *Tamerlane*, *The Miser*, *Zara*, *The Wife's Relief*, *The Beaux Stratagem*,.

Afterpieces: *Harlequin's Vagaries* (6), *Harlequin Restor'd* (4), *The Chaplet*, *The Virgin Unmask'd*, *The Honest Yorkshireman*, *Miss in her Teens*, *The Lying Valet*, *The Knights*, *Harlequin Dr Faustus*, *Damon and Phillida*, *Tom Thumb*, and an unnamed pantomime which ran for ten nights.

On June 18, the London company, which annually visited
Bristol about this time, gave a performance of *The Suspicious
Husband* and *The Devil to Pay* at Simpson's for the benefit of
Miss Hippisley. In the cast were Palmer, White, Mozeen,
Green, Barrington, Mrs Barrington, Mrs Green and Miss Pitt.

The advertisements for 1754–5 confine themselves to announcing one play each week. The following were in the
company:

Men	Women
Cooke	Miss Ibbott
Dancer	Miss Hippisley
Jones	Miss Roche
Falkner	Mrs Harvey
Fitzmaurice	Mrs Wye
Mason	Mrs Kennedy
Gates	Mrs Donaldson (formerly Miss Falkner)
Kennedy	

Further attempts at historical accuracy in costume are
recorded. Thus at the revival of Banks's *The Albion Queens*,
the characters were 'to be dress'd in old English dresses',
and for Gentleman's adaptation of *Richard II*, 'the principal
Characters' were 'dress'd in the Habits of the Times'.
Enthusiasm or finances did not often extend to the minor
roles, and we find that for *Henry VIII* 'the Dresses of the
three Principal Characters, the Coronation Robes, and all
other Decorations', only, were 'entirely new'.

On November 18 we read 'that the Tragedy of Osman, as
originally presented here with great Applause, is, by particular
Desire, preparing for Presentation some Day next Week'.
Gentleman's tragedy was duly given on November 28 with
a fresh prologue. It was announced on December 2 that his
new tragedy *Zaphira* 'is now in Rehearsal at the Concert
Room, near the Parade, and will be speedily presented there'.
The actual date of production is not recorded but Gentleman
tells us that 'it was better represented and better received than
the Sultan though with less profit to me': The first night of his

Richard II was on April 14, 1755, for the benefit of Miss
Ibbott, 'with a Prologue by the Shade of Shakespeare and a
New Epilogue'. Of this he says that there were 'too many
characters of importance, to be adequately supported by a
country company (for such Bath might then be called). The
play was, however, well received: indeed the performance
of Miss Ibbot, the best *declamatory* actress I ever heard, contributed much to the piece's reputation'.[1] John Brown's
tragedy *Barbarossa*, on the same theme as *Zaphira*, appeared
in Bath on February 6 only three weeks after its presentation
at Drury Lane, and is twice mentioned in the bills. Other
plays this season were:

Elizabethan: *Hamlet*, **Henry VIII* with its processions (5),
The Merchant of Venice described as a tragedy, **The Chances*.

Restoration: *Virtue Betray'd*.

Eighteenth century: Jones's **The Earl of Essex* (2), *Tamerlane*, *The Mistake*, *Love Makes a Man*, *The Beggar's Opera*.

Afterpieces: *The Spell, or Harlequin Salamander* (4),
Harlequin Restor'd, *Harlequin's Vagaries*, *The School Boy*.

On May 10, 1755, Simpson died. The theatre was then for
the next and last season under the management of Thomas
King, who was only twenty-five years of age. He had, as we
have seen, played in Bath in 1751, and had also been with the
Bristol Company. 'On an application from the proprietors
of one of the theatres at Bath, Mr King undertook to be
manager and principal performer there: both which stations
he filled greatly to the satisfaction and profit of the proprietor, and much to his own reputation. His commencement at Bath was in September 1755; and then it was that
the public, in that part of the world, were regaled with the
joint efforts of Mr King and that excellent actress Mrs
Abington, then Miss Barton, in Ranger and Clarinda,
Benedick and Beatrice, Tom and Phyllis, etc.'[2] Gentleman,
who rejoined the company for the season, found 'his
spirited performances drawing better audiences than ever

[1] Preface to *The Modish Wife*.   [2] *Biographia Dramatica*.

had been known there before', and that his 'regular, yet mild and gentlemanlike management, rendered the theatre much more agreeable than to me it ever had been, and to the proprietors much more profit'. So with a good actor and a great actress to lead the company, Simpson's went down in a blaze of glory. Among Miss Barton's parts were the following: October 18, 1755, Clarinda in *The Suspicious Husband* (first appearance in Bath); November 29, Silvia in *The Recruiting Officer*; December 6, Lady Fanciful in *The Provok'd Wife*; December 11, Lady Sadlife in *The Double Gallant*; May 15, 1756, Beatrice in *Much Ado*. King played Ranger in *The Suspicious Husband*, Archer in *The Beaux Stratagem*, Iago, for the first time, Touchstone, Brazen in *The Recruiting Officer*, Tattle in *Love for Love*, Brute in *The Provok'd Wife*, for the first time, Atall in *The Double Gallant*, Shylock, Don John in *The Chances*, for the first time, Young Mirabel in *The Inconstant*, Wildair in *The Constant Couple*, Romeo, Lopez in *The Mistake*, and Varanes in *Theodosius*.

The company consisted of:

Men	Women
King	Miss Barton
Quelch	Miss Ibbott
Lacey	Miss Baker
Pitt	Miss Cockayne
Sullivan	Miss Hippisley
Morgan	Miss Roche
Fitzmaurice	Mrs Mozeen
Harper	Mrs Cartwright
Gates	
Cooke	
Kennedy	
Jenkins	
Mason	

The Dancers had returned to York.

After January 10 the company left Bath: 'We hear that the Company of Comedians at Mr Simpson's Theatre, are (at the Request of great Numbers of the Gentry residing in Exeter) going to perform at the Theatre there, 'till the Spring Season.'[1] They resumed acting in Bath on April 21 and gave their last performance at the theatre on Saturday, May 29. They performed three times a week, the charges being boxes 3s., pit 2s., front gallery 1s. 6d., side gallery 1s.

Maddox appeared again this season and was given a benefit on December 3, it being the last time of his performing in the West of England: 'Particularly he will turn round in full Swing, ballance a Coach-Wheel; and play with twelve Balls.' For this great occasion ladies and gentlemen were requested to send their servants by 4 o'clock to keep places. For Morgan's *The Sheep Shearing*,[2] taken from *The Winter's Tale*, with music by Arne, 'Part of the Pit will be rail'd in, where Servants will be allowed to keep Places'. Tickets could be had of King, who played Autolycus, at his lodgings near the Cross Bath.

For the benefit of the General Hospital *Oroonoko* was given by 'Persons for their Diversion'. We do not know the result of this amateur effort.

The newspapers have full advertisements for this season, giving lists of plays done at both theatres during the week, so that the following table is a fairly complete one of the season's repertoire.

Elizabethan: *As You Like It* (4); *Romeo and Juliet* (3); *Henry VIII* (3); *Othello* (2); *The Merchant of Venice* (2); *Much Ado* (2); *Hamlet*; *King Lear*; *King John*; *The Royal Merchant* (2); *The Chances*.

Restoration: *The Provok'd Wife* (3); *Theodosius* (2); *The Constant Couple* (2); *The Orphan*; *Venice Preserv'd*; *Love for Love*; *The Mourning Bride*; *Oroonoko*.

Eighteenth century: *The Suspicious Husband* (6); *The Beaux Stratagem* (4); *The Earl of Essex* (3); *The Double*

[1] *Bath Journal*, January 10.
[2] It is advertised as performed at London and Dublin 'with universal applause'.

Gallant (3); *The Inconstant* (3); *The Recruiting Officer* (2); *The Busy Body* (2); *The Conscious Lovers* (2); *The Provok'd Husband* (2); *Tamerlane* (2); *Zaphira* (2); *The Beggar's Opera*; *She Wou'd and She Wou'd Not*; *Zara*; *A Bold Stroke for a Wife*; *The Mistake.*

Afterpieces: *The Spell, or Harlequin Salamander* (12); *The Whim, or Harlequin Triumphant* (11); *Harlequin Restor'd* (9); *Harlequin's Vagaries* (7); *The Lying Valet* (5); *The Sheep Shearing* (2); *Chrononhotonthologos* (2); *The Knights* (2); *The Mock Doctor* (2); *The Apprentice* (2); *The Devil to Pay* (2); *The King and the Miller of Mansfield*; *Miss in her Teens.*

The overwhelming popularity of the pantomimes in comparison with the farcical afterpieces is here well demonstrated. Fleming[1] has, indeed, noted that though performances in general were 'very middling', the pantomimes at Simpson's were 'well conducted'.

This was the end of Simpson's as an independent theatre. John Palmer who, by buying up the rest of the shares, had made himself proprietor of Orchard Street, at last obtained a contract with the proprietors of the old theatre whereby, in return for £200 a year, they agreed to refrain from theatrical performances.[2] Simpson's was still used as a music room for occasional concerts and oratorios and, whilst Orchard Street was being renovated from October 1766 to April 1767, again housed the city comedians.[3]

In 1820, the Lower Rooms, as they were then called, were burnt down, and the Royal Literary Institute, incorporating that part of them saved from fire, arose on the site. That, in its turn, has been demolished and that side of Terrace Walks now forms part of the public gardens.

[1] *Op. cit.* vol. III, p. 35.
[2] *The Bath and Bristol Guide*, p. 20; Fleming, *op. cit.* vol. III, p. 35.
[3] *Bath Chronicle*, October 23, 1766, April 2, 1767.

Chapter X

THE BRISTOL COMPANY'S
ACCOUNT BOOK

In the strong room of the Bristol Public Library there is a fascinating manuscript that, with the exception of G. T. Watts who quotes a page of it in his *Theatrical Bristol*, historians of the Bristol theatre and writers on eighteenth-century strolling companies seem to have neglected. It is the account book of the Jacob's Wells Theatre from 1741 to 1748. From its pages much is to be learnt about the running of a country company in the mid-eighteenth century. A study of the lists of expenses and the treasurer's occasional comments—accounts were more human and less accurate in those days—transports one to a bustling, candle-lit, theatrical world in which the customs of Shakespeare's day jostle incidents that might happen on the twentieth-century stage.

The company was a mixed one from the London theatres which came to entertain the Bristolians in the cramped quarters of Jacob's Wells during the summer vacation, from June to the beginning of September. Among the great names are those of Macklin who played there in 1741, Mrs Pritchard 1742–7, and Henry Woodward 1744–7. An entry made by Woodward in the account book on August 26, 1747, throws curious light on the method of giving notice. It reads: 'I think it necessary according to Stroling Custom to set down my Warning; that you may provide with another Person in my stead for the Ensuing Season. H. Woodward'. To this another hand has added 'N.B. a Stroling Speech becomes a Stroler'.

From nine to twelve actors and from six to eleven actresses formed the company, the numbers increasing with the years. They were recruited by Mrs Hippisley, wife of the Bristol manager and famous comedian, in London. 'Mrs Hippisley's Bill for Wine and Eating at a meeting of the company in London' was £1. 0s. 6d. on one occasion, 18s. 5d. on another and only 7s. 6d. on a third, entries which set for us the convivial scene at which final arrangements for the season were made.

The company was possibly given a reminder for there is an item: 'Frank for calling the People in London 5s.', and Frank was paid one week's wages, 15s., before the house opened. Another man, Bethorn, was paid 12s. 6d., and lodging for both cost 12s. Frank appears to have been general handyman and there are other payments to him for porterage and the like. On one occasion the treasurer noted among his figures with engaging humanity: 'Frank's wife is Brought to Bed of a Girle.' 'Hughs's man Anthony' also flits in and out the pages and is accorded various small payments.

The transport of goods to Bristol was made by waggon. It is possible that the company paid towards the heavy cost as we find an entry 'Mr Wiltshire's Clerk for carriage of goods to and from Bristol £12. 2s. 9d. Recd Co. £11. 16s. 3d.' Carriage payments varied in other years from £9. 15s. 9d. to £2. 15s. 0d., but no mention is made of any contribution from the company. In addition to the carrier's bill there were small payments for haulage and porterage: 'To Quay for porterage 3s. 10½d.', 'Frank for porterage 12s. 9d.', 'Bringing trunk from waggon 1s.'. In 1742 the hire of a coach from Bath and the breaking of the coach glass cost 7s. 6d. When the company was ordered by the Duchess of Norfolk to perform at the Long Room, coaches and chairs cost £1. 8s. 0d.; on another occasion 1s. was paid for a chair for one of the actresses.

Let us now consider the company's earnings and expenses. An ordinary evening's takings averaged at first about £10. The three lowest amounts taken during the period were £3. 14s. 0d. for *The Stratagem* and *The Virgin Unmask'd*,

£4. 17s. 6d. for *The Constant Couple* and £5. 5s. od. for *The Busy Body*. Plays that fetched over £20 on non-benefit nights were:

		£	s.	d.
1741.	Provok'd Husband	26	15	0
1742.	Orphan; Metamorphosis	33	4	0
	As You Like It	30	8	6
	Stratagem	22	11	0
	Tempest	20	5	6
1743.	Royal Merchant; Virgin Unmask'd	23	14	6
1744.	Provok'd Husband; Virgin Unmask'd	29	9	6
	Henry V	25	7	0
	Country Lasses; Devil to Pay	23	2	6
1745.	Fair Quaker of Deal	34	10	6
	As You Like It	27	5	6
	Conscious Lovers	23	8	6
	King Lear	23	8	0
	Committee	23	5	6
	Bold Stroke for a Wife	21	11	0
	Recruiting Officer	21	3	6
	As You Like It	20	13	6
	Othello; Hob	20	12	0
	Venice Preserv'd	20	3	6
1746.	Committee	27	19	0
	Committee	27	9	6
	Non-Juror	23	14	0
	Hamlet	22	17	6
	Measure for Measure	21	9	6
	Orphan	21	0	0
	As You Like It	20	10	6
	Non-Juror	20	10	0
	As You Like It	20	7	0
1747.	Merry Wives	24	7	6

From this list it will be seen that Shakespeare was well able to hold his own in popularity, a fact confirmed by the number of times his plays were chosen for benefits. Besides those listed the following were played either in proper form or in adaptations then current: *Macbeth, The Merchant of*

Venice, Henry IV, Richard III, King Lear, Timon of Athens, Julius Caesar, Much Ado.

After 1743 much bigger amounts were taken and most performances could boast a figure over £15. By 1747 the bookkeeper felt it incumbent upon him to apologise for a house of £7. 18s. od. by writing 'Dismal wet night' over the entry, though this had been quite a normal sum in preceding years. Expenses increased too. Whereas for the first three years they were usually between £3 and £5 a performance, from 1744 onwards they rose to between £5 and £8. It was the business of the treasurer to arrange and distribute the expenses. Thus he would wait for a successful night to settle big bills such as carriage, and sometimes he would divide the burden of such bills between the proceeds of two nights. Here is a typical balance sheet from a performance of *The Orphan* which took £15. 12s. 6d.:

	£	s.	d.
Rent	5	0	0
Musick		10	6
Candles		8	3
Printer		12	6
Stage keeper		3	6
Properties		1	0
Dancers	2	2	0
Bill sticker		2	0
Bill porter		2	0
Door keeper		2	6
Women's dresser		2	6
Men's dresser		2	6
Prompter		4	0
Taylor		2	6
Miss Stephens		4	0
Gallery door keeper		1	0
Remains	5	11	9
18 shares at 6s.	5	8	0
		3	9

Expense items may be considered under headings of (1) personnel; (2) advertisement, printing and copying; (3) properties and wardrobe; (4) rent, lighting and staging. Transport has already been considered.

(1) *Personnel*. The music was paid from 10s. to 13s. 6d. in the early years and as much as £1. 7s. 0d. in the later. There is an item for wine at several practices, and another for 12s. for the musicians' dinner. When the entertainment consisted of dancing, the dancers were paid one or two guineas. They may have been hired locally or brought from London but they did not participate in the sharing system.

The stage-keeper's wage varied from 3s. to 5s.; the door-keeper normally earned 2s. 6d. but sometimes on benefit nights 5s. In 1748 two door-keepers were employed. The gallery-keeper's wage was 1s. and there were also two in 1748. From 1743 onwards there was a stage door-keeper employed at 1s. 6d. and a scene man at 1s. The men's and women's dressers received wages varying from 1s. to 5s., but 2s. 6d. or 3s. 6d. was the normal fee; sometimes the men's dresser earned more than the women's; sometimes the other way about; occasionally an extra dresser was called in. The prompter was paid 4s. in 1741, 3s. in 1742 and then is not mentioned until July 1744 when he was reduced to 2s. 6d. In 1742 the prompter had a boy who was paid 2s. though in later years he was only paid anything from 6d. to 1s. 6d. On one occasion the prompter was given 5s. for reading the part of Pistol. Finally there was sometimes a boy at the door for a few pence. Link boys are frequently put down for 1s. 8d., 2s. or 2s. 10d., links at 3s.

There were in addition odd performers such as the black boy for *Oroonoko* who earned 1s. 2d., and a dwarf for the entertainments who received 2s. a performance.

(2) *Advertisement, printing and copying*. 'Bills' are an item constant in the accounts of all performances. They cost from 9s. to 14s., but there were occasionally extraordinary bills,

whilst on benefit nights the cost was often over a £1 and as much as £1. 15s. 6d. The bill-sticker and the bill-porter were indispensable adjuncts to the company. Their wages were usually 2s. each, but they were paid as much as 4s. each. The porter was once reduced to 1s. 6d. and occasionally made 5s. In July 1744 'Mr Hippisley paid the Porter at yᵉ Exchange for the Bills to be sett up there 10s. 6d.', a payment renewed in 1747. For advertising *The Recruiting Officer* in the *London News* and a post letter the charge was 3s. 5d. Hippisley's advertisements in the *Bath Journal* cost 2s. 6d. whilst in 1748 there are several entries for 10d. against the same newspaper.

The printer's account for one year amounted to £2. 12s. 6d., for another only to £1. 0s. 0d., but he was no doubt sometimes paid from stock, as one entry reads 'Printers Bill over and above wt is paid by the Book'.

It was part of the prompter's business to copy plays and parts, and one evening he is assigned 5s. 2d. for writing. At other times he is not specifically mentioned though he probably did the work. A payment of 8s. 6d. is recorded for writing *The Merchant of Venice* and of 3s. 6d. each for *Henry V*, *Measure for Measure* and *The Anatomist*. One Mr Lish earned 5s. for writing music and he, or another, 10s. 6d. for writing the music of *Pyramus*; but whether this was for copying or composing it is impossible to say. Binding the *Macbeth* music cost 2s., the book of *The Beggar's Opera* 1s. 6d. and a cast book 7s. 6d.

(3) *Properties and wardrobe.* Properties are either listed as such or amusingly specified. Thus a 'Fryar's beads' and 'A beard for the Jew' in *The Merchant* cost 1s. 6d. each, 5 yards of crêpe for Calista's veil £1. 0s. 0d. and Ophelia's coffin 5s. with a rope for the trap at 2s.! 14s. 5d. was paid for a table and four chairs for *Macbeth*, 3s. for plates and a saucepan for the entertainment, 16s. for foils, and £1. 7s. 0d. for nine glass lanthorns. There are items for paint at Bath 9d., and another year for painter and paint 17s. 8d. A curious entry

for Witcraft for 6d. and again Whitecraft [Witchcraft?] 1s. is puzzling. The sword cutler was paid 7s. 6d. one season, 6s. 6d. another.

For plays like *Macbeth* or *The Recruiting Officer* the services of a drummer were required and he was paid 1s. a time. *Othello* had news and drum 2s. probably for the herald's proclamation, Act II, Sc. ii, and *Julius Caesar* a trumpeter for 1s. as well as a drummer. There were big bills from the tailor and the mantua maker. The tailor charged 1s. for attendance at performances. One dress cost £1. 0s. 0d., a new dress for Mrs Pritchard £1. 15s. 5d. and a ghost dress was rather expensive at £2. 2s. 0d. Teague's waistcoat was made for 7s. 6d. and three cloaks in *The Committee* for 4s. 6d. The mantua maker's bills rose to as much as £2. 0s. 0d. Altering Mrs Woodward's gown cost 1s. 6d.; the milliner charged 7s. 6d. for a hat for Mrs Pritchard, and a pair of shoes were bought for Miss Mullart for 3s. 6d. On one occasion 7s. 6d. was paid to the wardrobe mistress in London, at other times payments were made to Caston, Rich's wardrobe-keeper, probably for the loan of costumes. There is an occasional mention of small washing charges. In the later years a guinea, or a guinea and a half, was put aside on most performances for clothes; twenty-four or twenty-five guineas being spent during a season.

(4) *Rent, lighting and staging.* Rent was, of course, one of the heavy expenses. The company paid £37 for the theatre for a season of eleven to twelve weeks. In 1747 it had risen to £58. The treasurer settled in instalments of anything from £2. 0s. 0d. to £4. 4s. 0d. a performance, so that all was paid up before the benefits started.

Candles cost from 8s. 3d. to 12s. 4d. a night, usually more on the opening night than on succeeding ones. That lamps were also employed is evident from a payment to the tinman for mending the stage lamps. Other workmen employed to look after the stage were the carpenter, who has an item of 4s. 3d. for the traps and a large bill for £5. 18s. 1d. the

following season; the plasterer 10s. 1d., the upholsterer
£1. 16s. 2d., the cabinet-maker £1. 2s. 6d. Frank, too, was
paid 7s. for 'Stage Money and Wax'. The green room had
to be cleaned from time to time and a charwoman was paid
from 1s. to 3s. for this. There is one item for 'Bags, Tape and
Tacks for the Boxes 6s. 2½d.'. There were a few incidental
expenses as two payments made to charity, one of one
guinea, the other of two. Small sums were lent and perhaps
never returned. A note was made one night that the Duke of
Leeds and his company had not paid for entry, but this was
adjusted a week later when he paid a guinea. Ale and wine
are sporadic items, and one entry records an error of 1s. 6d.
at the Bush Tavern. Lastly the barber's attentions were
sometimes needed. He charged 12s. for four nights and
6d. for Mrs Pritchard!

How did the actors fare with their shares after these
expenses had been deducted from the total receipts? Frequently no shares were given, the profits either being too
small or being used to pay outstanding bills. Thus on one
occasion, though the good sum of £16. 14s. 0d. was taken,
no shares were paid out. Again when *The Provok'd Husband*
fetched £26. 15s. 0d. and net profits were £21. 10s. 9d.
only 5s. shares were distributed, the surplus of £16. 10s. 9d.
going into stock. Any surplus after shares had or had
not been distributed, as finances demanded, went to clear
the stock debt. About the end of July or the beginning
of August this stock debt was settled and any money that
remained was divided into additional shares. On August 17,
1743, for instance, there is an entry: 'Settled stock debt.
Hen. Woodward, S. Hale & shar'd 14 shillings at ye
same time.' In 1744 the total receipts in stock were
£66. 16s. 5d. of which Mrs Pritchard received £50. 0s. 0d.,
carriage bills took £9. 5s. 11d. and 21 shares were divided
at 7s.

The number of shares given does not tally with the number
of actors and actresses whose names are recorded as forming

A PAGE FROM THE ACCOUNT BOOK OF THE
JACOB'S WELLS THEATRE, BRISTOL

the company, but is sometimes so near it that it does not seem possible that four 'dead' shares were allotted, as elsewhere, to the manager for his scenery and wardrobe. The lists of members of the company are not always complete. Thus in 1741 the names of Mrs Pritchard, Lowe and Mrs Hippisley are omitted although they all had benefits and must therefore have been acting during the season. It is probable that they did not partake of shares but were engaged on some special terms. Yet other actors were on a salary basis: in 1743 Fawkes and Miss Mullart were paid per performance, in 1747 Hacket, Mrs Vallois and Miss Mullart together received 10s. 6d. to appear, and in 1748 Dighton and Stephens the treasurer received 5s. each, Mrs Bland and Mrs Vallois 4s. and Miss Mullart and a boy 2s. 6d. for every performance in which they took part. Sometimes the wages of the 'hirelings', as they were called, were lumped together as 'salaries'. 'Salaries' rose from 11s. 6d. in 1745 to £1. 3s. 0d. in 1748. Mrs Pritchard seems to have contracted for £50 for the season and, if her benefit did not bring this sum, it had to be made up by the company. Thus in 1743 her benefit brought in £44. 19s. 6d. gross, and £8. 16s. 10½d. was taken from stock to make the benefit up to £50 clear.

On benefit nights 5s. shares were usually distributed. Actors occasionally forfeited shares. We read that 'Mr Stoppelaer forfeit'd being absent Rehearsal', and, for a reason not given, Green's share was stopped in 1744. In this year too, 'Mr Hale Recd yᵉ Shares for the Clothes etc.' on one account, and was thus reimbursed for money he had expended on the wardrobe.

In 1741 an actor received only £8. 14s. 0d. in shares for the whole season; in 1748 the amount had risen to £27. 7s. 0d. Even this was little enough and is evidence to what extent an actor had to depend upon his benefit. Some large amounts were netted at benefits by the more popular and famous players:

Year	Actor	Play	Gross receipts		
1741.	Macklin	*Beggar's Opera*	£52	0	0
1742.	Hippisley	*Way of the World*	55	6	6
	Woodward	*Careless Husband*	52	10	0
	Cashell	*Pilgrim, Lying Valet*	51	8	6
1743.	Cashell	*Merry Wives, Hob*	61	16	0
	Hale	*All for Love, What D'ye Call It*	57	0	0
	Rosco	*Fair Quaker, King and the Miller*	52	0	0
1745.	Woodward	*Measure for Measure*	64	13	6
	Rosco	*Tamerlane*	63	8	6
	Watts	*All for Love*	50	10	0
1746.	Mrs Hale (recently widowed)	*Distress'd Mother*	63	0	0
	Rosco	*Double Dealer*	50	0	0
1747.	Rosco	*Conscious Lovers*	76	2	0
	Watts	*Twin Rivals*	60	0	0
	Mrs Pritchard	*George Barnwell, Miss in Her Teens*	51	7	0
	Watts	*Tunbridge Walks*	67	15	0
	Rosco	*Non-Juror, Miss in Her Teens*	62	14	0
	Berry	*Henry IV, Miss in Her Teens*	60	4	0
	Mrs Green	*Conscious Lovers*	52	4	0
	Winstone	*Mourning Bride*	52	0	0

When Rosco drew £76. 2s. 0d. to the house—the biggest amount recorded during these years—the enthusiastic treasurer scored 'wonderful' across the page! The lesser actors, especially those who shared their benefits, did not fare so well. Thus Woodburn and Green's night made only £14. 16s. 6d. of which £10. 13s. 2d. went in expenses and shares to the company. When Mrs Egerton, Mrs Vallois and Miss Mullart shared their £8. 17s. 8d. profit, Mrs Egerton received half the total, the others each a quarter. An actor sometimes shared his benefit with the company; on such an occasion expenses were usually first deducted and 5s. shares given to all, then the remainder of the proceeds was halved between the actor and the company as nearly as possible. Thus Winstone received £8. 0s. 0d., and the company divided the other half into further 8*s*. 9*d*. shares totalling £7. 4*s*. 7½*d*. When, however, Anderson shared, some of the expenses were taken from the company's half of the profits only.

The actor sometimes arranged to pay the manager a lump sum out of his takings. Watts paid him ten guineas, out of which were taken expenses and shares at 6*s*. Mons. and Mdlle Michel gave the company £10, by agreement, from their benefit and kept the residue.

For Hippisley's benefit in 1747 the following note is made:

	£	*s*.	*d*.
72 Box tickets at 3*s*.	10	16	0
46 Pit tickets at 2*s*. 6*d*.	5	15	0
Money	11	18	6
Expenses	9	15	6

One Mr Hook is rather a mystery. His name does not appear in the list of actors and his benefit was by desire of Sir R. Cann. On that occasion twenty-two shares were divided instead of eighteen, but the extra four shares were evidently not taken up as the bookkeeper puts down in his stock account that year on the credit side '4 Dead Shares at Mr Hooks Benefit £1. 0*s*. 0*d*.' Hook's name appears again under the date July 19, 1748 when his benefit is put down as 'on Compulsion'.

This is one of the book's illusive references that must remain perforce to tantalise the reader. Our bookkeeper has raised the curtain a little on the conditions under which an actor laboured and performed his task in the provinces. We should be ungrateful were we not to pardon him his occasional allusive vagueness.

Chapter XI

THE KENTISH CIRCUIT, 1723–1744

The activities of the Kent companies had their centre in Canterbury. Unlike the Mayor's Court books in Norwich the Burmote books in Canterbury have almost nothing to tell us of the players. No doubt players visited the town and received permission from the mayor to act, but there is no mention of them. Even when we know from newspaper sources that the players were there, no record of the fact is to be found in the Burmote minutes. Only under the date April 16, 1723, is there a laconic entry: 'No Playes &c. It is ordered by this Court that no Stage players, Mountebankes, Poppit shewes or other publick Playes or Games shall be shewn or used in this City or the Libties thereof without the Leave and Consent of the Court Burghmote of this City by an order in that behalf.'[1]

This is the first date after 1660 for which I can find any allusion to the visits of players.

Where local records and also books on local history are so scant in their references, we have to rely for information almost solely on announcements in the local newspaper, *The Kentish Post or The Canterbury News Letter*. Though the paper started its career in 1723 copies of the earlier years are not extant in the Canterbury Library or the British Museum, and the first available notice is for January 29–February 2, 1726:

We hear, that in a short time will be Acted at the Theatre in Highstreet in this City, the Entertainment of the Necromancer, or Harlequin Dr. Faustus. Scene 1. A Study, the Doctor dis-

[1] *Burmote Minutes*, 1695–1744, p. 683, seen by kind permission of the Corporation of Canterbury.

cover'd setting [sic] at a Table in a thoughtful Posture: he rises as the Musick changes, uses Magical motions and an infernal Spirit appears, and tempts him to sign a Paper: and not prevailing, transforms himself into Lucifer, who brings in the Spirit of Helen: the Doctor gazing at her, signs the Paper, which vanishes: after which, attempting to approach Helen, the Phantom's Head flies off: Lucifer laughs, as having deceived him: the Scene closes. Scene II, a House, a Wood at a distance, wherein is represented several Magical Humours of the Doctor. Scene III, The Scene draws and discovers the Emperor Charles V and his Empress as to see some of the Doctor's Cunning, who waves his Wand and light Furies enter, who join in Antick Dance: It thunders, a Clock strikes and a monstrous Dragon appears: the Doctor is brought in by a Demon and devour'd by the Monster: the Curtain drops, which concludes the Entertainment.

This typical eighteenth-century pantomime, with its music and magic, its succession of scenes and transformations, had been brought out at Lincoln's Inn Fields in 1723.

The opening performance took place on February 7: 'This Entertainment was never perform'd in this Country before: All the Scenes, Cloaths and decorations being entirely New.' The play which preceded it was Banks's *Virtue Betray'd*: 'King Henry the 8th to be Dress'd after the true ancient Manner, answering the Character.' Other plays given during the season were *Oroonoko* and *The Rival Queens* 'in rich Persian Habits'. On February 26 to March 2 it was announced 'that the Dramatick Performance, that was sometime at the Theater in High-Street, Canterbury, at the particular desire of several Gentlemen and Ladies will remove to the Saracen's Head in Ashford; and that on Monday the 7th Instant, will be acted a Play, call'd the Unhappy Favourite or the Earl of Essex, in rich Modern Dresses, intermix'd with several Dances.' It is noteworthy that as early as this an attempt was made to dress Henry VIII historically, though *The Earl of Essex* was performed in eighteenth-century costumes. From later advertisements we learn that the Canterbury theatre was in the yard of the

Crown Inn which used to stand on the site of the present *Kent Messenger* office. The Saracen's Head is still a well-known hotel at Ashford.

In April 1726, the ubiquitous Thomas Keregan[1] turns up in Canterbury with a company of comedians. He had with him Orfeur who was later in his York Company. Keregan had arrived by April 6, but 'by Reason of Passion Week... will not begin to Act till Monday next'. He presented *The Rival Queens* and *Love and a Bottle* for the first time here with entertainments for the benefit of Orfeur. The performances began at 6 p.m. It is uncertain whether it was Keregan or another that presented on June 2 a new farce 'never Acted before, wrote in Canterbury; call'd, The Fortunate Hop-jobber, with the Comical Humours of the Tyers and Pickers'. This is the one piece of purely local interest of which we find record during the whole period. It does not seem to have been printed, nor does it figure in any list I have seen of eighteenth-century plays.

We first meet with Dymer's Company, which was to cover the Kent circuit for many years, in January 1728. They gave a six weeks' season at a theatre in Watling Street, now untraceable, in Canterbury. We hear of three plays being performed: *All for Love*, *The Committee*, and *The Provok'd Husband*. After *All for Love*, an announcement stated, 'will be performed several Surprizing Postures by Mr Shadrick who belongs to Dr Smith', and a song by Mr Duree. *The Committee* was given for the benefit of the 'Master of the Play-house',[2] and was followed by 'an entertainment by 4 Tradesmen, all separate, viz. Mr Stringer, Mr Adams, Mr Pembrook, and Mr Everden is to Sing a Song upon the Stage to entertain the Company'. The Kent circuit, as we shall see, was notable for its encouragement of local amateur talent. Besides Dymer there were in the company Williams, Mrs Butcher, and her daughter. From Canterbury Dymer

---

[1] See Chapters III and VI for his activities in Norwich and York.
[2] Lane had this title in 1731, see post, p. 223.

went to Dover where he gave 'the new play' *The Provok'd Husband*, *The Beggar's Opera*, 'having several times before, acted it with great Applause and Success', and *The Mourning Bride*. It is amazing how soon after its original performance in London *The Beggar's Opera* everywhere penetrated to the provinces.

Dymer returned to Canterbury on May 31 and played *The Beggar's Opera* every night for a week in June. 'They have already acted it here', comments the *Kentish Post*, 'with great Satisfaction to the Auditors. It has been Play'd in London 58 Nights.' Dymer took Macheath and Mrs Middleton Polly. One Wells had his benefit with 'Mrs Slamekin', who evidently thought she was better known under the name of her part in the opera than under her own. Other plays given were *The Fatal Extravagance*, *The Busy Body*, *The Provok'd Husband*, *Hob in the Well* and *The Stage Coach*. In July the company took *The Beggar's Opera* to Sandwich, and in August to Deal where they met 'with very good Encouragement'.

We next hear of them in October 1729 when they travelled from Ashford to Dover. They returned to Dover in December and reopened with Coffey's *The Beggar's Wedding*, a new ballad opera which had been given in Dublin and then in London in the spring of that year.

At Faversham we hear of one of the frequent amateur performances for which Kent was outstanding, a company of townsmen designing to act 'the Tragedy of Arden at the Roe-buck joining to that Place' on January 2, 1730. Whether this was the Elizabethan play or not we have no means of telling. Local interest in the Arden story caused it to be acted with great success in many forms during the period.

Meanwhile Dymer progressed from Dover to Deal and from Deal to Sandwich. At this last he played *The Busy Body*, *King Lear* and *Oroonoko* 'and will then shut up till the Holy-days; and then open with the Beggar's Wedding and Timoleon'. On Easter Monday he performed 'that Excellent

Play' *Cato*, and on Tuesday 'that diverting Comedy' *The Recruiting Officer*; Wednesday *The Beaux Stratagem* was given and finally Martin's 'new tragedy' *Timoleon* was presented on the Friday. On the Tuesday, which was Assembly Night, Dymer visited Canterbury 'to pay his Respects to the Gentlemen and Ladies, to know if it be their Pleasure to give him any Encouragement to perform here in the Spring'. He evidently received the encouragement, as his company, after a final performance at Sandwich on April 17, proceeded to Canterbury the following week, 'to entertain that City with some of their best Performances'. There they showed *The Beggar's Wedding* 'with all the Songs and Decorations, as it was perform'd in the Hay Market'. One evening was given over to the Freemasons, Dymer playing Archer and Lane Scrub in *The Beaux Stratagem*, 'with an Addition of the Free Mason's Prologue and Epilogue by Mr Lane, as it was spoken at the Theatre Royal, at the Request of their present Grand Master, His Grace the Duke of Norfolk'. At a subsequent performance[1] of *The Careless Husband*, for the benefit of Mr and Mrs Lane, a new prologue and epilogue were sent down on purpose from London, 'to be spoken by Mr Lane and his Wife in praise of Free Masonry'. Apart, however, from these and a very few other occasions the masons do not seem to have supported the drama in Canterbury as they did in some other provincial centres.

On May 13 the play of *Love for Love* was announced 'at the New Play-house in this City'. Whether this was a third theatre or only the Watling Street in contradistinction to the High Street one, we have now no means of ascertaining. On June 3 for the benefit of Warren and Scudamore *Hamlet* was given with Warren as Hamlet 'with two new Songs by Mrs Bennett, and a new Song of Old Similies by Mr Scudamore'.

The season at Canterbury was followed by a highly successful one at Margate. The company played there Mondays, Wednesdays and Fridays, 'And for the Conveniency of the

[1] On June 8.

Country Gentlemen and Ladies, they resolve to begin Exactly at 6 o'Clock'. This shows that they depended as much on the surrounding country gentry as on the townspeople. They intended to make only a short stay but, such was the encouragement they met with, 'that notwithstanding the Play-House is very large it will not contain the Company that Resort there. They will continue there a Fortnight longer, and then go for Romney in the Marsh, from thence to Tunbridge Wells.' We do not know where this large playhouse was situated or whether it was that barn in the Dane which Winston says Smith's company used later.[1] Among the plays given were *The Busy Body, Jane Shore, The Provok'd Husband, Hamlet, A Bold Stroke for a Wife* and *Oroonoko*.

In September we find the company as far afield as Rye, where we hear they 'have met with good Success' and 'are like to continue in that Place some Time, and that when they go from thence, they intend to go to Maidstone'. On their way they took in Tenterden, finally opening in Maidstone in November. We have the circuit for this year (1730) almost complete as follows:

January	Deal
March	Sandwich
April–May	Canterbury
June	Margate
	Romney-in-the-Marsh
	? Tunbridge Wells[2]
September	Rye
October	Tenterden
November–December	Maidstone

It is a large area to cover.

---

[1] *The Theatric Tourist.* The Dane would have been on the outskirts of the village.

[2] It is probable that the company never reached Tunbridge Wells, which would have been ridiculously out of the way between Romney and Rye.

In Maidstone the company stayed until February, after the fair, doing 'very good Business'. *Hamlet* was advertised twice, and *The Orphan* and *Woman is a Riddle* make their appearance in the repertoire. The company now called itself 'The Kentish Company of Comedians'.

From Maidstone they journeyed north to Rochester where 'Mr Dymer has so great Encouragement...that he is obliged to remove to a larger House in East-gate, which he will open this Night with the Comedy of The Fop's Fortune, at the Request of the Gentry of that City'. This is the subtitle of Cibber's *Love Makes a Man*. 'The Jubilee', also advertised, was no doubt Farquhar's *Constant Couple or a Trip to the Jubilee*. *Tamerlane* was another addition to the company's repertoire.

It was the turn of Deal to stage an amateur performance. On April 27 and May 3, 1731, 'some young Gentlemen and Ladies of this Place' organised performances of *The Orphan* which 'met with an universal and uncommon Applause each Time, from every Spectator'. However, the paper prints some verses occasioned by the fact that some persons had spoken against it. One idly wonders whether *The Orphan* was considered by them an unsuitable play for the young to act, or whether it was merely a case of the Puritan conscience protesting against any dramatic performance.

We come on Dymer's Company again at Sittingbourne in June where they acted *Tom Thumb* every day from two to six o'clock during the fair, and a full play every night. Thence they removed to Dover, and in August we find them in Folkestone on their way to Ashford, where they intended to play for three weeks, every night but Saturdays. Dymer was heralded as having 'as good a Company (or better) than ever he had in Kent'. At Ashford he produced 'that excellent Moral Play' *The London Merchant*, as well as *Othello*. He brought the former to the Watling Street Theatre in November, 'and it was so moving as to draw Tears from most of the Audience'. It was several times repeated by request 'to the great Satisfaction of all Degrees of People who have seen it'. It was also acted by another company at the same time in Faversham 'before the Mayor, Jurats, Commoners, Towns and Neighbouring Gentlemen with very great Applause'.

Dymer's season in Canterbury lasted until after the first week in February 1732 and 'met with all the Success they could desire'. *The Jew of Venice* was revived after a two years' absence. *Tamerlane* had 'the principal Characters...new dress'd in very rich Habits', and *The Constant Couple* was accompanied by 'a New Prologue, address'd to the Ladies, by an unknown Hand, to be spoke by Mr Dymer'. On the last night, for the benefit of Lane, Master of the Playhouse, Mallet's *Eurydice*, which had been some time in rehearsal, was brought out. To spice the performance there were 'several Dances between the Acts by Gentlemen of this City for their own Diversion', as well as the customary farewell epilogue by Dymer. On another occasion the son of the dancing master Oliver performed 'several diverting Dances between the Acts'. In the company were Mr and Mrs Buck,[1] whom we have met at Norwich, Ager[2] and Williams. Some kind of improvement was made in the playhouse, for the advertisement on January 24–February 2 adds 'Conveniences are made that Gentlemen and Ladies may not be too much crowded'. It looks as though Dymer was doing very well indeed. He next took *The London Merchant* 'with new Cloaths and Scenes' to Deal, and thence to Sandwich and Tenterden, at which last they acted every night during fair week. In May they were at Cranbrook fair.

In September the great event was the opening of the new playhouse at Maidstone erected in the yard of the Star Inn, then owned by one Holmes. 'The Charge being so great' the notice ran 'the Prices will be as follows, viz. Pit 2s., 1st Gallery 1s. 2d., Gallery 6d.', which shows that the prices must

[1] See *ante*, p. 54.
[2] Possibly the Ager who had managed the York Company.

have been unusually cheap before. 'On Tuesday next [29]',
it was further announced, 'Mr Dymer will open at his New
Theatre in Maidstone with The Careless Husband, and the
Opera of Damon and Phillida; the Cloaths being all new,
and very rich. And he will play every Night during the
Fair.' It was a huge success: 'We hear from Maidstone, that
since Mr Dymer has erected his new Booth at the Star in
that Town, for Theatrical Performances, there have been the
greatest Audiences that ever were known, the Country
Gentry coming in from all Parts; and that he will continue
there till Christmas.' Persons of distinction from the country
bespoke The Old Batchelor, and The Fair Penitent was played
with the new entertainment of The Devil to Pay. For
Dymer's benefit the same tragedy was followed by another
new entertainment entitled The Burgher Master Outwitted; or
The Loves of Harlequin and Columbine, in which Eaton from
Lincoln's Inn Fields was Harlequin, and Mrs Linnett from
Goodman's Fields Columbine. By December 23 the com-
pany had completed a long series of benefits 'to their great
Satisfaction', and 'on Thursday Night a certain Gentleman
of that Town gave an Entertainment of The Careless
Husband, for the Diversion of the Freemens Wives'. On
December 28 the company opened in Canterbury at 'the
Old Theatre', 'having obtained not only the Leave of Mr
Mayor, but...great Encouragement from the Gentry'. The
old theatre may or may not have been the one in the High
Street. During Lent the company played Mondays, Thursdays and Saturdays, since playing on Wednesdays and Fridays
was forbidden during the fast. When the Freemasons bespoke
The Recruiting Officer it was announced: 'The Body of
Gentlemen belonging to the above mentioned antient Society
will honour the Performance in the proper Dresses belonging
to their Order.' The Pilgrim, after 'having been some Time
in Study', was brought out before Easter, and The Mock
Doctor was the new entertainment. Among plays performed
were King Lear, All for Love, The Spanish Fryar, bespoke by

the Mayor and Aldermen, and *The Beaux Stratagem*, with the
subtitle of 'The Litchfield Landlord'. In the company were
Warren, Brassey and Mr and Mrs Achurch.[1] The first-named
took his benefit and farewell, 'being the last Time of his ever
appearing on any Publick Stage', in *Love Makes a Man*. The
company, having 'met with good Encouragement' in
Canterbury, opened at Dover on April 25, 'having obtained
Leave of the Mayor of that Place to play there'.

But the knell of their monopoly in Kent was sounded in
the following paragraph from Canterbury in the *Kentish
Post* of June 13-16, 1733: 'We are inform'd from London,
that during the Vacation of the Theatres there, a Company
of Comedians selected from both the Royal Playhouses,
design to entertain this City (for a short Time) with a Sett
of the best Plays, Tragedies, Comedies, and Operas, and
some that have not been perform'd here by any Company.'
The company, which opened at the Watling Street Theatre,
consisted of the Hallam family (i.e. Mr and Mrs Hallam,
A. Hallam, W. Hallam, Young Hallam and Miss Hallam),
Mr and Mrs Dyer, Winstone, Hewson, Roberts, Ridout,
Harrington, Maxfield, Miss Oates, Mrs Forester, Mrs Salle.
They covered, during their stay, Canterbury race week
when the local season was at its height.

A light is thrown on conditions prevailing when Dymer
visited the town by the notice, inserted by the Londoners in
the newspaper after a few weeks' experience: 'This Company
has always been accustom'd to begin at regular Hours; which
we find proper to give particular Notice of, as well from the
Inconveniences that the former Comedians in this respect
have occasion'd, as on Account of the Number and Length
of the Entertainments.' Since similar notices occur for many
seasons we may conclude that audiences were not quick to
change their bad habits. Performances began exactly at
seven; charges were pit 2s., first gallery 1s., second gallery 6d.
The London company brought out where they could a

[1] For their subsequent careers in York, see Chapter VII, passim.

local flavour. When *Henry IV* was given they added to their advertisement 'who lies interr'd in the Cathedral of this City'; and one of the attractions of the entertainments between the acts of *Venice Preserv'd* was the singing of The Canterbury Ballad by Miss Oates, 'Printed Copies of which will be given gratis to all Gentlemen and Ladies in the PIT that please to have them'; at the end of the play Miss Oates rendered a song by Flackton, a local bookseller.

Shakespeare played a big part in the repertoire. *Macbeth*, which had not been performed for many years, was given with Roberts in the title role and Mrs Hallam as Lady Macbeth, with the original songs and music, the vocal parts being rendered by Hewson, Mrs Forester, Mrs Salle and others. Roberts played Lear and Miss Oates Cordelia in Tate's version which was advertised as 'concluding with their attaining the Crown, as a Reward of their Virtue, and a general Punishment of all the Vicious Characters'. This no doubt seemed to the players sufficient refutation of the charges of immorality continually levelled at the stage. In *Richard III* Miss Hallam junior played the Duke of York, and it was she who was chosen to speak the epilogue of thanks to the town.

The only other trace we find of Dymer in 1733 is at Maidstone in September and October. The first day of the fair he put on 'That much admir'd Comedy' *The Miser*, 'the Cloaths being exceeding Rich and New', with new entertainments of dancing by M. Lavour and Eaton. Later *The Jew of Venice* was given 'at the Request of the Boarding School, for the Entertainment of the young Ladies, their Number being at this Time very great'. It is curious how even then this play was a popular one with schools.

There is a gap in the newspapers for 1734 and 1735.[1] In 1736 the first item of dramatic interest is from Faversham: 'that Mr Henry Collyer with his Puppet Show has acted ARDIN for several Nights with great Applause being perform'd

---

[1] Dymer paid a visit as far north as Ipswich this year (see *ante*, p. 97).

after a curious manner; as well as the Harlot's Progress. He designs next for Maidstone.' On May 26–9 an announcement appears from Canterbury, 'that a very good Company of Comedians from London will be here in a few Days, to entertain the Town as usual, with several new reviv'd Plays, and a new Pantomime Entertainment, during the Summer Season'. The company of 1736 was completely different from that of 1733 and consisted of Berry, Giffard, Lyon, Woodward, Mechlin (Macklin), Stoppelaer, Penkethman, Marshall, Tench, Miss Tollett, Miss Norman, Miss Norris, Miss Hughes, Mrs Mechlin (Macklin). They played on Mondays, Wednesdays and Fridays at 'the Playhouse'. This was probably no longer the Watling Street Theatre but the upper rooms over the Butter Market. The double-storied market house, which used to stand outside Christ Church gate, was built at a cost of £400 at the expense of John Somner in 1664. The upper rooms were originally used to house grain for the poor. Somner had the building on lease from the corporation and, at his death, it passed through various hands to one Lucy Lukin. She appointed trustees of the profits which were to be handed over to the poor of St Dunstan's parish. But one William Somner put in a claim to the market house, and it is in a document[1] in the Canterbury Library, in which one of the trustees engages with his colleagues to share the expenses of contesting that claim, that we first hear how 'some of them have been at great expences in repairing and supporting the said Building and in making the rooms thereof Comodious for a play house into which the same hath lately been converted'. As this document is dated October 1, 1734, it seems likely that the Butter Market was being used by the comedians in 1736, although the first reference to it as the theatre over the Butter Market does not occur until 1738.

Unfortunately no print or picture seems to exist of this building, and we have to be content with the scant informa-

[1] Bundle XIII.

tion given by William Gostling that 'it was supported by handsome pillars of oak'.[1] The great event of the season of 1736 was the production of Fielding's *Pasquin*, trumpeted as 'play'd at the Theatre in the Haymarket *three score Nights successively, to crowded Audiences*, and with *vast Applause*', with the following cast: Trapwit—Berry, Fustian—Giffard, Sneerwell—Lyon, Place—Woodward, Fox-chace—Macklin, Tankard—Stoppelaer, Mayor—Penkethman, Mayoress—Miss Tollett, Miss Mayoress—Miss Norman, Miss Stitch—Miss Norris, Firebrand—Marshall, Queen Commonsense—Miss Hughes, Law—Berry, Physick—Macklin, Ghost of Tragedy—Tench, Ghost of Comedy—Penkethman, Third Ghost—Stoppelaer, Harlequin—Woodward, Queen Ignorance—Norris.

Also new to the town were *The Confederacy* and *Harlequin Dr Faustus; or The Lively Skeleton* 'with Musick, Scenes, Machines, and other Decorations properly adapted'. The Macklins chose *The Constant Couple* for their benefit, Macklin appearing as Wildair and his wife as Lady Lurewell.

No players seem to have come from London in 1737, but Dymer was in Sittingbourne during the fair in May where he gave Havard's *King Charles the First* two months after its appearance at Lincoln's Inn Fields. Thence he toured to Dover and in December reappeared in Canterbury with Mr and Mrs Scudamore, Mr and Mrs Tenoe and Oliver jun. in his company. We have an advertisement for December 19 when he gave *The Spanish Fryar* and *The King and the Miller* with the following entertainments: a dialogue between Mr Clarenbull and Mr Lade, the Satire on all Trades by Dymer and Tenoe, humorous songs by Mr Rowles of Ashford, new dances by Oliver, a comic dance by two young gentlemen of the city entitled Mad Moll, and an epilogue by Scudamore. The company performed at 6 p.m. 'precisely', and a note to a later advertisement advises that 'Particular Regard will be had both to Perfectness and Performance,

[1] *A Walk in and about the City of Canterbury*, 1825, p. 80.

and keeping the House warm'. It looks as though Dymer
was having to meet a demand for a higher standard of acting
from audiences who had now seen the London players.
During the winter of 1737-8 Kent was taken by storm by
Henry Collier's puppets called 'the Saxonian novels'. When
they gave their Liliputian play at the Cock without Westgate
in Canterbury, the house was 'so crowded with Company,
as well as from the Country as the City, that they will not
go from thence till the beginning of next Week, but continue acting of Arden all this Week'. The puppets penetrated
to country houses and small villages and everywhere drew
crowds. They gave *Whittington* at Bridge Hill House 'to
near a Thousand People from the neighbouring Parishes;
and all Persons, both Rich and Poor, said it was wonderfully
beyond all others that ever was in that Part of the World:
Several Persons collected something extraordinary to encourage him, and desir'd it should be publish'd.' People, we
are told, flocked ten miles to the puppets which gave performances twice nightly. Other puppet shows attempted
imitations and Collier was compelled to put a notice in the
newspaper: 'It is reported that every Poppet Show in Kent
tells the Country People they have the Liliputian Figures
&c, but his Figures are just 18 Inches high, and he sends
printed Bills to every Place where he comes; and performs
no Play that ever was perform'd in Kent before.' The
advantage of the small figures was that it enabled more
to be on the stage at the same time. Fifty or sixty figures
were shown in one night and fifteen or twenty together
'which is as many as three common Poppet Shows have
in all'.

The players must have enviously regarded the overwhelming popularity of the puppets. Collier was able to
cater for the poorer yokels in the smaller villages at much
cheaper prices. Two or three country families, for example,
could join together and hire the show at a guinea an evening.
Perhaps they did good to the players in their way, encouraging

an interest in local stories like Arden, and giving remoter places a taste for the drama.

In 1738 Canterbury was visited by a London company from the end of May to mid-August. Hall, Rosco, Ridout, James, Hale, Havard, Mullart, Woodward, Anderson, Baker, Tenoe, Mrs Mullart, Mrs James, Miss Mullart, Miss Brunette, Miss Wright, Miss Bennet and Mrs and Master Ferg were the actors and actresses. Again they announced: 'This Company being too well acquainted with the ill Consequences of beginning late, are determin'd to begin punctually at the Hour advertis'd.' At their benefit 'Mr Rosco and Mr Havard humbly hope those Gentlemen and Ladies who favour them with their Company, will be pleased to be at the House by Seven, that the Play and Farce may be ended at a proper Time.' Ordinary charges were boxes 2s. 6d., pit 2s., first gallery 1s. and second gallery 6d.; but the boxes were raised to 3s. on one or two special nights.

The Double Dealer, Theodosius, The Tanner of York, Agamemnon, The Virgin Unmask'd, Sir John Cockle, The Mistake and The Beggar's Wedding were all advertised as new or never here. Of the pantomimes: 'We hear the Pantomime Entertainment of Harlequin Dr Faustus (with the Alterations and Amendments) was perform'd…with the utmost Decency and Decorum, and met with a general Approbation'; Witchcraft; or Harlequin Restor'd, and Harlequin Sorcerer were new. In the latter was introduced 'the favourite Scene of the Skeleton, the Restoration of Harlequin, and several entire new Scenes of Action'; further, 'As this is absolutely the last Night of playing in Town, particular Care will be taken that the Play and Entertainment may be conducted with the strictest Decency'. The Mayor and Corporation gave the seal of their approval by a bespeak of The Spanish Fryar. Othello, with Hall as Othello, Rosco as Iago and Miss Brunette as Desdemona, King Lear, Henry IV Pt. I, and Hamlet were the Shakespearean plays. A benefit was given for the two children, Master Ferg and Miss Wright: 'As the Children have had the Happiness of being indulg'd in their Performance, 'tis humbly hop'd that the Gentry and others of the Town will be so good as to incourage them at their Benefit with their Company and Interest, as being Children and Strangers, and not capable of making an Interest for themselves so well as the rest of the Company.'

Strolling and visiting companies made good use of the children of their families. At the age of five they usually made their appearance on the stage in children's or pages' parts, or in *Tom Thumb*, and spoke the epilogue at their parents' benefit or the epilogue of thanks on the last night. They were the times' equivalent of Shirley Temple, and equally popular.

The boys of King's School, Canterbury gave, too, a yearly play. In 1737 it had been the *Andria* of Terence 'before a numerous Audience, with great Applause'. The following year it was *Henry IV Pt. I* which, by the desire of the performers, was acted for a second time for the benefit of Rosco. This actor had presumably stayed on to coach the boys.

The theatre over the Butter Market is first specifically mentioned as housing the feats of a German strong man on September 30–October 4, 1738. At the end of the year Godwin's troupe of rope dancers and tumblers from Sadler's Wells performed in Canterbury 'with the greatest Satisfaction to all'. A benefit was given on January 15, 1739, for Mrs Reverant, a German rope dancer, when it was announced that 'The Gentlewoman has only a Benefit for her Trouble'. To her exercises on the stiff rope were added entertainments called *Love for Love; or, The Batchelour's Last Shift*, and *The Miser Outwitted*. The prices were less than for the dramatic companies, the charges being, boxes 1s. 6d., pit 1s., middle gallery 6d., upper gallery 3d. In February the rope dancers betook themselves to Faversham fair.

The London company in 1739 was as follows: Rosco,

Winstone, Cross, Mullart, Beckham, St Nicholas, Green, Havard, Stephens, Mozeen, James, Vaughan, Hamilton, Miss Burgess, Miss Bennet, Miss Hamilton, Mrs Vallois, Mrs Mullart, Mrs James and Masters J. and W. Hamilton.

A most interesting 'Catalogue of Tragedies, Comedies, Operas and Farces, performed by the said Company during this Summer's Season at the Theatre in Canterbury' appears in the opening announcement:

Tragedies: *Agamemnon, All for Love, Albion Queens, Cato, Distress'd Mother, Earl of Essex, Fair Penitent, Fatal Extravagance, George Barnwell, Hamlet, Henry IV Pt. I, Jane Shore, Julius Caesar, King Charles the First, King Lear, Macbeth, Mourning Bride, Mustapha, Othello, Oroonoko, Orphan, Richard III, Spanish Fryar, Theodosius, Timon of Athens, Tamerlane, Venice Preserv'd.*

Comedies: *Woman Keeps a Secret* [*Wonder*], *Bold Stroke for a Wife, Amorous Widow, Busy Body, Beggar's Opera, Careless Husband, Constant Couple, Committee, Conscious Lovers, Confederacy, Double Dealer, Double Gallant, Grief à la Mode* [*Funeral*], *Fair Quaker, Gamester, Inconstant, Love Makes a Man, Love's Last Shift, Love for Love, Miser, Match in Newgate* [*Revenge*], *Merry Wives, Man of Taste, Old Batchelor, Pilgrim, Provok'd Wife, Provok'd Husband, Royal Merchant, Relapse, Recruiting Officer, Sir Courtly Nice, Stratagem, Kind Impostor* [*She Wou'd and She Wou'd Not*], *Squire of Alsatia, Tender Husband, Tunbridge Walks, Twin Rivals, Way of the World, Æsop.*

Farces: *Cheats of Scapin, Contrivances, Country House, Damon and Phillida, Devil to Pay, Flora, Honest Yorkshireman, Intriguing Maid, King and Miller, Lottery, Mock Doctor, Stage Coach, School Boy, Lover's Opera, Sir John Cockle, Toy Shop, Tanner of York, Virgin Unmask'd, What D'ye Call It, Wedding.*

An immense repertory out of which any play could be performed, so it was stated, at three days' notice, or a play, not inserted in the list, at a week's. Unless there was a bespeak the company played on the usual Monday, Wednesday and Friday beginning 'always...punctually at Seven o'Clock except in the Race Week, and then exactly at Eight'. James was evidently the manager of the company, since it was he with whom one communicated if one desired a particular play, and it was at his lodgings that 'Places for the Boxes and Stage' were to be obtained. Once again on occasions the boxes and stage were raised to 3s.

Of interest this season was the production of a new pantomime called *Harlequin Triumphant; or the Yeoman Outwitted*, in which Vaughan played Harlequin, Mrs Hamilton Columbine and James the Clown. It was announced that 'The Company having been at a great Expence in providing Habits and other Decorations for the Pantomime, and having but a short Time to continue here before the Opening of the Theatres in London, we are obliged next Week, in order to defray the Charge, to play every Day, except Saturday; and care will be taken that every Performance be conducted with Decency and Regularity.' The pantomime was given later with alterations and the addition of the Skeleton Scene by desire. *The Fair Quaker* was revived after sixteen years for the benefit of Rosco and Winstone, 'and particular Care is taken to have it perfect: And Mr Rosco humbly (to avoid Offence) hopes, whatever Commands the Gentlemen or Ladies may have, that they'll be pleas'd to let him know 'em in Time'. *The Twin Rivals* made its first appearance with James as Teague, followed by *Chrononhotonthologos*, 'All the Characters dress'd in Roman Shapes'. Shadwell's version of *Timon of Athens* was revived after twenty-five years with the following cast: Timon—Havard, Alcibiades—Cross, Apemantus—Stephens, Nicias—Winstone, Phaex—Rosco, Cleon—Mullart, Ælius—Beckham, Diphilus—Vaughan, Demetrius—Green, Page—Master Hamilton, Thais—Miss Burgess, Chloe—Miss Bennet, Melissa—Mrs Vallois, Poet—James, Evandra—Mrs Mullart.

At the benefit of Cross and Miss Burgess *Julius Caesar* was presented with the following cast: Brutus—Stephens, Cassius—Rosco, Anthony—Havard, Caesar—Mullart, Casca—Winstone, Octavius—Cross, Trebonius—Green, Cinna—Mozeen, Soothsayer—Beckham, Cimber—Vaughan, Lucius,

Page—Master Hamilton, Calphurnia—Mrs James, Portia—
Mrs Mullart, Cobler—James.

Cross and Miss Burgess apologise for 'troubling the
Town with a second Benefit; which we wou'd not have
presumed to do, had not the first been so very small: But
being encouraged by several Gentlemen and Ladies, who
have kindly promised to use their Interest for us, we make
this second Attempt, and humbly hope for the Indulgence of
the Town, which shall be always gratefully acknowledged.'
Printed copies of the prologue addressed to Canterbury,
written for and spoken at their first benefit, were given out,
free of charge, at the doors.

Godwin's medley of entertainments came on from Ramsgate to Canterbury during the Christmas holidays. Prices
were further reduced to boxes 1s., pit 6d., middle gallery 4d.,
upper gallery 3d., 'Servants and others to the best Advantage'.
He showed the history of Whittington in waxworks, 'Where
you'll see the Morocco Court almost devour'd by Rats and
Mice', and performed Hob in the Well.

In 1740 the company from London opened in Faversham
'At a new Play-House in Church Lane'. They stayed but a
week, acting every day. Their opening night was by command of Lord and Lady Teynham, and, on their closing one,
they gave Carey's Nancy as performed at Covent Garden,
'With all the Musick proper to the same'.

They opened in Canterbury on July 28, and two days after
revived the Cibber-Shakespeare Richard III which had not
been seen for several years: Henry VI—Harrington, Prince
Edward—Miss Ferguson, Duke of York—Miss Mullart,
Richard—Roberts, Buckingham—Mullart, Richmond—
Neale, Stanley—Rosco, Norfolk—Beckham, Catesby—
Winstone, Mayor—James, Lieut.—Vaughan, Queen Eliza-
beth—Mrs Mullart, Anne—Mrs Roberts, Duchess of
York—Mrs Marshall. Mrs Beckham and Mrs James were
also in the company.

A feature of this season is the several letters to the Kentish

Post written by the actors. Thus John Roberts wrote to the gentlemen and ladies:

The Piece I first design'd for my Benefit not being entirely ready to be exhibited with that Regularity and Perfection suitable for the Entertainment of such Spectators as I have formerly had the Honour to be grac'd with the Presence of, in this Town; judg'd it necessary to change to the above Comedy &c [*Love Makes a Man* and *Flora*] which (as being a well allow'd decent and diverting Play, and as compleatly within the Bounds of our Performance as I cou'd pick out) I am assur'd will be an agreeable Amusement, and thereupon humbly hope to be indulg'd with usual Favour and Encouragement.

Harris James writes apologising that the 'present Condition' of Mrs James prevents his personal application at his benefit. The benefit was announced for him and 'the Good Woman in the Straw', a term for in childbed much in use in theatrical companies.

A communication from William Mullart reads:

I think it incumbent on me, for the many Favours I have receiv'd (conferr'd on self and Family) more especially for the Great Encouragement of my last Benefit, to return my most hearty Thanks—and humbly hope this publick Acknowledgement will be candidly accepted from

Yours (as in Duty bound)
WILLIAM MULLART.

James also thanked for attendance at his benefit, expressing his obligation 'particularly to the Good Lady who espous'd my Play'. On this occasion 'By Order of the Gentlemen no Servants are to be admitted on the Stage'. Also 'The Night will be illuminated with the Silver Rays of Cynthia'. Otherwise the season has nothing noteworthy.

In 1741 the company consisted of Taswell, Hallam, Mullart, Neale, Rosco, Winstone, Lacey, James, Beckham, Blogg, Davis, Mrs Bellamy, Miss Dodson, Miss Ferguson, Mrs Mullart, Miss Davis, Miss Georgina, Madame and Mdlle

Roland and Mons. Nivelon. They advertised that they would open with *All for Love* on June 3: 'All the Characters properly drest in entire new Roman Shapes', but they were obliged to postpone playing until June 8 'on account of new painting the Scenes and other Decorations, which cou'd not possibly be got ready as was intended'. Further difficulties beset them, and on June 17-20 they put a notice in the *Kentish Post*: 'Our Company not being together till now, we cou'd not with so much Certainty assure the Town, we intend to perform such Plays as are advertis'd, Mondays, Wednesdays and Fridays, during the Season, except the Interposition of any Lady's particular Commands.'

Mdlle Roland from Covent Garden gave dancing lessons and was prepared to stay in town if encouraged. On her benefit she announced that she had taken a house for teaching purposes and hopes that the town 'will be so good as to come to her Benefit to encourage her Stay'.

The company boosted *Sir Courtly Nice* as being 'esteem'd a Masterpiece of Dramatick Poetry for the Opposition of Characters it contains, by King Charles the Second, by whose Command and Assistance it was wrote'. The afterpiece on this night was Carey's *The Dragon of Wantley*, which had been played sixty odd nights successively at Covent Garden. *All for Love* was revived after twenty years 'decorated with a compleat Set of Roman Habits never seen on any Stage' with Hallam as Mark Anthony, Mullart as Ventidius, and Mrs Mullart as Cleopatra. *The Rehearsal* was given its first performance at Canterbury, being advertised as acted at Covent Garden over 100 times. On this occasion it was announced: 'None can possibly be admitted behind the Scenes, by Reason of the extraordinary Business of the Piece.' It seems to have been welcomed in Canterbury and was given at least three times.

Hardly a season passed without a performance of *Macbeth*, and this was no exception. It is of interest, however, because the Witches, played by Davis, Shore and James, were differentiated from the Singing Witches played by Mrs James, Miss Davis and others. New pantomimes were *The Gardener and his Wife* with Mons. Nivelon as Harlequin, and *The Rambling Lovers: or a New Way to Play an Old Game*, in which Harlequin was played by M. le Blanche, Columbine by Mdlle Roland and the Clown by James.

At Rosco's benefit play, *The Spanish Fryar*, it was announced that 'This is the last Play which will be acted till after Bartholomew Fair; and that there will be no Play (but this) till Monday the 31st of August; and that Mr Rosco has taken Care this Play shall not be alter'd.' The actors were contracted to Hallam at the fair, but returned after a fortnight for another week's playing.

In 1742 another company exhibiting German puppets toured Kent, playing *Arden, Crispin and Crispanus*, and *Virtue Rewarded* from *Pamela*. Collier's puppets were still active in the Isle of Thanet, but he was now forced to eke out a livelihood by selling haberdashery, cutlery and books. It is impossible to tell whether a performance of *The Lewd Wife; or the true and antient History of Mr Arden of Faversham* and *The Bilker Bilk'd* advertised for performance at Sandwich on Easter Monday, by particular desire of several gentlemen in the country, was given by puppets or live actors. No company from London appears to have visited Canterbury in 1742, and many of the actors went instead this, and succeeding years, to Bristol.

In 1743 an amusing incident is recorded in connexion with the High German puppets: 'On Friday there was but a very slender Audience the Craft being inform'd that Crispin was to be hang'd, and that it was all a Burlesque; but some of them seeing it was perform'd just to the History of Crispin and Crispanus and in so curious a Manner far surpassing their Expectation there was Five Score and Ten on Saturday night.'

And now the field being once more clear Dymer reappears on the Canterbury scene in March and April. He gave a benefit for 'as many Boys as the House will amount to over and above the common Charge, to have a Years Schooling in Reading, Writing, Spelling, and Accompts; Pens, Ink, Paper, a Bible and Spelling Book Gratis', on which occasion he himself played Careless in *The Committee*. By desire of several ladies and gentlemen he introduced Thomson's *Sophonisba* to Canterbury, followed by *The Burgomaster Trick'd*.

In May Dymer was in Dover but returned to Canterbury in July for race week, playing *Sophonisba*, *Venice Preserv'd*, *Rule a Wife* and *Love's Contrivance*. Thence he went to Maidstone. In December Canterbury saw 'The so much Fam'd Piece of Machinery, consisting of large Artificial Wax Figures, five Foot high, which have all the Just Motions and Gestures of Human Life', and which played at the theatre *The Unhappy Favourite*. A comp'ny was playing in Canterbury at the turn of the year. That it was not Dymer's is evident from a simultaneous news item that Dymer was removing from Maidstone to Rochester. The newspapers are not complete for 1744 but the company was still, or again, in Canterbury in May. The new company may have been that subsequently known as Perry's but, as no names of actors are given, this must remain a conjecture. Dymer henceforward is heard of no more in this district,[1] and with his disappearance ends a chapter of the theatrical history of Kent.

[1] *The Theatric Tourist* says he managed a company, which played in an inn in Chichester, until 1764.

Chapter XII

THE KENTISH CIRCUIT, 1744–1765

As the British Museum and Canterbury Library possess only odd copies of the *Kentish Post* for 1744, our knowledge of this dramatic season is limited. But we know that the Londoners resumed their visits, after two years absence, with a company which included Macklin, his wife and daughter, Mr and Mrs Mills, Malone and Vaughan. Macklin played his famous Shylock, and Sir Francis Wronghead in *The Provok'd Husband*; Miss Macklin, a child, played the customary Tom Thumb. *The Relapse* was said to be given for the first time. The prices were as usual except that we first hear of pigeon holes which cost 1s. along with the first gallery. On August 15–18 the *Kentish Gazette* announced 'that the Company of Comedians, from London, can continue acting in this City but a Fortnight longer, being obliged to attend the Play-house above [Drury Lane], during which Time the Publick may be certain of their performing every Monday, Wednesday, and Friday. Benefits being fix'd for those Days during their Stay'.

The company in 1745 was recruited from Drury Lane only and embraced Havard, Bridges, Morgan, Lacey, Malone, Vaughan, Simpson, Blakes, Usher, Bransby, Mrs Elmy, Mrs King, Mrs Havard, Mrs Vaughan, Mrs Bridges, Mrs Simpson and Miss Budgel. A number of Shakespearean plays were performed: *King Lear*, *Hamlet*, *Julius Caesar*, *Henry IV Pt. I*, and *Macbeth*. The season opened with *The Beggar's Opera* with Blakes as Macheath and Miss Budgel as Polly. For Vaughan's benefit a pantomime called *The Cheats of Harlequin*, of which he was the author, was staged. Vaughan was a dancer as well as an actor and was the company's

Harlequin. On the last night a benefit was given for Lacey, Usher, Mrs King and the late Mr Mullart's[1] children. An attempt was made to stop gate crashing with the notice: 'No Servants will be admitted but in Livery'.

The following year (1746) the Macklin family returned supported by Taswell, Blakes, Simpson, Kennedy, Malone, Vaughan, Winstone, Miss Royer, Mrs Butler, Mrs Simpson and Mrs Vaughan. Among the parts played by Macklin were Peachum, Shylock to Mrs Macklin's Portia, Mock Doctor, Sir John Brute to Mrs Macklin's Lady Brute, Daniel in *Oroonoko*, Jobson in *The Devil to Pay* and Tom in *The Conscious Lovers*. Miss Macklin sang for the first time on the stage and also took the part, in boy's clothes, of Collin in the musical dialogue of Collin and Phebe. Winstone acted Richard III, and Vaughan played Launcelot Gobbo in *The Merchant of Venice*. Vaughan's pantomime was revived under the title of *The Wedding: or, The Cheats of Harlequin*, Mrs Vaughan being his Columbine.

For the summer season of 1747 there appeared a new company of comedians which included Hayward, Clarke, Blogg and Mrs Freeman. This was the company afterwards known as Perry's. Indeed, though their names do not happen to appear, the Perrys were probably even then members of the troupe. They gave the ever popular *The Beggar's Opera* with Blogg as Macheath and Mrs Freeman as Polly; *Othello*; 'the last new Farce' *Miss in her Teens* 'perform'd thirty Nights successively at…Covent Garden'; *Tunbridge Walks*, and *The Lying Valet*.

In January 1748 the young gentlemen of Dover gave a performance of *Cato* 'with universal applause'. The company of 1747 reappeared in Canterbury in the summer, and we have a more complete list of its comedians, among whom are the Perrys, Hayward, Clarke, Godwin, Freeman, Blogg, Daniel, Palmer, Bruodin, Mrs Godwin, Mrs Freeman and

[1] This is strange as Mullart's name appears in the company list at Bristol in 1746.

Master Perry. They opened in July for race week and continued playing well into October. The company encouraged amateur efforts for which, doubtless, they were well paid. A gentleman of the city played Trueman in *The London Merchant*; 'a gown'd Person for his Diversion' took on Puff in *Miss in her Teens*, and, at the performance of *Hamlet*, Hamlet, the Ghost and Horatio were 'attempted by three Gentlemen of the City'. This last was repeated by particular desire. On September 21, and for two following performances, *Othello* was acted by gentlemen, when prices were advanced to pit and boxes 5s., first gallery 3s., upper gallery 2s., and on the last night even the galleries were 5s.; no persons were admitted without tickets. The profits from this play were to be given over to the building of an assembly room[1] so that 'it is hop'd that Gentlemen and Ladies in the Country will send for their Tickets soon'. Doubts had evidently arisen, as they were frequently to do in the future, about the security of the playhouse, and the advertisement adds: 'The Play-House hath been survey'd, and is reported to be in very good Repair. The Doors will be open'd at Six o'Clock exactly.' Such was the success of this venture that the same gentlemen performed the following month in *Macbeth* for the benefit of Mr and Mrs Freeman who, we may surmise, had coached them. The prices on this occasion were reduced to boxes 5s., pit 3s., first gallery 2s., upper gallery 1s.

Other details of interest for this season are that Clarke played Lappet in *The Miser* 'after the Manner of Mrs Clive'; the child, Master Perry, spoke the prologue and epilogue at his parents' benefit; Freeman wrote a new prologue to *Othello* on the occasion of his benefit; special songs were introduced by Blogg and Daniel into their parts of Sir John Loverule and Jobson in *The Devil to Pay* at their benefit; and no persons were admitted behind the scenes at the special performances of *Hamlet* mentioned above.

[1] Francis Whitfield's assembly rooms, at the corner of St Margaret's Street, were opened in 1750.

In January 1749 the triumphant gentlemen of the city acted *The Miser* and *The Lying Valet* for the benefit of one New-house 'Now a Debtor in Westgate Gaol, Canterbury'. Godwin, who was in Canterbury with his Sadler's Wells troupe, was presumably the leading spirit on this occasion since the advertisement states: 'This Performance is given Gratis by Mr Godwin, in Hopes to release Mr Newhouse from his Confinement, and who humbly begs the Interest of his Friends'. Prices this time were normal.

In February Godwin's company performed *The Beggar's Opera* 'with all the Songs adapted to it' together with a pantomime entertainment from *Perseus and Andromeda* and rope dancing by Mrs Godwin. This was on the occasion of the proclamation of the peace of Aix-la-Chapelle and was timed to 'begin as soon as the Fireworks are over'. Boxes were 1s., pit 6d., gallery 3d. Godwin returned from London in March 'to divert the Town with that famous Entertainment of Harlequin's Escape into the Bottle'. This he introduced into *The Burgomaster Trick'd*, as at Covent Garden, and gave with it a comedy entitled *Scapin Metamorphos'd: or, The Spaniard Bit*. The doors were opened at 6 p.m. for a performance at 7 p.m. He advertised: 'As Mr Godwin has put himself to a great Expence in going up to London to get this Entertainment, he hopes the Town will honour him with their Company; for his Stay will be but two Days.' The town did, for the next week we find the announcement: 'Mr Godwin having met with great Applause by exhibiting his Pantomime Entertainment of Harlequin's Escape into the Bottle, stays in Town (by particular Desire) 'till Monday Night, which will positively be the last Night of acting.' At Faversham *Arden*, with singing and dancing between the acts, was revived every night for a week at the Dolphin[1] in June, the principal parts being played by local people, the others possibly by Perry's Company.

For the last time a company of comedians from London

----

[1] This inn still exists.

usurped Canterbury for the summer season. They were Craven, Dancer, Furnival, Malone, Cushing, Goodall, Simpson, Mrs Simpson, Mrs Cushing, Mrs Beckham, Miss Morrison and Master Simpson. The Butter Market Theatre was 'new Painted, and neatly Fitted up with an entire new Set of Scenes'.

The difficulty remained of getting the audience to come to time: 'Being determin'd to begin exactly at Seven o'Clock, we hope that those Ladies and Gentlemen that intend Us the Honour of their Company, will be punctual to the Hour'.

The great event of this season was the production of *Romeo and Juliet*, never seen here, 'Alter'd from Shakespear, as it was perform'd last Season at the Theatre Royal in Drury-Lane, with great Applause'. This was the Garrick version with the additions to the tomb scene. The other new play presented was Moore's *The Foundling*.

'Mr Perry's Company of Comedians', now first called that, was at the Sign of the Harp in Begin Street, Dover, in November, playing *Arden of Faversham* every evening during the fair. In January 1750 Perry brought them to Canterbury for two weeks on his way to Rochester. Master Perry jun. was playing Tom Thumb. *Richard III* was also given: Richard—Freeman, Prince Edward and Duke of York—Masters Perry, followed by *The Virgin Unmask'd*. In February and March Perry was at the George Inn, Milton near Sittingbourne and after eight performances of *Arden* he announced that he would continue playing it every day for a week and no longer, as he was due to open with it at the Globe, Chatham. Whether his play was the Elizabethan tragedy, or the version brought out at the Haymarket in 1736,[1] or a local adaptation of the story we do not know.

In the meantime Canterbury was being regaled in March by the Grand Turk from Sadler's Wells in tight and slack rope performances. Among 'several other very surprizing Balances' he 'wheels a Wheelbarrow with a Child in it upon the Slack Rope'. He was supported by the conjuring tricks

[1] See Nicoll, *Eighteenth-Century Drama*, 1700-1750, p. 365.

of Yates and the singing of Mrs Yates for whom a benefit was given on March 27; pit 2s., first gallery 1s., upper gallery 6d.

Perry was in Ashford with *Arden* in May and came to Canterbury for race week in August playing *The Foundling*, *The Albion Queens* and *Richard III*.

There is nothing of dramatic interest in the newspapers for 1751 until November, and it does not seem as though Canterbury had either a winter or a summer season. In November Perry was in Sandwich during fair time and produced Havard's *King Charles the First* with the following cast: King Charles—Freeman, Duke of York—Master James Perry, Duke of Gloucester—Master R. Perry, Bishop Juxon —Ingall, Duke of Richmond—Perry, Marquis of Lindsey— Vaughan, Cromwell—Barton, Fairfax—Beeston, Bradshaw —Barnard, Queen—Mrs Freeman, Princess Elizabeth—Mrs Barton, Lady Fairfax—Mrs Beeston.

In December there appeared at Canterbury a new company, which was eventually to monopolise the Kentish circuit until 1765. The company was under the management of one William Smith, who came to be known as Canterbury Smith. *The Theatric Tourist*, speaking of his activities in Margate, says that he was an Essex wool-comber, that he conducted theatres at Margate, Canterbury, Dover, Deal, Maidstone, Faversham and Rochester and that he paid occasional visits to Tunbridge Wells, where however Peters, a member of the company, succeeded him in 1753. It was in this company that Roger Kemble, future father of a famous brood, started his theatrical career. The story is related by Lee Lewes in his *Memoirs*:[1]

In the course of his peregrinations he stopped sometime at Canterbury,[2] where he ingratiated himself into the good esteem of many of Smith's company of comedians, then performing

---

[1] Vol. I, p. 86.
[2] Cf. *Eccentricities of John Edwin*, vol. II, p. 158, where Kemble is said to have been a barber at Barnet and Rochester, whence he 'went to Deal, and commenced Actor'.

there; and conceiving it to be an idle, pleasant life, he soon formed a very tender connexion with the celebrated Fanny Furnival, who was then performing there. The lady was struck with Roger's nose and athletic make;...In return for his tender affection she flattered him with the promise of making an actor of him, and no woman on the British stage was better qualified for giving instructions in theatricals, at that time Ann. Dom. 1752. She was far superior to any of her predecessors, possessing an elegant figure, an uncommon share of beauty, a perfect knowledge of every part she undertook and an execution scarcely excelled by any actress of that day, Mrs Pritchard and Mrs Cibber excepted...it is singular that under all the disadvantages of private character, she was invited to the first families in every town the company visited, in consequence of her being a polite and agreeable companion, and superior in merit to all her theatrical sisters.

It took her seven weeks to drum the part of Kite in *The Recruiting Officer* into Kemble's head and, when he made his début, 'so coldly was he received in it, that notwithstanding Mrs Kemble was Smith's principal support, he could not be prevailed upon to allow her husband any encouragement'; so the pair left to trudge their way to join another company in Coventry. The first part we find Kemble, or Campbell as he was called in the company, playing is Furnish in *The Miser* on December 16. He also took the roles of Tamerlane, Richmond in *Richard III*, Porter in *The Constant Couple*, a Citizen in *The Roman Father*, Paris in *Romeo and Juliet*, Blandford in *Oroonoko* and Plume in *The Recruiting Officer*; some of them quite large and important parts. Mrs Kemble was seen as Mrs Wisely in *The Miser*, Arpasia in *Tamerlane*, Queen Elizabeth in *Richard III*, Horatia in *The Roman Father*, Belvidera in *Venice Preserv'd* and Jane Shore; she also sang the vocal parts in *Romeo and Juliet*.

The other members of Smith's company for his winter season at Canterbury, December to March 1751–2, were: Brooks, Willoughby, Brassey, Peters, Jones, Gately, Mrs Tyler, Mrs Peters, Mrs Smith and Mrs Willoughby. He opened on December 16 with *The Miser*; Mrs Kemble and

Mrs Willoughby supplying the entr'acte singing. His performances began at 6, then at 6.30, and finally at 7 as the days lengthened, and he renewed the plea for punctuality 'for we shall, as 'tis our usual Custom, begin punctually at that Hour'. No persons were to be admitted behind the scenes. In mid-December he paid a flying visit to Deal but returned to Canterbury after Christmas with *Richard III*: King Richard—Smith, King Henry—Brooks, Buckingham—Jones, Richmond—Campbell, Stanley—Willoughby, Mayor—Brassey, Catesby—Peters, King Edward—Mrs Willoughby, Duke of York—Mrs Peters, Queen Elizabeth—Mrs Campbell, Lady Anne—Mrs Tyler, Duchess of York—Mrs Smith.

In January Smith brought out, by particular desire of Sir Edward Hales Bt., Whitehead's *The Roman Father* with the following cast: Horatius—Smith, Hostilius—Brooks, Publius—Jones, Valerius—Willoughby, Citizens—Campbell, Brassey, Gately, Horatia—Mrs Campbell, Valeria—Mrs Tyler, Vocal parts by Mr and Mrs Peters and Mrs Willoughby. That the play was a success is proved by the notice at its second performance: 'Whereas a great Number of Ladies and Gentlemen &c. in this City and the adjacent Villages cou'd not get Room on Monday Evening to see the above mention'd Play, we (by their Desire), take the Advantage of this Publick Paper to advertise it again.' *Romeo and Juliet* with the additional scene was given the week following: Romeo—Smith, Mercutio—Jones, Friar Laurence—Brooks, Capulet—Willoughby, Benvolio—Peters, Paris—Campbell, Montague—Brassey, Peter—Gately, Balthazar—Mrs Willoughby, Juliet—Mrs Tyler, Lady Capulet—Mrs Peters, Nurse—Mrs Smith, Vocal parts by Mrs Campbell, etc. It, too, scored a success and the same advertisement was inserted two days afterwards when the play was repeated. People had evidently been enthusiastic enough to crowd to the theatre before the doors were open, as announcements thereafter point out that they do not open until 4 o'clock (3.30 on the last night) for a 6 o'clock performance.

Amateur co-operation continued to be encouraged. A gentleman of the town played Damon, in *Damon and Phillida*, for his diversion, another acted Castalio in *The Orphan* and the Master in *The Toy Shop*.

Among the plays given were *Venice Preserv'd*, Pierre—Smith, Jaffeir—Brooks, Belvidera—Mrs Campbell, *Jane Shore*, and *The Unhappy Favourite*, Essex—Smith, Queen Elizabeth—Mrs Smith.

After the positively last night had been announced, a further performance was given for the benefit of two debtors. The play was *The Stratagem: or, The Litchfield Landlord* with the following cast: Archer—Jones, Aimwell—Peters, Scrub —Smith, Mrs Sullen—Mrs Smith.

In the meantime we come across Perry's Company at Ramsgate where, on February 21, they played *Richard III*: Richard—Freeman, Henry—Brown, Richmond—St John, Stanley—Barton, Tressel—Perry, Mayor—Barnard, Catesby —Mrs Vaughan, Prince Edward—James Perry, Duke of York —Richard Perry, Queen Elizabeth—Mrs Freeman, Lady Anne—Mrs Barnard, Duchess of York—Mrs Perry.

Mrs Vaughan was often seen in men's parts. In Shakespeare's plays especially the large number of characters constituted a difficulty for travelling companies and frequently necessitated a resort to the practice of putting women in minor male roles. During the whole period in the circuit I have found the following Shakespearean characters taken at one time or another by women:

Macbeth: Fleance, Donalbain.
Henry IV: Prince John, Blunt, Westmoreland, Vernon, Douglas, Poins, Gadshill, Oxford, Francis.
Richard III: King Edward, Duke of York, Catesby, Ratcliff, Lieutenant Brackenbury.
Romeo and Juliet: Balthazar, Benvolio.
Hamlet: Osric, Guildenstern, Rosencrantz, Bernardo.
Othello: Duke, Montano.
King Lear: Cornwall, Burgundy, Albany.

Perry's company was at the Red Lion Playhouse, Sitting-bourne, from May 18 to June 7, after which they removed to 'Margate Spaw'. They arrived in Canterbury for the race week in August when they presented *The Fair Parricide*: Blandford—Johnson, Cranmore—Hayward, Goodman—Freeman, First Gentleman—Downing, Second Gentleman—Sampert, Steward—Clarke, Maria Blandford—Mrs Free-man, Maid—Mrs Barnard.

This play was printed in 1752 but this is the only record we have of its being acted. In fact the *Biographia Dramatica* says it was 'never acted, nor intended for the stage'. A note speaks of the 'great Inconveniences' which 'accrued from the Company's beginning so late last Season' and expresses a determination to reform.

Othello was given with Paddick as Othello and Mrs Too-good as Desdemona and was followed by an exhibition of rope dancing by an equilibrist from Sadler's Wells. The company was still in town in October when *The Beaux Stratagem* was given for the benefit of Perry and his two sons; the two sons played the Ghost Scenes from *Hamlet*.

Smith's company was in Canterbury at the end of November 1752. The Freemans and Mrs Vaughan had joined them from Perry's Company and other new recruits were Browne and Walker. The Kembles of course had left and so had the Willoughbys and Jones. *Romeo and Juliet* was given 'With the usual Solemnity'. *Hamlet* too was granted at least three performances with the following cast: Hamlet—Smith, Ghost—Brooks, King—Browne, Polonius—Brassey, Horatio—Walker, Player King—Freeman, Osric—Mrs Smith, Guildenstern—Mrs Vaughan, Gravediggers—Peters, Gately, Queen—Mrs Freeman, Ophelia—Mrs Peters, Player Queen—Mrs Tyler.

Other Shakespeare productions were *The Jew of Venice*, with Mr and Mrs Smith as Shylock and Portia, *Richard III* (3 times), and *Henry IV* with Smith as Hotspur. The great effort of the season was the presentation of *Theodosius* for the benefit of the Smiths in May. The advertisement runs:

The Opening of the Play will consist of more Variety and Grandeur than we have ever exhibited on this Stage. The Altar will be more magnificent than before. The azure sky will likewise be enlarg'd upwards of eight Feet. In the Centre of the Sky will be represented a transparent Bloody Cross. On the right Side of it will be pictur'd kneeling Constantine the Great, on the left Side a Dove and under it will be inserted the Inscription in Golden Letters, signifying thou shalt o'ercome in this. The principal Characters in the Play will be dress'd in new Roman and Persian Habits.

In February 1753, and thereafter, a celebrated equilibrist gave performances on the slack wire after the manner of Maddox. The stage too was improved: 'The Theatre is to be greatly illuminated by a large Number of additional Lights; the Boxes will be ornamented with several Trophies of Musick; and the Stage decorated with a Set of new profil'd Scenes, painted by Mr Nichols, in the Style of those at the Theatre in London.'

Two otherwise unknown afterpieces called *The Intriguing Footman; or the Miser Bit* and *Harlequin Captive; or the Pantaloon Bit* were produced. In *Pygmalion; or Harlequin's Enchantments* Freeman was Harlequin, Mrs Peters Columbine, and Smith Clown. Macheath was twice played by a gentleman of the town and Puff, in *Miss in her Teens*, by a young man. Browne and Walker had a second benefit owing to the failure of their first.

Perry was meantime at the Star, Maidstone, where he too gave a production of *Romeo and Juliet* with procession and solemn dirge, and a new prologue and epilogue by Downing. The procession prevented the admittance of gentlemen behind the scenes. The cast was: Romeo—Hayward, Mercutio—Martin, Friar Laurence—Downing, Capulet—Barnard, Montague—Perry, Tybalt—Sunderland, Paris—Crisp, Benvolio—Mitteer, Peter—Master J. Perry, Page—Master R. Perry,

Juliet—Mrs Fisher, Lady Capulet—Mrs Boucher, Nurse—
Mrs Perry. It is to be noted that the Perrys were now taking
old parts. *Romeo and Juliet* was given again by desire of the
Commonalty Club: 'The Doors to be open'd at Three, and
shut up at half an hour after Five' so that a great crowd was
evidently expected. It was performed six nights. An apology
is inserted in the *Kentish Post* for February 10–14 because
timely notice of the last performance had not been given
to country ladies and gentlemen in that paper, it being 'too
late to send it by Friday's Carravan'.

Tunbridge Walks and *Miss in her Teens* were given at
the Mayor's bespeak; on another evening a gentlewoman of
the town played Lady Townly in *The Provok'd Husband*. The
last we hear of Perry in Maidstone is on February 19.

Smith returned to Canterbury for the winter season 1753–4
at the beginning of December and stayed until May. He had
several new actors: Farrell, Clark, Osborn, Waller, Granger,
and his own young son hopefully named Master Garrick
Smith. He had parted with Browne, Walker and Mr and
Mrs Peters.[1] Master Garrick Smith made his début as the
Duke of York in *Richard III* on December 5. The 'new
profil'd Scenes' necessitated the constant reminder that no
persons could be admitted behind 'on account of shifting
the Wings'. A minor disaster is recorded in a notice inserted
in vain in several successive *Posts*: 'Lost out of a Waggon on
Monday Night the 26th of November, between New
Romney and Canterbury, several Wigs, contain'd in a Deal
Box: Whoever will bring 'em, or cause 'em to be brought
to Mr Smith's Lodgings, at Mr Andrews's, a Taylor, in Prince
of Orange Lane, Canterbury, shall for their Trouble receive
Half a Guinea. No greater Reward will be given.' Suddenly
the strolling life is vivid before us. *Romeo and Juliet*, *Hamlet*,
Richard III continued in favour and were joined by *Henry IV
Pt. II* and *Othello*: Othello—Freeman, Iago—Smith, Roderigo
—Granger, Lodovico—Brooks, Brabantio—Farrell, Cassio

[1] See *ante*, p. 244.

—Clark, Gratiano—Waller, First Senator—Osborn, Second Senator—Brassey, Desdemona—Mrs Freeman, Emilia—Mrs Smith.

On January 21 Rowe's *The Royal Convert* with the local sub-title of 'The Reign of Hengist King of Kent' was brought out: 'In which will be represented three Saxon Deities, Woden, Thor, and Friga, standing behind three Altars, according to the ancient Custom of the Saxons. Also a solemn Procession at the time Hengist designs to sacrifice his Brother for renouncing Paganism and turning Christian. The cruel Preparation ordain'd by the Princess Rodogune to rack Ethelinda on a Wheel: Her and the Converts' happy Delivrance. Concluding with the Death of the King and the Enthroning of Aribert and his Queen.' Thus were eighteenth-century audiences harrowed. Smith played Hengist, Mrs Freeman the baleful Rodogune and Mrs Tyler the long-suffering Ethelinda. On the fifth night there was introduced 'besides the usual Solemnity, An entire NEW ANTHEM, written and compos'd by a Gentleman for the Procession'. The next new play was Jones's *The Earl of Essex* with Freeman in the title role and Mrs Freeman as Queen Elizabeth. This couple also played Beverley and Mrs Beverley in the production, this season, of Moore's *The Gamester*. New afterpieces were *The Artful Wife*,[1] *The Coquette; or Love in a Mist*,[2] and a pantomime called *The Genius; or Harlequin Restor'd*, in which Master Smith played Genius, Mrs Tyler Columbine and Farrell Pantaloon. This last was given many nights, later, as was so usual with these entertainments, with alterations and an additional scene.

We hear the last of Perry's company in April acting at the Town Hall in Ashford *Venice Preserv'd* with Priuli—Perry, Jaffeir—Fisher, Pierre—Perry jun., Bedamar—Barnard, Renault—Wignell, Captain—Master Richard Perry,

---

[1] This may have been taken from William Taverner's full-length comedy of the same name; otherwise it seems to be unknown.

[2] Probably Cunningham's *Love in a Mist*.

Belvidera—Mrs Fisher. The elder son was now taking young men's parts and perhaps it was he that some time after the close of our period ran a company in Kent.

Smith now held undisputed sway. He was in Margate in June and July and intended to come to Canterbury for race week but we have no record of his actual visit. In November he was at the Ship in Faversham, and here we find Mr and Mrs Eden in the company. His audience could not always be sure of a performance for at 6 o'clock he either began the performance or, if the attendance was meagre, shut the playhouse doors.

His 1754-5 sojourn in Canterbury was uneventful and shorter than usual, lasting only from December 26 to March. Browne had rejoined the company, which, however, had parted with Farrell, Osborn, Waller, Brooks, Granger and Gately. The Edens took over from the Smiths the parts of Iago and Emilia and they also played Legend and Mrs Frail in *Love for Love* and Falstaff and Lady Percy in *Henry IV Pt. I*. The company was short of actors and Mrs Eden played Capulet whilst her husband undertook Friar Laurence in the ever popular *Romeo and Juliet*. Bespeaks were given by a Society of Gentlemen and Sir Edward Hales Bt. Browne spoke a prologue by Garrick in the character of a country boy, and Freeman rendered the corresponding epilogue as a fine gentleman. Such occasional addresses became popular, and these and similar ones are frequently to be found in the programmes of ensuing seasons.

February 27 was advertised as the last night, March 6 as positively the last night, but playing continued until March 17 when *The Royal Convert* and *The Artful Wife* were given for the benefit of one Daniel Warmer, a local debtor, who 'humbly hopes that the Ladies and Gentlemen &c. will be kind enough to encourage the Night's performance to help him out of his present Calamity'. The company is found in Sandwich in April and in Margate in July when one Crispe, who may have been the actor of that name from Perry's

Company but of whom we do not hear further, played Ballance in *The Recruiting Officer*. On July 21 the company opened at Canterbury and were to play every night during race week. They did not advertise further and are next heard of in Dover in October where they 'fitted up the Play-House in a very commodious Manner'. 'There will be four fires in the House to keep it warm' ran one notice, and another forbade entrance behind the scenes on account of the shifting the wings. The new scenery was evidently not confined to Canterbury but was also used on tour. The company stayed in Dover until the end of December and began the New Year 1756 in Canterbury. There they continued playing until May. Two Brownes, Richard and William, were now acting and Mrs Vaux was responsible for singing between the acts and for vocal parts such as Ophelia and Polly. At her benefit, which was also a bespeak by the officers, she rendered 'an Epilogue of Thanks, as originally sung by Mrs Clive'.

The cast for *Hamlet* was now as follows: Hamlet—Smith, King—Eden, Ghost—Freeman, Laertes—W. Browne, Polonius—Brassey, Horatio—Clark, Player King—R. Browne, Osric—Mrs Smith, Rosencrantz—Mrs Vaughan, Queen—Mrs Eden, Ophelia—Mrs Vaux, Player Queen—Mrs Tyler.

The Rival Queens was the one new production and this does not seem to have been a great success as I can trace only three performances. The famous trio was played by Eden as Alexander, Mrs Freeman as Roxana, Mrs Tyler as Statira. New entertainments were *The Fond Husband: or The Intriguing Wife*, and *The Press-Gang; or Love in Low Life*, 'As it was perform'd at the Theatre-Royal in Covent Garden several Nights this Season'. The Brownes specialised in prologues and epilogues: R. Browne spoke an epilogue in the character of a drunken sailor, on another occasion used as a prologue, W. Browne an epilogue on nobody. Master Garrick Smith also delivered an epilogue after the play on two occasions. A band of German music was an additional attraction between the acts on another night. The company returned to Canterbury at the end of July for race week.

We cannot trace them in 1757 before March, and they continued in Canterbury until May. They had lost Brassey and Mrs Vaux and there is no mention of the Brownes, but they probably still belonged since there is a Mrs Browne now in the troupe. Richardson and Maxfield were additional actors. Richardson took over such parts as Laertes, Benvolio and Fantome in *The Drummer*, Maxfield played Stanley in *Richard III*, Indent in *The Fair Quaker*, Polonius, and Capulet. Mrs Browne was given Ophelia, and Jiltup in *The Fair Quaker*.

The Mayor and Corporation bespoke *The Spanish Fryar*. No new play seems to have been attempted, but *Harlequin Shipwreck'd: or, Oberon King of the Fairies* was a popular new pantomime. *The Vintner in the Suds* comes out under a new title: *The White Fox Chace: or The Vintner in the Suds*.

Maidstone saw in June a company brought from London by Wignell,[1] now an under actor at Covent Garden, which included Morgan, Smith, Haughton, Clough, Jones, Buck, Castle, Tate Wilkinson, Barrington, Hull (later), Miss Morison, Miss Bradshaw, Mrs Roberts, Mrs Wignell, Mrs Haughton, Mrs Barrington, Miss Hallam. Wignell told Tate Wilkinson[2] that he was erecting a wooden booth in Maidstone. It was as usual in the Star Yard where Dymer's booth had probably fallen into disrepair or had been destroyed. Wilkinson mentions that the players had not been to Maidstone for some years and in fact the last visit of which we have evidence is that of 1743. Wilkinson joined the company by sailing to Gravesend, thence taking the stage coach to Chatham, and a post chaise to Maidstone. Garrick had recommended him to practise on the provincial boards so that he would acquire 'freedom and ease on the stage'. Wilkinson has described in his *Memoirs* the failure of the enterprise:

[1] He had been in Perry's Company. See, *ante*, p. 251.
[2] *Memoirs*, vol. I, p. 123.

'The little motley troop from London certainly deserved
more attention and encouragement than was bestowed' he
says, and continues: 'In Douglas, (without a joke) I was very
well received; but not even my Orestes, nor Mrs Barrington's Andromache, could attract a sufficient audience.' *The
Beaux Stratagem*, with which the company opened, did not
bring more than £5 to the house and the audience was often
so sparse that the actors dismissed. Some weeks their shares
did not amount to 6s. To stimulate interest they started their
benefits early but poor Wilkinson's benefit of *The Distress'd
Mother* only brought him 1s. 6d. and two pieces of candle, 'a
dismal Banquet', he comments, 'for Prince Orestes'. Wignell,
because he was a good stroller, punctually paying his bills
and understanding the art of application and solicitation, was,
however, certain of a good benefit. So too were the Barring-
tons, who were able to make a big show, amazing 'the eyes
and ears of the little streets with a very handsome one horse
chair' in which every noon they 'took a genteel airing'. The
other members of the troupe grew restive and demanded
that the trio share their benefits. This was agreed to and as
the benefits fetched £19 or £20 the actors went home with
a guinea or two in their pockets. Of this disastrous season
one advertisement occurs, by which we learn that the company played three times a week and that 'the greatest Care
will be taken that the several Performances may be conducted with Decency and Decorum'.

In October Maddox, the famous rope dancer from Covent
Garden, paid a visit to Canterbury. He played three times a
week, giving different items at each performance, and he
charged the same as the players. He was supported by Mr
and Mrs Dennis, singers, and by Waters the Clown. From
Canterbury he went to Dover.

We do not hear of Smith's company during the whole of
1758 and it is unlikely that there was any season in Canterbury this year. The famous Mrs Charke, daughter of Colley
Cibber, arrived in the city on August 26, 'with a Design,

next Week (for one Night only) to entertain the Ladies and Gentlemen here with a Comic Medley; after which will be a Ball'. On August 30–September 3, the *Kentish Post* says: 'We hear that the Worshipful Mayor of this City has been so obliging as to grant Mrs Charke the Liberty of the Town-Hall for her Dissertation and Auction on Wednesday next; after which will be a Ball. Tickets 2s. 6d.' On September 23–7 we hear 'that Mrs Charke's worthy Friends of this City have requested her to exhibit her Medley of Entertainments, with Additions at the Play-House in Canterbury, on Monday the second of October next. After which there will be a Ball'. Charges were pit 2s., first gallery 1s., upper gallery 6d. On September 27–30 she addressed the following letter to the printer:

Sir, I shall take it as a Favour if you'll insert my grateful Acknowledgments to my worthy and much esteemed Friends in this City, for the favour lately conferr'd on me at the Town Hall, and a further Proof of their kind Regard, in requesting my Exhibition, with a Ball, on Monday Evening next, at the Play-House; which fixes me with the highest Sense of Obligation.

Their obedient humble Servant

CHARLOTTE CHARKE.

Mrs Charke was followed by Mrs Midnight from the Haymarket, who exhibited 'her Jubilee Concert and Oratory' at the playhouse. A typical entertainment consisted of vocal and instrumental music 'interspers'd with the Old Woman's Oratory', an oration called 'The Tea-Pot and Scrubbing Brush' by Mrs Midnight, a mock concert, and a pantomime called *The Novelty: or The Adventures of Harlequin*. Gaudry and Miss Lenton assisted with the songs. Prices were the same as for plays. At her benefit Mrs Midnight imitated Mrs Cibber, Mrs Bellamy and Miss Nossiter in 'the Garden Scene' from *Romeo and Juliet*, and Garrick in a 'new bombast prologue'. The epilogue by Smart of Cambridge she spoke riding on an ass. The pantomime was called *Les Charpentiers* and in it a funeral procession to the monument of the Luns[1] parodied that of *Romeo and Juliet*. It looks as though Mrs Midnight was not a great success, since, she states, she 'has no other Advantage for her Performances than the Benefit of this Night only', and in January Jobson's 'Grand Medley of Entertainments' joined her and gave her another benefit. Jobson had 'operatical moving Figures' and showed 'Mr Punch and his merry family' in *The Necromancer*, as well as eight Lilliputians in a country dance. He played up to a local interest too when he demonstrated six figures, ringing bells by clockwork. 'We defy all Men to shew the like' he boasts. Charges were reduced to pit 1s., first gallery 6d., upper gallery 3d.

In February 1759 a company, probably Smith's,[2] appeared for one night only. Smith was definitely in Canterbury for a short season in March. The Brownes had rejoined the company, and Lambert, Mrs Clark and Mr and Mrs Southgate were new recruits. Smith's daughter played the Prince of Wales in *Richard III*. The Freemans, the Edens and Mrs Tyler had gone. Smith was gradually giving up the young and strenuous parts. He now played Tybalt in *Romeo and Juliet* with Southgate as Romeo, Mrs Browne as Juliet, W. Browne as Mercutio, and Mrs Smith as the Nurse; in *Richard III* he merely played the Mayor; in *Venice Preserv'd* he took Pierre, the Southgates acting Jaffeir and Belvidera, but in *All for Love* he still played Anthony to Mrs Southgate's Cleopatra. This last was given 'With the Supper as it was originally perform'd' for the benefit of the Smiths; Garrick Smith spoke a prologue and Smith himself an epilogue 'in the Character of Mr Foote on his Arrival from Paris to London'. Lambert, at his benefit, recited *Tit for Tat; or, a Dish of Mr Woodward's Chocolate*. Actors' monologues, such as those of Foote and Woodward, were as popular in

---

[1] Pseudonym assumed by John Rich, originator of the pantomime.

[2] The prologue in character of a country boy and the epilogue in character of nobody were given.

the provinces as in London, and were frequently reproduced by local comedians. *Arden of Faversham* was brought out on March 22 with success; if, as is most likely, this is Lillo's version it predates the Drury Lane production of July 7. *The Country Lasses, King Lear, The Revenge* and *Venice Preserv'd* were revived. *The Country Lasses* must have been a failure, since the Southgates, for whose benefit it was given, had, on the advice of their friends, a second benefit night.

The company disappears until September when we find them at Dover presenting *King Lear* with the following cast: Lear—Smith, Edgar—Southgate, Gloster—Maxfield, Bastard—Clark, Kent—Brocas, Albany—Ranger, Cornwall—Mrs Smith, Cordelia—Mrs Clark, Regan—Miss Smith, Goneril—Mrs Vaughan, Arante—Mrs Brocas. Charges were boxes 2s., pit 1s. 6d., first gallery 1s., upper gallery 6d.

By February 1760, the company was in Canterbury where they continued until March. Mr and Mrs Brocas and Ranger were new actors. Mrs Smith was evidently dead as Smith shared his benefit with his daughter. Prices for boxes were reduced from 2s. 6d. to 2s. When *King Lear* was performed for the benefit of the Southgates, Southgate put a note in the newspaper 'that great Care will be taken in conducting this Play, and our utmost Endeavours to render the Performance agreeable'. For *Richard III*: 'Several of the principal Characters will be dress'd in entire new Dresses.' Townley's *High Life Below Stairs* was presented this year for the first time. The season ended early in March, and Canterbury was next regaled in August by the feats of the equilibrist Saunders from Covent Garden, supported by a company from the Haymarket. Among the supporters were Miss Macklin, Miss Kezia, Mrs Browne, Madam German, Hussey and Balthesar: 'New Musick, Dresses and Scenes' were promised at normal prices. Tickets were to be had at the theatre, where places for the boxes could be taken. After a flying visit to Margate, Saunders returned to Canterbury in September. The last night was for the benefit of Miss

Macklin and, after 'many amazing additions' was 'to conclude (by Desire) with a Vocal Concert perform'd by Twelve Cats (as exhibited at Paris, in 1752 with great Applause) they all sit in the Orchestre, and alternately Sing, and then join all in the Chorus; there will be additional Musicians to attend the Concert'. For this strange entertainment[1] 'Ladies and Gentlemen are desired to send Early to keep Places, as 'tis thought the House will be pretty full'. Saunders was in Ramsgate in November, where the charges were pit 1s. 6d., first gallery 1s., upper gallery 6d.

When Smith's Company reappeared in December 1760 it had suffered considerable changes. Mrs Blanchard, Mrs Fairbairn, Miss Harrington, Mrs Richardson and Miss Gaudry were now in the company, and a mysterious Liddale from London acted throughout the season for his diversion. Among his parts were those of Marplot in *The Busy Body*, Ghost in *Hamlet*, Shift and Mrs Cole in *The Minor*, Richard III, Archer in *The Beaux Stratagem*, Lear, Sealand in *The Conscious Lovers*, Raymond in *The Spanish Fryar*, Osmyn in *The Mourning Bride*, Marcus in *Cato*. Mrs Blanchard took older women's parts such as Queen Elizabeth in *The Unhappy Favourite*, the Queens in *Hamlet* and *Richard III* and Zara in *The Mourning Bride*. Mrs Fairbairn played the Duchess of York in *Richard III*, Goneril, the Nurse in *Romeo and Juliet*; Miss Smith was now the leading lady playing Ophelia, Cordelia, Juliet, and Cleopatra in *All for Love*. Smith resumed Romeo but allowed Liddale to play many of his parts. The names of the Southgates, the Clarks and Mrs Vaughan have disappeared.

What was new was mostly in the way of entertainments. *Harlequin in Bondage; or the Pantaloon Bit*[2] and Foote's *The Minor* were the chief of these. The latter was performed with

---

[1] Probably suggested by the feigned concert between two cats in burlesque of the Italian opera in Foote's *The Knights*.

[2] Probably a revival or revision of *Harlequin Captive; or The Pantaloon Bit*. See, *ante*, p. 249.

additions of Foote's mimicry, and a scene out of his *Taste* became a popular diversion between play and farce. For *Romeo and Juliet* 'the Procession and Dirge will be represented this Time much grandeur [*sic*] than it has ever been before upon this Stage'. It was followed by a song written by Liddale and sung by him in the character of a drunken landlord accompanied by several freemen. Miss Smith on this night spoke an epilogue in the character of a Freemason's wife. The last night was Liddale's for the benefit of a Mr Mors. Mitchell and Hill's *The Fatal Extravagance* was given its first performance in Canterbury, followed, not only by *The Cheats of Scapin*, but by *Chrononhotonthologos*, an interlude by Murphy, and a poem on the new King (George III) written by Mors, recited by Liddale. No wonder that the latter hoped the audience would come early 'on Account of the Variety of Entertainments which is to be exhibited'. He also asks to be excused from a personal visitation 'but shall endeavour on the Night to make himself as agreeable as possible'.

In April one Thompson came to the theatre with feats of conjuring and a Prussian Punch and family.

Smith was acting at the 'Large theatrical Barn behind the Six Bells' in Sittingbourne in May. He played every night during the fair, and three times a week for the rest of his stay. Newcomers were Gibbs, Harrison, Fitzgerald, Blogg,[1] Mrs Fitzgerald and Miss Seymour. At the beginning of July the company went on to Margate where they asked humbly for encouragement 'as the Company will, by due Application, endeavour to make their Performances entirely satisfactory'.

At Dover, too, in October, Smith speaks of 'the very great Expence' the company was put to 'and the Company will, by their Assiduity, endeavour to make their Performances agreeable'. Similar announcements became an almost constant feature, a fact which leads us to suppose that business

---

[1] He had been in Perry's company, *ante*, p. 240.

was not very good. The failure of benefits and the continual changes in the personnel of the company confirm this. Mr and Mrs Brocas, Ranger and Miss Gaudry had now left and we are greeted by still more new names when the company reaches Canterbury in January 1762: Mr and Mrs Nepecker, Marten and later W. Richardson and Mitteer. Master Garrick Smith is replaced by Master Mate[1] and Master Browne. *King Lear* was given with the following cast: Lear—Smith, Edgar—Browne, Gloster—Maxfield, Bastard—Richardson, Albany[2] and Gent.-Usher—Nepecker, Kent—Gibbs, Cornwall—Blogg, Burgundy—Miss Harrington, Captain—Marten, Messenger—Master Mate, Cordelia —Miss Smith, Goneril—Mrs Richardson, Regan—Miss Seymour, Arante—Mrs Nepecker.

Hamlet with Hamlet—Smith, King—Browne, Ghost and Laertes—Gibbs, Horatio—Nepecker, Polonius—Maxfield, Osric—Blogg, / Marcellus—Marten, Bernardo—Mrs Nepecker, Guildenstern—Miss Seymour, Rosencrantz—Miss Harrington, Gravediggers — Maxfield, Marten, Queen — Mrs Blanchard, Ophelia—Miss Smith, Player Queen—Mrs Richardson.

Othello with Othello—Smith, Iago—Browne, Cassio— Nepecker, Roderigo—Gibbs, Brabantio—Maxfield, Lodovico—Marten, Montano—Blogg, Desdemona—Miss Smith, Emilia—Miss Seymour.

Mitteer first appeared as Pierre in *Venice Preserv'd* in May, Smith now taking Jaffeir and Miss Seymour Belvidera. Smith was still able to play Harlequin with his daughter as Columbine and Gibbs as Clown in *Harlequin in Bondage*. Colman's *Polly Honeycombe* appears to have been the one new piece given this season. *The Drummer* was graced 'With a new Prologue, relative to the Story of the Cock-lane GHOST as performed at Covent-Garden' spoken by Browne. This

---

[1] This may have been Charles Mate who succeeded to the management of the Margate Theatre in 1779 but who is said to have been a sailor.
[2] At a later performance played by W. Richardson.

comedy was also chosen as the Mayor's play. *Arden* still proved popular; *Jane Shore* was revived with Miss Seymour in the title role, and Master Browne played Tom Thumb at the family benefit. The Brownes were evidently local people as the address is given as 'Mr Browne's, Currier, North Lane', so was Blogg who had 'Lodgings in Lamb-Lane at Mr Blogg's Sen.'.

The company achieved several positively last nights. Marten, Mrs Fairbairn and Miss Harrington had a second benefit between them, having met failure respectively with *Henry IV*, *Jane Shore* and *All for Love*. Benefits were further given for 'John Holmes, Cooper, an Inhabitant of this City' incapacitated through lameness, and James Anderson, silk-weaver, a debtor in Westgate who begged encouragement 'that he may obtain his Liberty'.

The company then removed to Sandwich where they played in a barn by the side of the Olde New Inn. A most entertaining print, showing the exterior of the theatre before a rehearsal, is reproduced opposite. The company was in Dover in November. When Smith reappeared in Canterbury in January 1763 he had lost Gibbs, W. Richardson, the Nepeckers and Miss Harrington. No new recruits appear but Mate was now playing adult roles such as the Grave-digger in *Hamlet*, the Usher in *King Lear*, and Peter in *Romeo and Juliet*. One Bean of the city played for his diversion Falstaff in *Henry IV* and Boniface in *The Stratagem*. In the former Miss Fairbairn appeared as Prince John.

A new afterpiece, Fielding's *The Debauchees*, called by its sub-title *The Jesuit Caught*, was produced in February, and *The Picture* was revived after nine years' absence for the benefit of Miss Seymour who had failed with *Romeo and Juliet* 'from the Inclemency of the Weather'. The Mayor's play was *Richard III* followed by *The Lying Valet*. Doors this season were only open an hour or an hour and a half before the curtain rose.

From Canterbury the company visited Sittingbourne in

SANDWICH THEATRE, EXTERIOR

April and May, showing for the first time there *The Picture*
and *The Walking Statue*. In the cast of the ever popular
Arden we find the new names of Clarke, Naylor, Edwards
and Miss Thurnum; the last name does not appear again.
Marten and Mate had left.

In October the company was at the New Theatre, Globe
Lane, Chatham. The charge for boxes was 2*s*., for pit and
slips 1*s*. 6*d*., for first gallery 1*s*., for upper gallery 6*d*., and
tickets were to be had at the Old Globe. *Romeo and Juliet*
was given with the following alterations in the cast: Paris—
Blogg, Benvolio—Naylor, Montague—Edwards, Tybalt—
Clarke.

When the company gave this tragedy in Canterbury in
March 1764, Romeo was played by Browne, Smith taking
the Prince; Nepecker had returned as Laurence, Farrell as
Balthazar and a new actor, Porter, took Gregory. Mrs
Edwards, Mrs Blogg, Mrs Naylor first appear and Garrick
Smith returns in adult parts such as Poins, Gratiano in *The
Jew of Venice*, Gentleman Usher in *King Lear* and Harlequin in
Pygmalion. Miss Smith is now designated as Mrs Smith and
Miss Seymour appears no more. Smith gave up Othello to
Richardson but still played Lear and Shylock.

Colman's *The Jealous Wife* was brought out in March and
given three performances during the season. Colman's *The
Deuce is in Him* was the only other new production, though
there was a revival of *Edward the Black Prince* after nine
years.

By particular desire the company gave a one-night performance in Sittingbourne in July for the benefit of Mrs Smith.
They next appear in February 1765 in Maidstone with the
additions of Mulliner, Hamilton, Crosby, Mrs Williams and
Mrs Miney. They performed there a new pantomime called
Harlequin Mason. They begged leave 'to acquaint the Publick
in general, that they, as usual, shall with the Magistrates
Permission, &c. visit the Towns in the County as heretofore'. This announcement was inserted as a challenge to the

activities of a rival company, called the Chatham Company of Comedians, which first appeared in Dover in March and to which had deserted the Richardsons, the Naylors, Maxfield and Mrs Blanchard. Smith remained in Maidstone until June. During Lent he played Mondays, Thursdays and Saturdays, afterwards Mondays, Wednesdays and Fridays.[1] Prices were the same as in Canterbury but on the bespeak evenings of the Commonalty and Liberty Clubs we find the notice 'No Sixpenny Gallery To-night' and full price during the whole performance. A gentleman played Hastings in *Jane Shore* and an inhabitant of the town, Kite, in *The Recruiting Officer*. *Arden* was given 'as originally written', in opposition to the Chatham Company who advertised Lillo's version, and the season ended with benefits for charity children and for a former citizen of Canterbury in gaol for debt in Maidstone. On this latter occasion Beeston who had been in Perry's Company,[2] first appeared as Cato, and Graham as a Captain. The debtor, runs the notice, 'according to all account, is worthy of Compassion, therefore 'tis humbly hop'd that he will find a sufficient Number of humane Benefactors to relieve him from his dismal Situation'.

This is the last we hear of Smith. He fades henceforth from the advertisements. The Chatham Company went from Dover to Faversham and in September to Canterbury where they opened 'at a large Building in St Peters-Street, which is now fitting up in a commodious Manner'. Repairs were being done to the superstructure of the Butter Market Theatre by the Mayor and Corporation[3] to whom the building had reverted in 1764. At the St Peter's Theatre there were no boxes, the pit was 1s. 6d., first gallery 1s., upper gallery 6d. In the company were Richardson, Farrell, Taylor, Browne, Nelson, Rowley, Knowles, Mrs Richardson, Mrs Blanchard, Mrs Fairbairn, Mrs Taylor, Mrs Knowles and Miss Dale. At the beginning of October they moved back to the theatre

[1] Wednesday and Friday playing was forbidden during Lent.
[2] See, *ante*, p. 244.   [3] See Burmote Minutes, T. 25 June, 1765.

over the Butter Market. Judging by the number of second benefits their season was not altogether successful. They returned, however, in the winter of 1766–7, but, in race week of 1767, Mr Burton's 'real' Canterbury company appears upon the scene. This was under the management of that Thomas Burton, who, *The Theatric Tourist* tells us, was ostler at the Ship in Faversham and used to snuff the candles for Smith. He is said to have assumed the management from Smith so that we may conclude that Smith's era was at an end.[1]

The Butter Market Theatre, many times repaired and re-decorated, continued in use until 1789 and was pulled down in 1790, being replaced by Mrs Baker's Theatre in Orange Street.[2] But the rest of Canterbury's theatrical history, though neglected and remaining to be written, falls outside our period.

[1] *The Theatric Tourist* says that he continued in the East Kent circuit until 1768 but as we find Burton already in command in 1767, this may be added to Winston's numerous errors. E. C. Everard (*Memoirs of an Unfortunate Son of Thespis*, p. 89) joined the company of a Mr Smith 'called Canterbury Smith' in the early 1780's at Godalming where his share came to barely 8s. a week. This may have been our old friend or his son Garrick.

[2] Still existing as Reynolds's warehouse.

Chapter XIII

PENKETHMAN'S GREENWICH THEATRE

Greenwich fair, held at Easter and Whitsun, must have long
been a Mecca for strolling companies. That rogue and
comedian Jo. Haines, after his quarrel with Hart in 1672,
joined some strollers there 'where he both Acted and Danc'd
for some time' until, growing weary, he took his leave with
a lampoon which was first printed in *The Covent Garden
Drollery* (1672). They played then in a stable, with a
hayloft for dressing room and faggots for seats:

> I confess they had never a Scene at all
> They wanted no copy, they had th' originall;
> For the windowes being down, and most of the roof,
> How could they want Scenes, when they had prospect enough.

There was, however, no regular company or theatre in
Greenwich until the comedian William Penkethman conceived the idea of exploiting the place as a resort for actors
during the long summer vacation of the London theatres.
The first we hear of his venture is from *The Tatler*, April
16–19, 1709:

> We hear, Mr Pinkethman has remov'd his Ingenious Company
> of Strollers to Greenwich: But other Letters from Deptford say,
> the Company is only making thither, and not yet settled; but that
> several Heathen Gods and Goddesses, which are to descend in
> Machines, landed at King's-Head-Stairs last Saturday....It is
> credibly reported, that Mr D[urfe]y has agreed with Mr
> Pinkethman to have his Play [*The Modern Prophets*] acted before
> that Audience as soon as it has had its First Sixteen Days Run in
> Drury-Lane.

WILLIAM PENKETHMAN

Acting was in full fling by May 9 as we read in the *Daily Courant* of that date:

Mr Pinkethman In order to divert and oblige the Gentry and others at Greenwich, Deptford, Woolwich, Lee and other adjacent Places thereabouts has remov'd the most Famous, Artificial and Wonderful Moving Picture that came from Germany, and was to be seen at the Duke of Marlborough's Head in Fleetstreet, is now to be seen at the Hospital Tavern in Greenwich, next Door to his new Play-House, where variety of Plays are Acted every Day as in London.

Penkethman started, then, a strolling company weeks before the London theatre season had ended. On June 6 'at the desire of several Ladies in Greenwich and from London', he presented Baker's *The Fine Lady's Airs*, which had been produced at Drury Lane the previous winter, and on Monday June 20 Dryden and Lee's *Mithridates*.

The following year Penkethman developed his enterprise, putting it partly on a subscription basis, and bringing his company from the London theatres. He enlisted the patronage of Isaac Bickerstaff (Sir Richard Steele), who tells us in *The Tatler*, May 25–7, 1710 that:

The ingenious Mr Pinkethman, the Comedian, has lately left here a Paper or Ticket, to which is affixed a small Silver Medal, which is to entitle the Bearer to see One and twenty Plays at his Theatre for a Guinea. Greenwich is the Place where, it seems, he has erected his House; and his Time of Action is to be so contrived, that it is to fall in with the going and returning with the Tide. Besides, that the Bearer of this Ticket may carry down with him a particular Set of Company to the Play, striking off for each Person so introduced one of his Twenty one Times of Admittance. In this Warrant of his, he has made me an high Compliment in a facetious Distich, by Way of Dedication of his Endeavours, and desires I would recommend them to the World.

Bickerstaff attended a performance of *The Fond Husband* at the theatre on August 17 but has unfortunately left us no description of it.

Another preliminary announcement appeared in the *Daily Courant* on May 24 and succeeding days:

From Mr Pinkethman's new Theatre in Greenwich. Several Persons of Quality and others having already Subscribed there to please to take notice That all Subscribers Tickets shall pass to see any Play during the whole Season, till all Subscribers or their Friends have seen 24 Plays. He opens the 12th of June next with a new Prologue spoke by himself and a new Epilogue by him and Mr Bullock. He designs forthwith to Wait on the Nobility and others who have not already receiv'd Tickets, (and not yet Subscribed) to get their Subscriptions that he may provide a due Accommodation according to the Quality and Number of his Encouragers.

The opening was actually postponed until Thursday, June 15, when Penkethman played Don Cholerick for his own benefit, with Jubilee Dicky Norris as Sancho in *Love Makes a Man*. The advertisement states that this was the company's first performance at Greenwich and that it was wholly drawn from 'both Playhouses in London'. The following performed either regularly or occasionally during the season: from the Haymarket, Penkethman, Bullock sen. and jun., Thurmond sen. and jun., Husband; from Drury Lane, Elrington, Norris, Cory, John Leigh, Powell, Spiller, Carnaby, Cole, Cave Underhill, Freeman, and Layfield. Additional names which cannot be traced to London theatres at that time are those of Cross, Shepherd, Morris, Ryan, Bois, Verbraken and Pendry. There was a much smaller list of actresses: Mrs Granger, Mrs Sapsford, Mrs Kent, Mrs Spiller, Mrs Shepherd, Mrs Pollett, Mrs Baker, Mrs Powell, Mrs Baxter. Lacy Ryan, who three years later was to start his London career, appeared for the first time that is known on July 1 as Rosencrantz. He also played Indent in *The Fair Quaker of Deal* and Adrastus in *Oedipus*. George Powell was 'prevailed upon to act his own part of Sir Courtly Nice' on June 28 and remained with the company, playing Alexander in *The Rival Queens*, Prospero, Macbeth, The Gamester,

Oedipus, Florez in *The Royal Merchant*, Castalio in *The Orphan*, Willmore in *The Rover*, Brutus in the quarrel scene from *Julius Caesar*, Otrante in *The Maid in the Mill*, Aurenzebe, Old Marius in *Caius Marius* and Moneses in *Tamerlane*. Old Cave Underhill, who had just retired, 'to oblige Mr Pinkethman's friends', came to play Ned Blunt in *The Rover* at Penkethman's benefit on August 26.

The company acted three times a week: Mondays, Wednesdays or Thursdays, and Saturdays. The following performances are not given by Genest;[1] stars indicate first performances at Greenwich:

June 19. *Othello*	Othello—Thurmond, Iago—Shepherd, Cassio—Husband, Roderigo — Norris, Desdemona — Mrs Spiller
The Walking Statue	
June 21. **The Fatal Marriage*	Baldwin—Shepherd, Villeroy—Thurmond, Jacqueline—Leigh, Sampson—Spiller, Belford—Elrington, Isabella—Mrs Kent
June 24. **Venice Preserv'd*	Jaffeir—Thurmond, Pierre—Husband, Belvidera—Mrs Baker, Antonio—Penkethman
June 26. *Oroonoko*	Daniel—Penkethman
June 28. **Sir Courtly Nice*	Sir Courtly—Powell, Sir Thomas Calico—Penkethman, Leonora—Mrs Kent
July 3. *Tunbridge Walks*	Squib—Penkethman
July 8. *The Libertine Destroyed*	Don John—Husband, Comical Shepherd—Penkethman
July 10. *The Tempest*	Prospero—Powell, Alonzo—Cory, Ferdinand—Elrington, Antonio — Husband, Trinculo — Leigh, Ventoso—Penkethman, Mustacho —Spiller, Stephano—Shepherd, Hippolito—Mrs Kent, Caliban—Norris, Miranda—Mrs Baker, Dorinda—Mrs Shepherd
July 17. *The Fair Quaker of Deal*	Indent—Ryan

[1] *Op. cit.* vol. II, p. 468.

July 20.	*Epsom Wells*	Fribble — Penkethman, Bisket — Norris.
July 22.	The Emperor of the Moon	Harlequin—Spiller
July 24.	The Fair Quaker of Deal	
July 27.	The Recruiting Officer	Plume—Elrington, Kite—Spiller, Silvia—Mrs Spiller
July 29.	The Gamester	Gamester—Powell
	The Walking Statue	
Aug. 5.	The Island Princess	
Aug. 10.	The Fond Husband	Sneak—Penkethman
Aug. 14.	The Orphan	Castalio—Powell
	The Walking Statue	
Aug. 19.	The Mistake	Bft. Leigh—Toledo
Aug. 21.	The Gamester	
	The Walking Statue	
Aug. 29.	The Fond Husband	
Aug. 31.	Oedipus	Bft. Husband, Mrs Baker. Adrastus —Husband, Creon—Freeman
	The Falling out of Lovers is the Renewing of Love.	
Sept. 1.	The Mistake	
Sept. 20.	The Relapse	Bft. Mrs Sapsford. Foppington— Mrs Baxter, Clumsy—Shepherd, Lory—Norris
Sept. 28.	*Aurengzebe*	Bft. Penkethman, Powell. Aurengzebe—Powell

This last may not have taken place as it is advertised on the 23rd but not on the 27th.

Singing, dancing, rope dancing, and Harlequin entertainments took their usual place in the programmes. On August 19 Leigh provided for his benefit 'a new Consort of Musick, Compos'd of Trumpets, Hautboys, Kettle Drums, Double Courtal and Violins which will perform several select Sonatas before the Play begins', and which played on subsequent nights. Neither were machines lacking. *The Libertine Destroyed* was given 'With all the Sinkings and Flyings as were perform'd in the Play Originally', as were likewise *The Tempest* and *Macbeth*. *The Emperor of the Moon* had 'all

the Scenes and Machines. With a new invention first contrived by Monsieur St Everimont which Represents a Suit of
Hangings which in an Instant is transform'd to Men and
Women.' Such trappings no showman of the day could
afford to neglect.

Specially written prologues and epilogues were additional
attractions. Powell was responsible for one or two of these,
and he and Spiller recited an epilogue 'expressing the dreadful
hardships Lawyers and Players suffer in the long vacation'; a
little boy delivered Cibber's mimic epilogue burlesquing
Italian operas.

Subscribers' tickets gave admittance to any part of the house
during the season except on special occasions. One of these
was on August 5 when *The Island Princess* was performed:

> For the entertainment of Madam La Signiora Fount, Signiora
> Espagnola, Native d'Barcellone, di Cale Quallificatta (who will,
> in a particular manner, honour Mr Pinkethman that day, it being
> for his benefit, by appearing in her own Country Habit).... The
> Subscribers are desir'd not to bring their Tickets this Day, his
> Friends having promis'd to make this a Jubilee Day to him, and
> fill the House at the full Price, Mr Pinkethman being at a greater
> charge than ordinary. The Boxes will be open'd to the Pit, the
> Price of each half a Crown.

The ordinary prices were: boxes 2s. 6d., pit 1s. 6d., gallery 1s.
When 'Esquire Bickerstaff' honoured Penkethman with his
presence, however, in spite of an 'Extraordinary Charge'
for the special entertainments, Penkethman 'to oblige his
Friends,...lets 'em in at Common Prices', though subscribers
were once more excluded. Neither were they admitted to
Penkethman's benefit on August 26 when Underhill played
and the pit was again raised to 2s. 6d. On September 1
Penkethman announced that subscribers' tickets would pass
every day during the rest of his stay 'unless it be some
particular Actor's Benefit-Day', and on the 28th that they
were valid on benefit nights also; but then the season ended
on September 30.

The curtain rose at 5, 5.30 or 6 o'clock 'by reason that the Gentlemen and Ladies who come from London may have time to return again the same Night'. The newspapers often note the convenience of the tides: 'The Tide happens very luckily for Mr Pinkethman's Friends in London: it Ebbs to Greenwich from 10 in the Morning till 6 at Night; flows from 6 in the Evening till 11, it being Moonlight.'

Of the 1711 season we know less, since the advertisements that year do not give the casts. The fact that there was a regular summer season at Drury Lane must have rendered Penkethman's task more difficult. On Monday, May 21, at 5 o'clock, for the benefit of Mrs Baxter, *Pastor Fido* was acted by an entire cast of women, 'several People returning to London the same Night'. Penkethman's season does not seem to have opened until July 21, when *Othello* was given, by the same company, it is stated, as the previous year. We know from the benefits that Leigh, Husband, Thurmond jun. and Mrs Granger were of the company; additional names being those of Tenoe, Rainton, Mrs Lewis and du Brill, a dancer from the Brussels opera. Performances were given thrice weekly as before, and the last advertised was on September 20. Shakespeare, or adaptations of Shakespeare, were well represented in the repertoire, which included *Hamlet, The Jew of Venice* 'as it was performed before her Majesty on her birthday at St James', *Timon of Athens, or The Man-Hater* 'that excellent Moral Play', and *King Lear and his Three Daughters*. In addition to *King Lear* first performances at Greenwich were given of *Don Sebastian, Don Quixote* and *The Provok'd Wife*.

It is doubtful whether Penkethman thereafter continued his connection with the theatre. In 1712 on Monday, May 19, by subscription, a concert, vocal and instrumental, was performed 'by the best masters now in England', followed by dancing 'by greatest performers extant'. The concert was due to last from 5–8 o'clock and the tickets, price 2s. 6d., were 'deliver'd out at Mr Bewley's at the Royal Hospital

Coffee-House next Door to the Play-house...at Mr Pyne's at the Anchor, and the Chocolate-House upon Black-heath'. The following Wednesday *The Fatal Marriage* was to be acted and on Saturday, July 19, *The Loves of Baldo and Media*, after the Italian manner, was announced for performance by Leveridge and Mrs Lindsey, with a new prologue set to music; the boxes were laid open to the pit and the charge was 3s.[1]

No further trace of the theatre has come to light. It was probably pulled down soon after, for, according to Hasted:[2] 'An old house on the west side of the Hospital, when taken down early in the eighteenth century, was described as fitted up for a theatre.' As the Greenwich Rate Books only go back as far as 1750, it would seem impossible now to discover the site of the theatre with any certainty, but Mr S. C. Robinson, the Chief Librarian of Greenwich, thinks that it may possibly have been situated in the present Church Street, which runs down to the river west of the Hospital.

Penkethman, though he abandoned Greenwich, kept the idea of a summer theatre at the back of his mind and finally found a realisation for it in Richmond.

[1] *Spectator*, July 17.
[2] *History of Kent*, ed. H. H. Drake, Pt. 1, p. 103.

Chapter XIV

THE RICHMOND HILL THEATRES
1715–1768

The opening of Richmond Wells in 1696 set a seal on Richmond as a convenient summer resort for Londoners.

It was, however, the Prince of Wales's quarrel with his father George I in 1717 that brought the place its golden years of popularity. The Prince rented Richmond Lodge, which he subsequently bought in 1718, and there he and the Princess held a summer court to which the fashionable world flocked. But even before the quarrel Richmond had seen at least one dramatic performance,[1] that of Benjamin Griffin's tragedy *Injured Virtue*, an adaptation of Massinger and Dekker's *The Virgin Martyr*. This piece was played at the King's Arms Tavern in Southwark on November 1, 1714, and was advertised in the *Daily Courant* of that day as already printed. So that although the title-page bears the date 1715 it was evidently printed at the end of the previous year: 'As it was Acted at the Play-House in Richmond By his Grace the Duke of Southampton and Cleaveland's Servants.' It must, then, have been played in Richmond in the summer of 1714 though of the playhouse where it was acted we know nothing, and of the company only the names of the performers. Harper wrote and spoke the prologue, Mrs Deyman delivered the epilogue and the cast was as follows: Dioclesian—Durham, Aurelius—Bullock jun., Sapritius—Griffin, Theophilus—Harper, Antonius—Glover, Eumillius—Madox,

[1] Mr E. Beresford Chancellor surmised that there was an early theatre in Richmond on the evidence of the discovery on Hill Rise of a brass entry token stamped with a head of Charles II and the words 'Theatre Royal' and on the reverse 'Upper Gallerie 1671', but this was certainly a London theatre pass dropped by some careless gallant.

Priest of Jupiter—Gillo, Physician—Tollet, British Slave—
Alcock, Artimia—Mrs Deyman, Dorothea—Mrs Ellerson,
Hellena—Mrs Alcock, Calista—Mrs Lax, Christeta—Mrs
Smith. The play was dedicated to Henry Hyde Earl of
Rochester, who was Ranger of Richmond Park, because of
'The Encouragement you were pleased to give our Company
in general, and my self in particular, when the last Season we
had the Honour to Play before you at Richmond, and the
charitable Concern for, and kind Assistance of us now, since
the much lamented Death of Her Majesty[1]...had put a stop
to our Business'.

We hear nothing further of the drama in Richmond until
William Penkethman, seizing the opportunity that the
Prince of Wales's summer residence there offered, opened his
theatre on the Hill in June 1718. 'We hear', announces
Read's Weekly Journal for May 31, 1718, 'the famous Mr
Pinkethman is building a handsome Playhouse at Richmond,
for the Diversion of the Nobility and Quality that attend the
Court of their Royal Highnesses; and will begin to play
there soon after Whitsuntide, and shew the musical Picture
he has prepar'd of the Royal Family, the like of which has
never been seen in England.' Some further details of this
curious entertainment are given in the *St James's Evening Post*
for June 3, 1718.[2] Contiguous to the theatre, we learn, 'is a
room, handsomely adorned, where he will show his fine
musical Picture, in which the Royal Family are curiously
painted by the first Master of the Age; drawn from Elizabeth,
Princess of Great Britain, eldest daughter of King James 1st
and Frederick King of Bohemia, her husband, & originally
designed for the entertainment of Their Highnesses the
young Princesses'.[3] The picture was invented by Penkethman and painted by Pieter Tillemans of Antwerp and others,

[1] Queen Anne died August 1, 1714.
[2] Latreille, vol. 1, f. 293, Add. MS. 32,249.
[3] Anne b. 1709, Amelia b. 1711, Elizabeth b. 1713, daughters of the
Prince of Wales. The picture was no doubt a pointed illustration of the
Hanoverian succession.

and was later advertised as shown at Richmond before the Prince and Princess of Wales, 'to the entire Satisfaction of all the Nobility and Gentry present'.[1]

Saturday, July 19, was 'The First Time of Acting' at the new theatre. *The Spanish Fryar* and *The Stage Coach* were presented: 'The principal Comic Parts perform'd by Mr Pinkethman, Mr Bullock sen., Mr Norris, Mr Leigh, Mr Miller, and Mr Spiller, and other Parts to the best Advantage. With several Entertainments of Celebrated Dancing and Singing, which will be express'd in the Bills. Also a new Prologue by Mr Pinkethman. To begin exactly at 6 a Clock.'[2] The company was drawn from the actors of both London theatres and represented quite an array of comic talent. They acted every Saturday and Monday evening, so that performances did not interfere with the summer seasons held at the London theatres, until Monday, September 1, 'which is the last Time of acting till after Southwark Fair'.[3] Penkethman had a famous booth at the fair and the Prince of Wales one night at the Richmond Theatre 'was pleas'd to Enquire what Entertainments he and Mr Bullock had in Southwark Fair'.[4]

The following plays were presented at Richmond during this season:[5]

Saturday, July 26, Love Makes a Man with Penkethman in his original part of Don Lewis. This was by His Royal Highness's Command and was interspersed with dancing by the Moreaus, the Cookes, Pelling and Spiller 'Particularly an Italian Night Scene, between a Harlequin and a Countryman' (Cooke and Spiller). Pit and boxes were 'laid together'. (*Daily Courant*, July 25.)

[1] *Daily Post*, September 6, 1723, where the picture is described as 'All Moving and in Action, tho' painted on a Flat'.

[2] *Daily Courant*, July 17, 1718.   [3] *Ibid*. August 30.

[4] *Read's Weekly Journal*, August 23. Norris, Spiller, Pack, Leigh also had booths.

[5] Some of these are listed in Prof. Nicoll's Handlist of Plays, *Eighteenth-Century Drama, 1700–1750*.

Monday, July 28, *The Busy Body*, with Miller in the title role, and *The Stage Coach*. The performance, reported to have been excellent, began at 7 o'clock and was attended by the Prince and Princess and 'a very great Apearance of Quality and Gentry'. Penkethman spoke his epilogue riding on an ass and there was the usual dancing. (*Daily Courant*, July 26, 28, *St James' Evening Post*, July 26–9.)

Saturday, August 2, *The Committee*. Teague—Miller, Day—Penkethman, Mrs Day—Mrs Shepherd. (*Daily Courant*, August 2.)

Saturday, August 9, *Love for Love*. Angelica—Mrs Spiller, Sir Sampson—Bullock sen., Valentine—Leigh, Ben—Spiller, Scandal—Ogden, Tattle—Oates, Foresight—Shepherd, Jeremy—Williams, Mrs Frail—Mrs Finch, Mrs Foresight—Mrs Shepherd, Nurse—Mrs Elsam, Miss Prue—Mrs Moreau. The boxes were 4s., pit 2s. 6d., gallery 1s. 6d. (*Daily Courant*, August 9.)

Monday, August 11, *The Gamester*, with Leigh in the title role. (*Daily Courant*, August 11.)

Saturday, August 16, *Tunbridge Walks*, with Penkethman in his original part of Captain Squib, and *Hob, or The Country Wake*: Hob—Spiller, Friendly—Pack, 'In which he sings the Song of London is a fine Town'. (*Daily Courant*, August 16.)

Monday, August 18, *The Non-juror*, with the original prologue and epilogue. Both plays 'at common Prices'. (*Daily Courant*, August 16, *Read's Weekly Journal*, August 16.)

Saturday, August 23, *The Committee, Hob*. By Her Royal Highness's Command. The Prince and Princess of Wales attended this performance. (*Daily Courant*, August 22, *Applebee's Weekly Journal*, August 23–30.)

Monday, August 25, *A Duke and No Duke*. (*Daily Courant*, August 22.)

Saturday, August 30, *Oroonoko*, with Penkethman as Daniel 'and the diverting Entertainment of the Dancing Dogs, newly arriv'd from France, who have been shewn at Court with much success'. (*Daily Courant*, August 30.)

There is no record of any performances after Southwark fair, although the Prince of Wales did not return to London until November. Penkethman must have run his venture on a subscription basis, as he had previously done at Greenwich, for the *Daily Courant* for August 30 has a notice: 'The Tickets deliver'd to Subscribers will all be taken at this Play, or on Monday Night'. The theatre must have been a temporary one, for the next year Penkethman seems to have opened a new theatre with much éclat before the Prince and Princess of Wales[1] on June 6. This building was converted from a stable for asses, which were kept in Richmond for their milk, for riding, and for towing barges.[2] The prologue, which Penkethman spoke with an ass standing by him, 'at the opening his New Theatre' is printed in *Read's Weekly Journal* for June 13. It is worth reprinting at length both as a sample of Penkethman's humour and for the light it throws on his theatre and its construction:

> Hither I'm with my Adversary, come,
> To know from you, both his, and my own Doom.
> 'Tis said this Place belongs to Him, not Me,
> Which must determin'd be by your Decree.
> And to prepare you for this Grave Debate,
> His Case and mine, impartially I'll State.
> As all the World was first made out of Chaos,
> From a dark, dirty Barn I rais'd this Play-House.
> This End, where Palaces are seen to Day,
> And Tragick Kings their Regal Power Display;
> Was fill'd with unthrash'd Corn, and mouldy Hay.
> On those two Sides that now are fill'd with Beaus,
> Were Twelve Assnego's tied in goodly rows:
> This Plaintiff Ass was Lord of all the Race,
> And was in full Possession of the Place.
> Here, his Friends and Kindred with him Boarded,
> And here, their Store, for Years to come, was hoarded:
> Over his Head, I took the Tenement
> And to the Common him, and his, I sent.

[1] *Mist's Weekly Journal*, June 13.
[2] H. M. Cundall, *Bygone Richmond*, 1925, p. 54.

Not without Qualms from Conscience or from Nature,
For Dispossessing my poor Fellow Creature:
But He's return'd, and calls all this his Due,
And He must ha't, without great Help from you.
I've been for your Diversion, at Expence,
Which has not only run out all my Pence;
But into Debt I'm got so very deep
My Creditors assure me they can't sleep,
Unless you stretch forth your kind Hands, what think ye?
Becomes of them, this House, and Bankrupt Pinky?
I, in my turn, if I'm by you neglected,
For this Grave Spaniard here, shall be Ejected,
Who's but a Dull, Fantastick, Stubborn Tony,
For all he looks as wise as Alberoni.[1]
Yes, without you, this Painted, Gilded Play-House
Will dwindle to its first dark, dirty Chaos;
Down will the Stage come, down yon Azure Skye,
Where Clouds now move, there Corn once more will lye.
Cattle, where Beaus now sit, once more will Feast,
And what a change is that, from Beau, to Beast?
And as this Place once more will come to th' Ass,
Poor Penky'll be the Beast, that's turn'd to Grass.

This amusing prologue would lose a great deal of its point if we were to assume that the theatre was the same that had been in use the previous year; but it seems impossible to determine more definitely that it was a fresh building. Neither can we know more of the site than that it was below that of the later theatre on the Hill. Full details of the programme for the opening night are supplied by the *Daily Courant* for June 6:

By His Royal Highness's Command At the Opening of Mr Penkethman's New Theatre at Richmond, . . . will be presented the last new Comedy call'd Chit Chat.[2] To which will be added the Comedy in the last Act of the Island Princess, wherein Mr Penkethman and Mr Norris play their original Parts. Likewise

[1] Cardinal Alberoni whose *History* had recently been published.
[2] By Thomas Killigrew. It had been produced at Drury Lane in February.

a Prologue spoke by Mr Penkethman in Company of an Ass, Ground Landlord of the Place, upon a Writ of Ejectment, with 2 Entertainments of Dancing by Mons. and Madm. Sa[l]e, serious and comic, a Shepherdess, with the Turkey Cock, and a Mimick Song of an old Woman; and two Dances, viz. the Irish Trot, and the Turkey-cock Dance by Mrs Willis. To begin at 6 exactly.

The only two performances recorded this season are those for Monday, August 31 and Saturday, September 5 when, 'by particular Recommendation of some Persons of Quality', a previously unacted and anonymous comedy called *The Soldier's Stratagem* was presented. The first performance was enhanced by 'Dancing by Mr Moreau and Mrs Moreau, who likewise plays one of the principal Parts; being the first time of their appearing there this Summer'; on the second night for the benefit of the author *The Stage Coach* was added to the programme with Miller as Squire Somebody and dancing by Miss Scooling.[1] Both performances took place at 7 o'clock.

On July 6 Penkethman and Norris presented their burlesque of Addison's *Cato*. The story is told by Chetwood:[2] 'After the Death of that celebrated Author Mr Addison,[3] the merry Mr Penkethman, at his Theatre at Richmond, play'd the Tragedy of Cato, or, rather, defil'd those noble Sentiments of Liberty, out of such merry Mouths. Norris was ridiculously dressed for Cato, Penkethman Juba, low Comedians for the other Characters, and the two Ladies supplied by Men of the same Cast: Yet a blind Man might have borne with Norris in the Roman Patriot, for he spoke it with all the Solemnity of a suffering Hero; while Penkethman, and the rest of the motley Tribe, made it as ridiculous by Humour and Action: And yet some of the first Rank in the Kingdom seemed highly diverted, whilst others invoked the Manes of the dead Roman and Briton to rise, and avenge

[1] *Daily Courant*, August 31, September 5.
[2] *A General History of the Stage*, 1749, p. 198.   [3] In June, 1719.

their own Cause. I remember the next Morning the following
four lines were pasted on the Door of the Playhouse:

> While Greatness hears such Language spoke,
> Where godlike Freedom's made a Joke;
> Let such mean Souls be never free
> To taste the Sweets of Liberty.

An illustrious Nobleman, who had a Seat at Richmond,
seeing several People reading the Lines as he was riding up
the Hill, stop'd and perused them and said, in his usual grave
Manner—I wish the Poetry had been better.' Lady Bristol
was another protester, and she wrote from Richmond to her
husband[1] on July 7 that, after she had been told how nobly
Addison died, 'I had no patience to see his play burlesqued
as it was the last night for the entertainment of their Royal
Highnesses; I need not give any other description of it than
telling you who acted; Cato by Dicky Norris, Juba by
Penkethman, Marcia by young Wilkes, Lucia by Shepherd,
Porcius by Fieldhouse, and the rest suitable; their audience
was much too good for them, for there was a great many
people of quality.' These few lines only of the burlesque are
now extant:[2]

> *Portius.* It is indeed a damn'd dark cloudy morning,
> Yon Ass's bray portends approaching rain;
> The clouds big-bellied teem with drizzling showers,
> To wail the fate of Rome, our mother city
> And Cato's too, our old dejected dad.

We know nothing of the Richmond theatre for the next
two years, but in 1722 John Williams's *Richmond Wells* was
brought out there. The author's benefit night was on
Monday, July 23. *Richmond Wells* is a quite undistinguished
comedy of manners, with the usual array of gulls, cheats and

---

[1] *Letter-Books of John Hervey*, 1894, vol. II, p. 345.
[2] A. Barkas, *Richmond Notes*, vol. XVII, in the Richmond Reference
Library. The source whence they were copied is unknown. Cf. the
opening lines of *Cato*.

wits, but it has its interest because it gives us glimpses of
Richmond and its society. 'Why this', exclaims Gaylove, 'is
Richmond—the admir'd Richmond, the frequented Rich-
mond—the Seat of Pleasures, and Center of Delights, in a
Word Un petit Beau Monde...Here's Musick, Balls, Walks,
Dancing, Raffling, and, to crown all, a Play-house.' Later
he makes a comparison 'as glad of it, as she us'd to be of
going to Penkethman's Booth at Bartholomew-Fair; or as
she is now of going to his Play-House when he pleases to
entertain us'. The cast was as follows: Randome—Shepherd,
Loveworth—Chas. Williams, Gaylove—Wilks jun., Cheatly
—Oates, Tony Souscrown—Miller, Robin—Harper, Belinda
—Mrs Morgan, Mrs Fainal—Mrs Wetherilt. The prologue
was spoken by W. Wilks and the epilogue by Penkethman.
The author in his Preface makes bitter complaint of mis-
management and injustice. 'How scandalously', he laments,
'I was abus'd', and proceeds to specify that whole speeches
were cut out and acts left unfinished, despite his earnest
entreaties. The acting, he adds, was an affront to the assembly
of ladies and gentlemen 'who might with Reason expect
a better Performance from his Majesties Servants'. He
acknowledges his obligations, however, to 'the incompar-
able Mr Miller' who 'added more Beauties than I imagin'd so
mean a Part was capable of receiving', to William Wilks and
to Mrs Wetherilt 'for the Industrious Care she took to render
herself Mistress of her Part'. 'As for the other Woman', he
adds, 'I am a Stranger to her Merit, not having had her at
any Rehearsal, nor even seen her till about two Hours before
she appear'd publickly in her Character; This Misfortune I
must charge upon the Management, as likewise deficiency in
the Musick etc.' But Williams's chief grievance was against
Penkethman for whom he had written the part of Randome:
'that either he should be so destitute of good Nature, or I
of good Fortune, as not to be able by any Arguments or
Considerations, to gain him to Study and Perform it. I may
be so bold to say, that had he oblig'd me so far, the Character

(without derogating from Mr Sʜᴇᴘʜᴀʀᴅ's Deserts) would have appeared in a much greater Beauty.' Even allowing that Williams was smarting under a sense of injustice it looks as though the acting was not up to the standard of Drury Lane whence the actors were drawn, and that Penkethman's management was, to say the least of it, haphazard.

The last performance, and the only other one advertised for the 1722 season, was that of a new dramatic entertainment, never before acted, called *The Distressed Beauty; or The London Prentice*, on Monday, August 20. This was Penkethman's benefit night and was by the Prince's command; 'The Boxes', it is noted, 'will all be illuminated with Wax Candles'.[1]

The Distressed Beauty served afterwards at Southwark fair, and the following year Penkethman had descended to drolls. On Monday, September 2,[2] by the Prince's command, *Pyramus and Thisbe* by Shakespeare and Leveridge was given with Penkethman as Pyramus and Norris as Wall. This was followed by another droll, *The Blind Beggar of Bethnal Green*, as well as by rope and other dancing. Box tickets were to be had from Penkethman's house and places could be taken there. According to the *Daily Post* (September 5) the picture of the Royal Family was also shown to an audience of 'Nobility, Gentry, and Ladies upwards of 200, who all express'd a general satisfaction'. For 1724 we have much fuller accounts. On May 28, the King's birthday, Penkethman staged a demonstration of Loyalty, illuminating the windows of his house upon the hill and hoisting 'a fine silk Flag'. A new birthday song composed for the occasion was sung by Mrs Hill to the accompaniment of trumpet and hautboy, and 'The Gentlemen and Ladies were treated with wine etc. & the Commonalty with a Barrel of Ale'.[3]

---

[1] *Daily Post*, August 20. (Burney, *Theatrical Register*.)
[2] *Read's Weekly Journal*, August 31; Latreille, vol. ɪɪ, f. 97 v. wrongly gives Monday, September 7, which Nicoll emends incorrectly to September 9.
[3] Latreille, vol. ɪɪ, f. 112.

On Saturday, June 20 *Peele's Weekly Journal* reports: 'We hear that a select Company of Comedians from the Theatre Royal, design to perform Saturdays and Mondays at Mr Penkethman's Theatre in Richmond. They begin on Monday next with a Play of Sir John Vanbrugh's call'd The False Friend; with a choice Band of Musick and Entertainments of Dancing.' The following are the plays and casts for the season, the actors being drawn from both London theatres:

Saturday, June 27, The Drummer. Truman—Orfeur, Fantome—Chapman, Tinsel—Bridgewater, Vellum—Norris jun., Butler—West, Coachman—Harper, Gardiner—Norris sen., Lady Truman—Mrs Orfeur, Abigail—Mrs Gulick. Singing and dancing by Haughton, Bridgewater, Mrs Willis. (*Daily Post*, June 25.)

Monday, June 29, The Stratagem. Scrub—Norris, Archer—Bridgewater, Aimwell—Chapman, Sir Charles—Williams, Gibbet—Norris jun., Foigard—West, Boniface—Harper, Mrs Cherry—Mrs Roberts, Country Woman—Mrs Willis, Mrs Sullen—Mrs Haughton, Dorinda—Mrs Orfeur, Lady Bountiful—Mrs Gulick. (*Daily Post*, June 29.)

Saturday, July 4, A Duke and No Duke. Trappolin—Harper, Barberino—Roberts, Prudentia—Mrs Haughton. *Hob.* Concerto by Corelli, singing and dancing. (*Daily Post*, July 3.)

Saturday, July 11, The Busy Body. Sir Francis Gripe—Norris, Scentwell—Mrs Vincent, Charles—Williams. Entertainments between each act. (*Daily Post*, July 10.)

Monday, July 13, The Country Lasses. 'With the Original Songs and Dances, and other Decorations proper to the Play.' First time at Richmond. (*Daily Post*, July 13.)

Saturday, July 18, The Spanish Fryar. Fryar—Harper, Torrismond—Roberts, Bertran—Orfeur, Raymond—Chapman, Pedro—Williams, Alphonso—Norris jun., Queen—Mrs Gulick, Elvira—Mrs Haughton, Teresa—Mrs Vincent, Gomez—Norris sen., Colonel—Bridgewater.

Monday, August 3, A Duke and No Duke and The Stage

Coach. By their Royal Highnesses' Command, benefit Chetwood. Nicodemus Somebody—Miller. Singing and dancing. Tickets given out for *Merry Wives* taken at this play. (Burney, *op. cit.*)

On August 1 Penkethman celebrated the anniversary of the Hanoverian succession 'at his new House upon Richmond Hill...with his usual Rejoycings, his Flag spread, Musick, Bonfires, and his Windows finely Illuminated, and several Sorts of Liquors distributed among the Multitude without Doors: The People pleas'd to see such Loyalty, with Huzza's Dancing, and singing round his Bonfire (of the first Magnitude) contributed to the General Joy.'[1]

It is interesting to note that Penkethman's role as entertainer was not confined to the Theatre but that he seems to have been accepted as a kind of master of the ceremonies in Richmond society. On September 20, 1725, he died at Richmond and was buried in the parish church four days later.[2] By his will Penkethman, who styles himself 'of Richmond...Gentleman', confirms a deed of gift by which his property, probably including the theatre, passed to Anne Atkins 'of Richmond...spinster'.[3]

Thus ends the first period in the history of the Richmond Theatre.[4] Continuity is, however, preserved to some extent by the fact that the next venturer, Thomas Chapman, had been an actor in Penkethman's Richmond company in 1724. The *Daily Journal* for June 4, 1730, has news from Richmond dated June 1:

There is building, and almost finish'd here, a small, but very neat and regular THEATRE, a little higher on the Hill than where

---

[1] Burney, *op. cit.*

[2] *Parish Registers of Richmond*, J. Challenor Smith, 1905, vol. II.

[3] Somerset House, Romney, 217.

[4] In *Brice's Weekly Journal*, August 1, 1729, we read: 'Mr Rich, of the New Theatre in Lincolns-Inn-Fields, went down last Saturday to Richmond where, in the Gardens, he entertain'd the Queen and Royal Family with the Comedy call'd Hob, or the Country Wake.'

the late Mr Penkethman's stood. We hear it will be open'd next Week by a Company of Comedians from the Theatre Royal in Lincoln's-Inn-Fields and that their first Play will be the Recruiting Officer...and that they design to perform three or four Times a Week during the Summer Season, which we expect will be a very good one.

It is from *The Theatric Tourist* that we learn that this theatre was built by Chapman, 'an actor on the London boards, (to whom Ned Shuter was errand boy)', and, like Penkethman, a low comedian. His theatre was an immediate success, as we learn from the *Daily Journal* of July 14. 'We hear from Richmond...that the Company from the Theatre Royal in Lincoln's Inn Fields acting in the new erected Theatre there, meet with universal Approbation and Encouragement.' Plays and casts advertised this year are as follows:

Wednesday, June 24, The Busy Body. Sir Jealous Traffick—Bullock, Sir Francis Gripe—Smith, Sir George Airy—Chapman, Charles—Milward, Marplot—Morgan, Whisper—Haughton, Miranda—Mrs Morgan, Isabinda—Mrs Grace, Patch—Mrs Martin, Scentwell—Mrs Rice. Dancing by Mons. Nivelon, Mrs Ogden and others. Boxes 3s., pit 2s., gallery 1s. (*Daily Journal*, June 24.)

Thursday, June 25, The Beggar's Opera. (*Daily Journal*, June 24.)

Thursday, July 16, The Provok'd Husband. Lord Townly—Chapman, Manly—Milward, Lady Townly—Mrs Templer, Lady Grace—Mrs Grace, John Moody—Bullock, Myrtilla—Mrs Chapman.

Saturday, July 18, Love Makes a Man. (*Daily Journal*, July 15.)

Thursday, August 6, Love for Love. Benefit Milward. (*Daily Journal*, August 5.)

Tuesday, October 20, The Busy Body. Attended by Prince of Wales and Princess Caroline.

Tuesday, October 27, The Recruiting Officer. His Royal Highness's Command. (*Daily Journal*, October 26.)

Though the company was rather different from any under

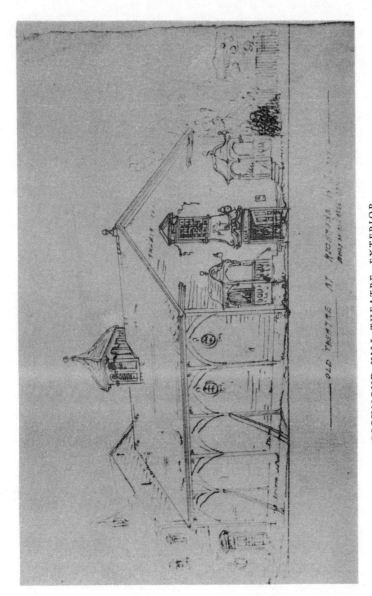

RICHMOND HILL THEATRE, EXTERIOR

Penkethman, Chapman, Bullock and Mrs Morgan alone reappearing, the repertoire shows surprising conservatism. It is to be noted that acting days were no longer confined to Mondays and Saturdays, and that the new Prince of Wales continued his father's patronage of the theatre.

The *Daily Journal* for June 8, 1731, reports 'that part of the Company from the Theatre Royal in Lincoln's Inn Fields will open their Theatre at Richmond the latter end of this week and being willing to give a general satisfaction they have strengthened their Company with several additional persons —particularly the pleasant and facetious Mr Hippisley'. The following plays were given; first performances in Richmond are starred:

Thursday, July 1, ★The Constant Couple. Sir Harry Wildair —Chapman. Dancing by Hippisley. (*Daily Journal,* June 30.)

Thursday, July 8, The Merry Wives of Windsor. Falstaff 'to be attempted by a Gentleman, being his first Appearance on any Stage'; Ford—Milward, Page—Ogden, Shallow— Chapman, Slender—Morgan, Caius—Hall, Host—Bullock, John Rugby—Smith, Simple—Woodward, Mrs Ford—Mrs Templer, Mrs Page—Mrs Grace, Anne Page—Mrs Morgan, Mrs Quickly—Mrs Martin, Sir Hugh Evans—Hippisley. Dancing by Smith and Mrs Ogden. (*Daily Journal,* July 7.)

Thursday, July 15, ★Love's Last Shift. Sir Wm. Wisewould —Hippisley, Sir Novelty Fashion—Chapman, Loveless— Milward, Armanda—Mrs Templer, Maid—Mrs Chapman. (Latreille, vol. II, f. 371.)

Thursday, July 22, ★The Conscious Lovers. Sealand— Haughton, Myrtle—Salway, Daniel—Young Woodward, Isabella—Mrs Rice, Lucinda—Mrs Chapman. (*Daily Courant,* July 21.)

Chapman was more enterprising this season and put on three plays that had never been acted at Richmond, though acting days seemed to have been confined to Thursdays. That Richmond was still a popular resort is proved by the fact that that year a new road in from the Hill was made for coaches and horsemen 'private and free from Dust'.[1] Indeed, stag hunting in Richmond Park was a favourite pastime of the Prince of Wales and other members of the royal family, who would often pay a visit to the theatre after their exertions. Thus, although there are no advertisements for the performance, we know that on Saturday, July 22, 1732, after a hunt, the Prince of Wales, Duke of Cumberland and Princesses Mary, Caroline and Louisa saw *The Careless Husband* at Richmond and then returned to Kensington at 11 o'clock.[2] On Thursday, August 17, for the benefit of the Morgans *Love's Last Shift* was acted 'By the Company of Comedians' with Chapman as Loveless and W. Bullock as Sir Novelty Fashion; Hall, Rosco, Haughton, Morgan, Bullock, Mrs Templer, Mrs Morgan, Mrs Grace, Mrs Martin and Mrs Chapman were also in the cast. The afterpiece was *The What D'ye Call It* in which Mrs Grace, Mrs Rice and Bardin also played. Morgan spoke a new epilogue riding on an ass. The usual charges of 3s. for boxes, 2s. for pit, and 1s. for gallery were made and the performance began at 6. The audience was reminded that 'The Night will be illuminated with the Silver Rays of Cynthia'.[3]

There is no further information until 1736. There may or may not have been performances in the intervening years but none is advertised. On Saturday, July 24, 1736, there was a stag hunt in the Park 'and in the Evening their Royal Highnesses the Prince and Princess of Wales, attended by several Persons of Quality, went to the Theatre at Richmond to see the Comedy of the Tender Husband and the Honest Yorkshireman (which was perform'd to a splendid Audience with universal Applause) and afterwards they returned to Kensington'.[4] Again on July 31, 'attended by several Persons

---

[1] *Daily Advertiser*, July 24, 1731.
[2] Barkas, *Richmond Notes*, vol. v. I have to thank Mr Piper, the Richmond Librarian, for permission to see these.
[3] *Daily Post*, August 16, 1732.
[4] *London Daily Post*, July 26.

of Quality and Distinction', they saw *The Funeral* and returned, this time, to Kew.[1] On August 14 they witnessed *The Squire of Alsatia* and *Damon and Phillida*,[2] and on the 21st the Princess saw *The Wonder* 'which was performed, with the Farce of the Devil to Pay to a numerous and polite Audience, with great Applause, for the Benefit of Mr Turbutt and Mrs Pritchard'.[3] By royal command at Chapman's benefit on August 28 *The Stratagem* and *Flora* were played, and tickets delivered for *The False Friend* were taken for this.[4]

There is another gap until 1740 when, on Saturday, August 9, the *London Daily Post* announces, for the benefit of Turbutt and Marten, *The Busy Body* once again, with Chapman as Marplot, and *The Devil to Pay* in which Sir John Loverule was to be played by a gentleman. The prices were as usual and tickets were to be had and places taken at the Three Compasses opposite the theatre. Nothing more then until 1743 when *The Beggar's Opera* was advertised for Saturday, July 30, to be played by a company of comedians from the 'Theatres Royal'.[5] By particular desire Lowe from Drury Lane played Macheath, 'Being the only Time of his appearing upon this Stage', Polly—Mrs Vincent, Peachum—Chapman, Lockit—Turbutt, Lucy—Mrs King. Tickets at the usual prices could be had either at the Three Compasses or at Mr Slater's, the Prince William's Head, upon the Hill. This was Turbutt's benefit and a crowd was evidently expected for 'Ladies are desir'd to send their Servants early to keep Places, to prevent Mistakes'.

On August 6, for Blakes's benefit, *The Careless Husband* was at first announced but gave place to *The Beggar's Opera* with Blakes as Filch. The afterpiece was *The Lying Valet* with Chapman in the title role and Blakes as Gayless.[6] The gallery is put at 2s. but this may be a printing error. In 1744

---

[1] *London Daily Post*, August 2.   [2] *Ibid*. August 16.
[3] *Ibid*. August 25.   [4] Latreille, vol. III, f. 297.
[5] Covent Garden, Drury Lane. *London Daily Post*, July 27 and 29, 1743.   [6] *London Daily Post*, August 3 and 6.

we have record only of the last night of acting on Saturday, September 8.[1] This was the first occasion on which the company adopted the usual method of evading the Licensing Act, and they advertised a concert between the divisions of which would be performed, gratis, *Richard III* with the following cast: Richard—Chapman, King Henry—Blakes, Buckingham—Philips, Richmond—Cross, Lord Mayor—Morgan, Lord Stanley—Naylor, Ratcliff—Berkley, Catesby—Shuter, Tyrrel—Blunt, Duchess of York—Mrs Egerton, Queen—Mrs Mullart, Lady Anne—Mrs Horsington, Prince Edward—Miss Ferguson, Duke of York—Miss Naylor. This was followed by the first performance in Richmond of *Chrononhotonthologos* with Philips in the title role and Shuter as the Cook. The performance is advertised as being at the Assembly Room but a news paragraph gives the theatre.[2] The occasion is noteworthy as being one of Shuter's first appearances on the Richmond stage. It is curious that Chapman should have chosen to play Richard III, a part wholly unsuited to his talents as a low comedian, but he was apparently addicted to attempting roles quite outside his range. For this Tom Davies takes him to task: 'At his own theatre of Richmond, where he had the double claim of manager and principal performer, he exerted his power, to the destruction of his own property, as well as of all propriety. Instead of Tom in The Conscious Lovers...he would needs assume the fine gentleman, in the person of young Bevil', and 'at Richmond, too, he strutted in the robes of King Richard III to empty benches.'[3]

Chapman was, however, sufficiently encouraged to revive *Richard III* the next year, when the following plays were presented by a company from both London theatres:

Saturday, July 6, Richard III. Richard—Chapman, King Henry VI—Cashel, Richmond—Cross, Buckingham—

---

[1] Genest incorrectly gives the month as July.
[2] *General Advertiser*, September 7 and 8.
[3] *Dramatic Miscellany*, 1784, vol. I, p. 166.

Philips, Queen Elizabeth—Mrs Vincent. (*General Advertiser*, July 5, 1745.)

Saturday, August 17, *The Way of the World*. Benefit Cross. Mirabel—Cashel, Fainall—Cross, Witwoud—Chapman, Marwould—Mrs Horsington, Millamant—Mrs Vincent, Lady Wishfort—Mrs Egerton. *The Walking Statue* not acted here for 10 years. Toby—Chapman. Tickets and places at Mr Chapman's and of Mrs Tomlin at the Three Compasses. (*Daily Advertiser*, August 15.)

Saturday, August 24,[1] *Macbeth*. 'With all the Original Musick, Songs, Dances and other Decorations.' Benefit Philips. Macbeth—Cashel, Macduff—Chapman, Banquo—Cross, Lenox—Goodfellow, Lady Macduff—Mrs Horsington, Seyward—Philips, King—Stoppelaer, Malcolm—Miss Ferguson, Donalbain—Shuter, Seyton—Martin, Fleance—Miss Morrison, First Witch—Miss Haughton, Second—Mrs Egerton, Third—Mrs Haughton, First Murderer—Lynham, Second—Brown, Hecate with songs—Stoppelaer, Lady Macbeth—Mrs Vincent. *The Mock Lawyer*. Not here for 10 years. Feignwell—Chapman, Cheatley—Shuter. 'With all the Entertainments proper for both the Play and Farce, viz. In Act III. The Witches Dance', and after the play, a hornpipe by a child of five. ' 'Tis humbly hop'd all Gentlemen and Ladies will be so good as to take Tickets, to prevent Mistakes, at the Door.' Boxes, stage, upper boxes 3s., pit 2s., gallery 1s. (*General Advertiser*, August 20, 22.)

Wednesday, August 28, *The Beggar's Opera*. Benefit Goodfellow. Macheath—Cashel, Peachum—Philips, Lockit—Marten, Mat o' the Mint—Goodfellow, Filch—Shuter, Mrs Peachum—Mrs Copin, Lucy—Gentlewoman, Polly—Mrs Vincent. *The School Boy*. (*Daily Advertiser*, August 25.)

Saturday, August 31, *Measure for Measure*. Benefit Cashel. Duke—Cashel, Angelo—Philips, Claudio—Cross, Escalus —Goodfellow, Provost—Marten, Lucio—Chapman, Isabella

---

[1] Genest incorrectly gives 25.

—Mrs Vincent, Mariana—Mrs Horsington, Juliet—Miss Haughton. *The Toy Shop*. Toyman—Chapman. (*Daily Advertiser*, August 29.)

Monday, September 9, *Don Sebastian. Benefit Chapman. *The Anatomist*, Mons. le Medecine—Blakes, Crispin—Chapman. Tickets and places for the Boxes to be taken of Mrs Chapman, Office Keeper, next door to the Theatre. (*Daily Advertiser*, September 7.)

Wednesday, September 11, The Busy Body. Benefit Marten, last performance of season. Sir George Airy—Cashel, Charles—Cross, Marplot—Chapman, Miranda—Mrs Vincent. *The Devil to Pay* Sir John Loverule with songs—Lowe, Jobson—Turbutt. 'Those Gentlemen and Ladies who intend to honour me with their Company (in order to prevent mistakes) are humbly requested to send for Tickets which may be had and places taken at Mr Ansel's, the George in Richmond.' (*Daily Advertiser*, September 9.)

Chapman also took his company over to Twickenham where he opened on Tuesday, July 23, with *The Conscious Lovers*; on August 13 he played *Richard III* for the benefit of Mrs Chapman, Master Shuter and Miss Morrison, the afterpiece being *Damon and Phillida*. He repeated *The Conscious Lovers* on September 3 with *The Toy Shop*; gave, on September 6, *Macbeth* and *The Anatomist* for the benefit of Cross, Philips and Mrs Vincent, and, on September 10, the last night, *The Beggar's Opera* and *The Anatomist* for Cashel's benefit.[1]

This notable season was much more ambitious than previous ones. Drama and tragedy held their own for the first time against comedy and farce, which hitherto had monopolised the repertoire. Shakespeare especially was, for the first time, well represented albeit, in two out of three cases, by adaptations. Shuter again played small parts with the company.

Advertisements of performances for the years 1746-53 have been collected from the *Daily Advertiser* by Mr Emmett

[1] *Daily Advertiser*, August 10, 31; September 5, 7.

L. Avery and reprinted in *Notes and Queries*.[1] It will suffice
here to summarise his findings. In 1746 the company opened
at Twickenham on Wednesday, June 4, and finished their
season at Richmond on Saturday, September 27, with a
performance of *The Beggar's Opera* in which Beard and Mrs
Dunstall made their first appearance on the Richmond
boards as Macheath and Lucy. On this occasion too Woodward played Corporal Cuttum and Harlequin Statue in a
pantomime of that name. The company divided its attention
about equally between the two theatres at Twickenham and
Richmond. First performances at Richmond were *Sir
Courtly Nice*, and *Phebe; or The Beggar's Wedding* on August 9,
The Lying Lover on September 1, *The Resolute Husband* on
September 13, and *The Silent Woman* on September 20.
Othello had its first performance at Twickenham on Sep-
tember 16: Othello—Cashel, Iago—Cross, Desdemona—
Mrs Vincent, Emilia—Mrs Bland. Also in the company
were Havard, Burton, Bridges, Morgan, Philips, Chapman,
Stoppelaer, Blakes, Shuter, Conyers, Beckham, Lowe, Ben-
craft, Mrs Havard, Mrs Bridges, Miss Ferguson, Miss
Morrison, Miss Haughton, Master Shuter.

Mr Avery remarks that he can find no advertisements of
the company's activities in 1747 before August 17; this was
doubtless because of the death of Thomas Chapman of a
fever on July 14.[2] Like his predecessor he is buried in the
parish church;[3] unlike him he left no will, but the administra-
tion of his goods was left to his widow Hannah.[4] The rate
books refer to the theatre as Mrs Chapman's music room
until 1756, when she is put down as the late Mrs Chapman;
in 1757 the rates were paid by one Perkins; in 1769 rent was
£16, and the following year the rates were paid by a Mr
Williams. By 1772 the building is referred to as the old
playhouse, and by 1774 the name Williams and the term

[1] 1937, pp. 290, 312, 328.   [2] *General Advertiser*, July 16.
[3] *Parish Registers of Richmond*, vol. II.
[4] Somerset House. Admon. Act. Surrey, July 1748.

playhouse both drop out.[1] Who ran the theatre on Chapman's death we do not know, but the season opened at Richmond on August 17 and came to an end on October 13. The company again divided their attention between Richmond and Twickenham. *The Refusal* given on September 12 and *The Wife's Relief* on September 19 had not been acted at Richmond previously. Two benefits, one at Richmond and one at Twickenham, were given for the widow Chapman. Lee made his first appearance at Richmond as Ranger in *The Suspicious Husband* on October 3, and acted Hamlet on the last night to the Ophelia of Mrs Vincent and the Polonius of Shuter. Others in the company were Morgan, Bridges, Burton, Gibson, Rosco, Hippisley, Paget, James, Storer, Dancer, Lynham, Mrs Bland, Mrs Vincent, Mrs Storer, Mrs Bridges, Miss Ferguson, Miss Morrison, and Miss Haughton.

The 1748 season opened at Richmond with a first performance there of *King Lear and His Three Daughters* on June 4, and *The Pilgrim* was revived, after ten years, on August 8. At Twickenham the company gave *Harlequin's Vagaries* for the first time and ended their season on October 5 with a benefit for Mrs Chapman. In the company this year were Cross, Storer, Bridges, Lee, Gibson, Ridout, Cushing, Morgan, Dunstall, Bencraft, Anderson, Mrs Vincent, Mrs Storer, Mrs Bridges, Mrs Cushing, Mrs Ridout, Miss Ferguson, Miss Haughton, and Masters Bennet, Cross, and Shawford. On August 11, 1748, Horace Walpole wrote to George Montagu:

Our great Company at Richmond and Twickenham has been torn to pieces by civil dissensions, but they continue acting. Mr Lee, the ape of Garrick, not liking his part, refused to play it, and had the confidence to go into the pit as spectator. The actress, whose benefit was in agitation, made her complaints to the audience, who obliged him to mount the stage; but since that he is retired from the company. I am sorry he was such a coxcomb for he was our best.[2]

[1] Barkas's *Richmond Notes*, vol. v.
[2] *Letters of Horace Walpole*, ed. Toynbee, vol. ii, p. 331. Lee, an actor from Drury Lane, was acting again for his benefit on September 7.

On September 3, Walpole wrote of another visit:[1]

I am just come from the play at Richmond, where I found the Duchess of Argyll and Lady Betty Campbell, and their court. We had a new actress, a Miss Clough; an extremely fine tall figure, and very handsome: she spoke very justly, and with spirit. Garrick is to produce her next winter;[2] and a Miss Charlotte Ramsay, a poetess, and deplorable actress. Garrick, Barry, and some more of the players were there to see these new comedians; it is to be their seminary.

London managers evidently did not fail to grasp the obvious opportunities presented by a summer theatre for trying out new players.

Both theatres continued in 1749, but Mr Avery quotes the following note to show that the Twickenham venture was far from flourishing:

As the indifferent Success generally met with here will not suffice to defray the nightly Expences of performing at this Theatre, we shall trouble the Town with a Play but once a Week, except desir'd, which shall be constantly on Tuesdays, when the Company will endeavour to the utmost of their Power to please, and hope those Gentlemen and Ladies who are kind enough to think so will not let them leave the Town losers.

Another notice offers apologies that the company had dismissed and caused disappointment to some patrons, and promises thereafter to play every time they advertise. The season lasted from June 12 to October 2. *Lethe* and *The Albion Queens* were plays new to Richmond, and *Tunbridge Walks* was revived. We do not know who the manager of the company was, but he had a benefit on September 16, and Mrs Chapman had hers on the last night. The company included Lee, Naylor, Eden, Scrase, Shuter, Costollo, Philips, Wildair, Gibson, Arthur, Bennet, Dunstall, Delane, Oates, Graven, Lacey, Mrs Vincent, Mrs Bennet, Mrs Cowper,

---

[1] *Op. cit.* p. 337.
[2] Miss Clough does not, however, appear in Drury Lane casts 1748–9.

Mrs Mathews, Mrs Ridout, Mrs Dunstall, Mrs Ogilvie, Miss Haughton, Miss Ferguson, Miss Falkner, and Miss Young.

In 1750 the company opened on June 16. They continued to confine their operations at Twickenham to Tuesday nights, but announced that they would never 'dismiss on any Occasion, being determin'd to perform every Night we advertise'. New pieces were *Merope* on July 14 and *Mock Pamela, or a Kind Caution to all Country Coxcombs*, an otherwise unknown piece, on August 4; *As You Like It* and *The Tender Husband* were the revivals. The players were Cross, Falkner, Bryan, Hackett, Shuter, Philips, Wildair, Castle, Paddick, Reinhold, Roberts, Lacey, Lee (only one performance), Mattocks, Ridout, Sherriff, Mrs Vincent, Mrs Toogood, Mrs Mathews, Miss Ferguson, Miss Young, Miss Haughton, Miss Toogood (who made her stage début as the Duke of York in *Richard III* on July 28), and Masters Brett and Mattocks. A playbill from this year of a performance of *Don Quixote Part II* and *Miss in Her Teens* which is reproduced by Crisp in his *Richmond and Its Inhabitants* (1866) can now be dated July 30. A note on it reveals that the practice of entering the theatre late at cheap rates obtained at Richmond as elsewhere, and ''Tis humbly hoped no Gentlemen or Ladies will take it amiss that nothing less than the full Price will be taken during the whole Performance'. There is extant, too, a song in praise of Richmond, written by Cross and sung by Wildair at the theatre this year.[1]

In 1751 the same arrangements continued. A young gentlewoman made her first appearance on any stage as Indiana in *The Conscious Lovers* on July 10 and her second as Miranda in *The Busy Body* on July 24; another lady played Polly in the *The Beggar's Opera* on September 14, the closing night. In the company this year were Shuter, Philips, Robertson, Francis, Marr, Cross, Mattocks, Shepherd, Lee, Sturt, Cooke, Storer, Brown, Lacey, Lowe, Mrs Bambridge,

[1] *Richmond Theatre Cuttings*, Richmond Public Library.

Mrs Robertson, Mrs Lee, Mrs Mathews, Mrs Price, Miss Davies, and Master Cross.

In 1752 the company played from June 13 to September 27. The new plays were *Zara*, *The Double Disappointment* with Shuter as Phelim O'Blunder, and *Don Quixote in England*; revivals were *A New Way to Pay Old Debts*, *The Silent Woman*, *A Duke and No Duke*, *The Gamester* and *King Lear* with Cooke in the title role and Miss Ibbott as Cordelia. The company consisted of Cross, Blakes, Philips, Burton, Macgeorge, Shuter, Ackman, Scrase, Vaughan, Davies from Dublin, English, Mrs Jones, Mrs Davies, Mrs Mathews, Miss Ross, Miss Ibbott, Miss Woodward, Miss Moore, Miss Helm and Miss Davies.

The following year, 1753, the company gave up their Twickenham theatre and confined themselves to Richmond. Advertisements run from June 23 to September 29. *The Fine Lady's Airs* on June 30 and Jones's *The Earl of Essex* on August 25 were new productions and *Macbeth* was revived with Dancer as Macbeth and Mrs Cowper as Lady Macbeth. A young gentlewoman who had never appeared on any stage played Miss Notable in *The Lady's Last Stake*, and Mrs Sullen in *The Beaux Stratagem*. In the company were Parker, Dancer, Sturt, Vernon, Murphy, Stoppelaer, Dennet, Howard from Covent Garden, Walker, Settree, Brudnal, Cross, Scrase, Burton, Ackman, Philips, Parker, Cross jun., Mrs Pye, Mrs Cowper, Mrs Mathews, Mrs Harvey, Mrs Pond, Miss Mills, Mdlle Hulette, Miss Pond, Miss Helm, Miss Davies, Miss Pope, Miss Ross and Master Vernon. We have met in other provincial centres a good proportion of the actors and actresses that figure on these lists; among them there were good all-round players who capably filled secondary positions in the London theatres, but the only famous name is that of Shuter; otherwise the company did not rise to first class talent.

Though the days of Richmond's glory had by this time departed, a 'brilliant Appearance of Nobility and Gentry' might still be seen at assemblies at the Wells.[1] But of the theatre we hear nothing further until 1756 when 'Mr Cibber ...opened at the...warehouse (late called the theatre) on the hill, an histrionic academy for the instruction of young persons of genius, in the art of acting; and purposes, for the better improvement of such pupils &c frequently with his assistants, to give public rehearsals without hire, gain or reward.'[2]

Evidently, in spite of the care taken to evade the Licensing Act, there had been trouble, and Theophilus Cibber was making another attempt to outwit the law by running a playhouse under cover of a 'Cephalic Snuff' business, with a dramatic school attached. Cibber had a success with at least one 'young person of genius', for, about this time, Foote saw Miss Barton, afterwards Mrs Abington, play Lady Pliant in *The Double Dealer* on her first summer excursion at Richmond, 'and was so unexpectedly charmed with her taste, humour, and fine conception of the part, that, after paying the highest compliments to her talents behind the scenes, he immediately introduced her to Mr Lacy, who engaged her for the next winter at Drury-Lane.'[3]

Cibber was drowned on his way to Ireland in 1758, and the history of the 'Histrionic Academy' remains a blank until Dibdin performed there in the summer of 1762. Dibdin has left us a picture of the company and of the light-hearted way in which they took their duties:

The company was pretty respectable, and well regulated by Burton and Bransby.[4] The whole business was a kind of summer frolic, for, whatever celebrated actors, and sometimes actresses, happened to be in town, they were sure, either for pleasure, or

[1] *General Advertiser*, July 28, 1751.

[2] Lysons, *Environs*, vol. I, p. 469, purporting to quote from *The General Advertiser*, July 8, 1756. This paper had given place to *The Public Advertiser* to which the quotation is, however, untraceable.

[3] Wm. Cooke, *Memoirs of Samuel Foote*, 1805, vol. II, pp. 20–1. She had already appeared at the Haymarket under Cibber's management.

[4] Two actors from Drury Lane.

from invitation, to take a trip to Richmond, and perform on a Saturday. We had, during that summer, Shuter, Weston, Miss Pope, and others, besides a detachment, occasionally, from Foote's troop, and sometimes a dancer or an opera singer. One circumstance that highly entertained me was, as they considered this as mere fun and recreation, there was no getting Shuter or Weston to perform their usual parts. Shuter chose King Richard...and Weston desired that his name might be advertised for a song between the acts[1]

although he had no voice and convulsed the house by his performance. Dibdin relates how on another occasion Shuter, though accustomed to play Falstaff, elected to essay the Prince of Wales to Scrase's Percy; Shuter was determined to make Scrase laugh, and, upon the latter's gravely uttering the lines: 'If I mistake not thou art Henry Percy', archly replied: 'No, I ent; you are Henry Percy.' Shuter was but continuing Chapman's tradition of playing unsuitable parts though, whereas Davies attributes Chapman's motive to vanity, Dibdin finds in Shuter's action only a sense of fun.

A new epilogue by Samuel Derrick, spoken by Miss Maclean at Richmond in the character of the Fair Penitent, was printed in the *Public Advertiser* on August 21, 1762; it starts off in jaunty, cynical Restoration fashion only to decline into a moralising tag. A company drawn partly, at any rate, from the Haymarket performed *Venice Preserv'd*, with Davis as Pierre at Richmond on Saturday, July 30, 1763. The afterpiece was Foote's *The Minor* in which Tate Wilkinson made his first appearance in Richmond and mimicked the actors of the company in the part of Shift. Wilkinson[2] has described how the following season:

From love of cash I performed five Saturdays for the sixth to be clear, at the old theatre on Richmond Hill: Mr Foote lent me his dresses, and my benefit was on Saturday, August 20[18], 1764, and was honoured with the sanction of the Duke of York. Lady

[1] *The Professional Life of Mr Dibdin.* Written by himself, 1803, vol. I, p. 38.
[2] *Memoirs*, vol. III, p. 247.

Petersham and a large party were there, and I was favoured with a brilliant appearance: Most of the little pit was laid into the boxes. The farce of the Citizen I had as a play, and I acted Young Philpot; Old Philpot, Mr Weston; with Tragedy A-la-Mode.

The New Theatre on the Green was opened on June 15, 1765,[1] by James Dance who called himself Love. Shuter and Davis continued to use for occasional benefit performances what is thenceforward known as the Old Theatre on Richmond Hill.[2] On August 17 the former played the title role in *The Busy Body* supported by Davis, Parsons, Gardner, Costollo, Preston, Miss Reynolds, Mrs Kennedy, Mrs Burden, and Mrs Parsons from the Haymarket Company. This was followed by entertainments by Shuter and *Miss in Her Teens* with Shuter as Fribble. 'Mr Davis', runs the advertisement, 'has had the House entirely repaired by Mr Joseph Thomas, Taylor, and Mr Lyons of Richmond.' There had been a clash with the management of the new theatre and Davis 'thinks it a Duty incumbent on him, to acquaint his Friends, that he sent a Message five Weeks ago to the Manager of the New Theatre, acquainting him, that his Benefit would be on the above Night, in order to re-imburse himself for the Repairs of the Old Theatre.'[3] The rival benefits gave an opportunity for a wag to print in the *St James's Chronicle* of August 27–9 verses called *The Devil*[4] *and Love*:

> A Legion in the Devil's Train,
> From Catherine-Street and Drury-Lane,
> And from the Golden-Cat,
> In Chaise-and-one and Chaise-and-two,
> Bawds, Whores, and Rogues, the Dev'l knows who,
> Came frying in their Fat.

[1] For its history see Frederick Bingham, *A Celebrated Old Playhouse*, 1886. 'It has long been lamented', says the *St James's Chronicle*, June 18, 'that the theatrical Entertainments there [at Richmond] were as inelegant as the Company was respectable.'

[2] The old theatre was used on August 1 for G. A. Stevens's famous lecture upon heads.

[3] *Public Advertiser*, August 17.   [4] Davis was known as Devil Davis.

> Love hearing this, commanded straight
> That for Recruits his Drum should beat,
> Himself great Serjeant Kite.

The following year Davis sensibly arranged his benefit for Saturday, September 20, the day after the new theatre had closed. Foote's Haymarket Company performed his new comedy *The Commissary*, in which the Westons, the Macgeorges, Palmer, Nelson, Murden, Davis and Mrs Worley had parts. A new occasional prologue was spoken by Davis. *The Lyar* was the afterpiece. The promoters announce that 'Care will be taken to have the House well aired, fitted up in a proper Manner, for the Reception of those Ladies and Gentlemen who intend honouring Mr Davis with their Company'.[1] The performance began at 7, but 'To prevent mistakes, those ladies and gentlemen who have taken places are desired to send their servants by five o'clock'.

During the season of 1767, Shuter made a more wholehearted attempt to keep the Old Theatre going. He opened on Saturday, June 6[2] with the usual concert, *The Suspicious Husband* and *Lethe*. Burton, Du-Bellamy, Ackman, Didier, Popperwell, Wright, J. Burton, Master Cape, Mrs Johnston, Mrs Du-Bellamy, Mrs Didier, Miss Pierce, Miss Helm and Mrs Dorman were in the cast. Shuter played the Old Man in the afterpiece and spoke a prologue, written by Colman, who resided at Richmond, and printed in the *St James's Chronicle* for June 6–9. Part of it runs as follows:

> Welcome ye Generous, Polite, and Fair,
> Who to our lowly Roof this night repair!
> Who come, invited by our humble Bill,
> To the Old Theatre on Richmond Hill;
> Where to those guests, whose Taste not over-nice is,
> We serve up common Fare—at common Prices!
> No Cornice here, no Frieze to feast your Eyes,
> No Galleries on Dorick Pillars rise;

[1] *Public Advertiser*, September 20, 1766.   [2] *Ibid.* June 4.

No gaudy Paintings on the Roof we deal in
To break your Necks with looking tow'ards the Cieling;
No Theatre we boast superbly built,
A Gingerbread Round O, a Cockpit gilt;
But a plain Booth, of Boards ill put together,
To raise a Stage, and keep out Wind and Weather.
Yet here shall Heroes in their Buskins stalk,
And Shakespeare's Ghosts in this small Circle walk!
Here Tragedy shall take three narrow Strides,
And laughing Comedy hold both her Sides:
Here shall the Moor say 'Haply for I am black!'
And here plump Falstaff—'Give me a Cup of Sack!'
Here Bobadil shall don his dirty Buff,
And cry—'The Cabin is convenient enough'.

 . . . . . .

Thus while You deign to visit our poor Cottage,
And kindly taste of our Dramatic Pottage,
We, all intent to shew our Zeal and Love,
Shall each a Baucis or Philemon prove,
And every Guest shall seem to us—a Jove!

The House is advertised as being 'compleatly fitted up for
the Reception of the Gentlemen and Ladies who will please
to honour the Performance with their Company'. The same
night the Theatre on the Green opened with the same play
followed by *The Devil to Pay*. Richmond had not room for
so much dramatic fare and though Shuter bravely advertised
Love in a Village for performance on June 13,[1] he was compelled on that day to insert a notice that 'The Opera of Love
in a Village, with the Farce of the King and Miller, which was
to have been given after the Concert at the Old Theatre on
Richmond Hill this Evening is obliged to be postponed for
some Time, on a very extraordinary Occasion'. The New
Theatre had triumphed and a prologue intended to have been
spoken by Mrs Love appeared in the *Public Advertiser* of
June 26 over the initials W.K. in answer to Colman's.

[1] *Public Advertiser*, June 8.

By opposition lately sore affrighted
We own, with gratitude, we see, delighted
Our rivals disappointed of their ends,
To alienate the favour of our Friends.
What could their musing Prologue-monger dream on,
By his strange tale of Baucis and Philemon;
Of heathen Jove, and such-like idle stuff?
True, to be sure! and probable enough!
But were it real, 'tis a fine example,
And of his taste, no doubt, a curious sample!

. . . . . .

Well must they know, who much frequented Plays,
Enacted up the hill, in former days,
How oft the same dragg'd on, nay, stood stock still
For want of something—worse than want of skill.
How ludicrous to see, altho' in sport,
The fields of Cressy and of Agincourt
Scarce big enough t'admit a warrior's stride—
Your heroes always straddle four feet wide.—

How can Harlequin, the prologue continues:

Escape pursuit by jumping—half a yard!
Yet have we seen that motley child of fun
Coop'd in a hutch, where he could skip nor run;
But fidgetted, his wrigglings to confine
From tripping up the tripping Colombine:
The stage so spacious, that three steps, at most,
Ran Agamemnon's Nose against the post;
While his fair consort, Madam Clytemnestra,
Hid, with her petticoat, the whole Orchestra!
Nor was the playhouse faultier than the play'rs.

. . . . . .

Oft, 'tis well known, the careless comic muse
Forgot to laugh—because forgot their cues.
Nay, we have seen a whole performance undone,
For want of chieftains, not arriv'd from London.

. . . . . .

Meanwhile poor Tragedy was forc'd to cry
And whimper sadly with a single eye;

The other turn'd incessantly to look,
Tearless and dry, intent upon the book:
The actor's parts by some pert prentice play'd,
Too fond of buskins e'er to learn his trade.
No wonder stage so small, play'rs so obedient,
Should render a new Theatre expedient.

But it was not quite the end. On September 26, after the season at the Green Theatre had finished, the Old Theatre opened its doors once more to actors from Drury Lane and Covent Garden, who presented *The Clandestine Marriage*[1] by particular desire. The last performance of all was that of *The Beggar's Opera* on Saturday, October 10, 'exactly at Six', with the following cast: Macheath—Vernon, Peachum—Massey, Lockit—Bates, Filch—Cushing, Mat—Banister, Player—Ackman, Lucy—Mrs Green, Mrs Peachum—Mrs Parsons, Diana—Miss Copin, Jenny Diver—Miss Pierce, Polly—Mrs Mattocks. The afterpiece was *The Virgin Unmask'd* with Cushing as Coupee and Miss Reynolds as Miss Lucy.

Thereafter the 'Histrionic Academy' became a Methodist Chapel,[2] and later a granary for the town corn chandler.[3] It was finally pulled down about 1826 to make way for York Place. Richard Crisp, writing in 1866, had spoken to aged people who recollected performances at the theatre in their youth, and many then still alive remembered the building which was 'a large timber built place'. Its site is said to have been on that part of the Hill, formerly known as Hill Rise, now numbered 10–28 Richmond Hill, which stands between the Vineyard and Lancaster Mews. This has been confirmed by a recent discovery: Messrs Drew, estate agents of Richmond, have found, and have kindly allowed me to see, a lease of the old playhouse dated March 1796, whereby Sir

[1] *Public Advertiser*, September 23.
[2] *A Sketch of the Life and Reminiscences of John Rogers*, 1889, p. 30.
[3] R. Crisp, *Richmond and Its Inhabitants*, 1866, p. 363. *The Theatric Tourist* states that Love bought part of the property.

John and Lady Sebright of St George's, Hanover Square, who held the premises by copyhold, rented 'All that boarded Building commonly known by the Name of the old Playhouse with a small Tenement and Yard adjoining situate in a Street called the Rise of the Hill' for twenty-one years to Samuel Smith, baker, at a rent of ten guineas a year. Smith's tenancy expired at Christmas, 1816. In the Richmond Library there is an unsigned and undated pen-and-ink sketch of the theatre from the collection of the late F. Brewer;[1] it shows a light-looking, barn-shaped structure, with a house attached at the rear, which has about its fantastic little tower and entrance porches an air of chinoiserie that would have made it a fitting setting for a 'summer frolic'. For, although great actors and actresses, and even, on occasion, great plays, appeared upon its boards, one's general impression is that of a haunt for drama on holiday. Three famous comic actors ran it in turn; burlesque was its constant tradition through the years, and about its proceedings there must always have been a haphazardness. Yet it served to entertain and delight a royal and gallant company in the days of Richmond's glory.

[1] I am unable to trace the origin of this. Mr T. H. Smith writes that Mr Brewer acquired it about forty years ago.

INDEX

I. PLAYS

[† indicates that I have not found mention of the play elsewhere.

* indicates that, as far as I know, the play has not been printed.

Subtitles are given only (1) for distinction when there is another play of the same name, (2) when the play is not otherwise known, (3) for cross-reference when the subtitle, as in many pantomimes, is used with different titles.

Plays performed under subtitles are referred to the main title. Type of play is given only when there is a need to distinguish plays of the same title.]

II. PERSONS, PLACES, SUBJECTS

[It is generally impossible to distinguish between actors of the same name since so few Christian names have come down to us. I have therefore listed actors of the same name under that name and subdivided into the companies in which they are to be found. Sometimes they are certainly, or almost certainly, the same actor who has changed his company, sometimes equally certainly not. But only when I have very positive evidence, such as clashing dates, or years too wide apart, have I made separate entries for the same name. There is the further complication that names were often erratically spelt in various ways so that the same person may be concealed under different entries. I have made a cross-reference when I have thought this to be the case. When the actor was attached to a local company I have put the company, when he was merely a visitor I have put the place only. I have only mentioned company or place at all when an actor of the same name is found in different ones and may therefore be a different person. In the case of theatrical families I have, out of strict alphabetical order, put the actor and his wife first and the children afterwards.]